PRAISE FOR

LIFER

"United States military combat veterans are national treasures—many call them heroes, which is precisely what they are. *Lifer* is the must-read story of one of those great American heroes—Master Sergeant Nathan Aguinaga (Retired)—who, for twenty years, served this great nation as a US Army Infantry paratrooper in the 82nd Airborne Division and a host of other assignments.

Highlights of his years of service to our country include a combat tour in Iraq, a year on the Korean DMZ, a tour on the drill field as a drill instructor and more. *Lifer* is an insightful behind-the-curtain look into the life and career of a US Army Infantry paratrooper and a must read for other combat veterans regardless of service."

—Colonel Carl D. Matter, US Marine Corps (Retired)

"Nate Aguinaga's *Lifer* is a gripping and inspirational journey, reflecting the resilience and dedication required of our soldiers. His stories are testaments of the enduring spirit and unwavering commitment of our nation's finest."

—Major Roberto Lainez, US Army (Retired)

"*Lifer* is a richly detailed story of one man's twenty-year career in the US Army, though he never intended to be a lifer. Chip on his shoulder? Big one. Rough and tough? Oh yeah. Polished yeller and screamer? Yup. Exactly the kind of man you want defending our nation and training others to do so as well. His story deeply details the endless training exercises, prepping, parachuting, hiking, diving, crossing rope bridges—doing everything possible—to be prepared to defend our nation and allies in Panama, Iraq, and the DMZ in Korea, among others where he served. The beauty of the story is that you are literally with him every step, push-up, jump, injury, battle, and shot along the way. The book is a great read that will help you better understand and appreciate how much soldiers prepare and train to put their lives on the line for us and each other."

—Bruce K. Berger, Author of *Brothers Bound* and *Fragments: The Long Coming Home from Vietnam*

"I believe there is no tougher job than that of a US Army noncommissioned officer (NCO). Being a 'lifer,' especially in demanding units like the 82nd Airborne Division in a time of war, takes a special kind of person. Nate's story is a must read. Follow him on his journey of love, life, and soldiering. You'll enjoy his humor, humility, and the 'tell it like it is' approach he takes to life and writing. Chute up and turn the page!

—Colonel Rob Cambell, US Army (Retired), author of *It's Personal, Not Personnel: Leadership Lessons for the Battlefield and the Boardroom*, and *At Ease: Enjoying the Freedom you Fought For*

"Echos of nostalgia. The Army's good, bad, and hilarious."

—Galen D. Peterson, Author of *Strike Hard and Expect No Mercy: A Tank Platoon Leader in Iraq*, REDCON ONE, and LIGHTING SIX

"What an astounding reflection of military service. Well-written and descriptive, Mr. Aguinaga masterfully tells his story. I have never served in the military; however, this story is told so well that I didn't need to have that prior knowledge to enjoy it. His attention to detail and authenticity are refreshing, allowing the reader to go on the journey with him."

—Mrs. Diana Kiser, EdS, eighth grade ELA teacher

"An amazing description of life in the Army by one of the most influential and dedicated leaders I had the privilege to serve with. Thank you 'Sergeant Augi!'"

—Lieutenant Colonel Jeff Huston, US Army (Retired)

"Sometimes we discover our path in life, sometimes we forge it, and sometimes we stumble onto it. For most of us, it's a combination of all three. I suspect Nate Aguinaga's journey to becoming a 'lifer' in the US Army was just that, a favorable and satisfying collision of opportunity, talent, and chance. However he got there, I'm grateful for his leadership and proud to have served alongside him and walked with him during his incredible journey."

—Colonel John Vermeesch, US Army (Retired)

"While life is often filled with obstacles, in the 82nd Airborne, Nate Aguinaga faced sink or swim challenges daily."

—Bob Dorgan, USN Veteran, author of *Sea Pay: an Enlisted Man's Naval Adventure.*

Lifer: My Epic Journey as a US Army Infantry Paratrooper
by Nathan Aguinaga

© Copyright 2024 Nathan Aguinaga

979-8-88824-409-8

All rights reserved. No part of this publication may be reproduced, stored in a retrieval system, or transmitted in any form or by any means—electronic, mechanical, photocopy, recording, or any other—except for brief quotations in printed reviews, without the prior written permission of the author.

Published by

3705 Shore Drive
Virginia Beach, VA 23455
800-435-4811
www.koehlerbooks.com

LIFER

MY EPIC JOURNEY AS A US ARMY INFANTRY PARATROOPER

NATHAN AGUINAGA

VIRGINIA BEACH
CAPE CHARLES

AS AN INFANTRY soldier, you'll serve in the field, working to defend our country against any threats on the ground. You'll capture, destroy, and deter enemy forces, assist in reconnaissance, and help mobilize troops and weaponry to support the mission as the ground combat force.

Feel sorry for yourself soldier and turn your back on this platoon, and I damn sure will turn my back on you—you will be on your own, kid.
—Sergeant First Class Aguinaga, Platoon Sergeant, 82nd Airborne Division

INTRODUCTION

MAKE NO MISTAKE about it. A "lifer" is a term used in all branches of the US Armed Forces. It basically refers to the fact that an individual soldier, airman, sailor, and marine will become a career servicemember with the goal of eventually retiring from the military with a great pension.

These are some of my personal experiences as a career soldier in the US Army Infantry, from the time I entered the service in 1990 until I retired in 2010. These stories will take you on my journeys from Infantry School, my time in some of the toughest Army Infantry units, drill sergeant duty, combat deployments, and dealing with all the hardships that came along with these challenges—not only for me, but for my family and friends as well.

I don't hold back when it comes to language and some other details that might be considered by some to be distasteful. I have never been one to sugarcoat the details, and I'm not going to start now.

I begin these stories in the early 1990s, when I was about twenty-one years old. During my final Army experiences, I was nearly forty. So please sit back and enjoy the ride. One thing I can promise—you will be entertained. Thank you for reading my story.

—Nate Aguinaga

CHAPTER 1

FIRST INFANTRY ASSIGNMENT
THE 82ND AIRBORNE DIVISION

I HAD RECLASSIFIED after my initial enlistment from 71L, administrative specialist, to 11B, light infantry. I was an E-4 promotable at the time, already Airborne qualified, and had two previous duty stations under my belt, including a combat deployment to Desert Storm. I had just completed a two-year station in Germany prior to arriving to Fort Bragg, North Carolina (known today as Fort Liberty) and was awaiting my upcoming date to attend infantry training at Fort Benning, Georgia (known today as Fort Moore).

During my first reenlistment in Germany I had requested to change over to light infantry, and be stationed at Fort Bragg with the 82nd Airborne. The reenlistment NCO (noncommissioned officer) told me to be careful what I wished for. My initial reaction was, *How the fuck would this guy know? He ain't even Airborne qualified.* I knew in my gut I had made the right choice because I was bored and wanted to see how the other side of the Army lived.

And man, did I find out. However, nothing ever came as a surprise to me.

I arrived in Fayetteville, North Carolina, in September of 1994. I took a taxi from the Fayetteville airport to Fort Bragg. I had flown in straight from Germany without taking leave between, which was usually the norm. Hell, I didn't even have any leave saved up and I was so excited to get to the 82nd that I didn't go home and see the family first. I was a young twenty-two-year-old full of energy and excitement, with a combat patch on my right shoulder.

I found out the next morning that all that didn't mean shit in this place, especially since my combat patch was earned in the 44th Medical Brigade, which is also a Bragg unit but stuck out in *pog land* on the other side of Bragg Boulevard. A *pog* (person other than a grunt) is any soldier or marine that is not an Infantryman. It is a derogatory term.

When the taxi dropped me off at the replacement battalion, I encountered a group of soldiers wearing civilian clothes, sitting at a picnic table while smoking and drinking beer. They told me to go up and sign in with the soldier on charge of quarters duty (CQ), who was just another replacement soldier himself.

I walked up to the second floor and signed in. It was after duty hours, so the CQ told me to go to a room and said there was linen in one of the wall lockers. I had arrived with nothing but two duffel bags. I didn't even own a suitcase, but back in those days, it was normal to just show up with duffel bags if you were single and a junior enlisted soldier. On a chalkboard in the hallway it said what time formation was the next morning and what the uniform was. The mess hall was already closed, so the CQ told me where the Airborne PX was and that they had a food court. I asked where the nearest phone was because I needed to call my parents and tell them I had arrived at Fort Bragg. There were a couple of phone booths outside the barracks. Wow, as I write this, it's hard to remember a time without cell phones; phone booths were your savior when you arrived at a new duty station with nothing but a wallet and some clothes.

As I walked to the Airborne PX for the first time in my life, I was amazed at the scenery along the way. Every unit area had pull-up bars and rock formation areas, edged with railroad ties. Anyone stationed there during this time remembers that if you were leaving the

Replacement Battalion, heading toward the Airborne PX, you would pass by the 82nd Military Intelligence, Signal, and Engineer Battalions. Then you'd come up on the 73rd Cavalry Regiment, which had a little Sherman armored vehicle in front of its headquarters (the Engineer Battalion had a little wagon in front of theirs). Then, for the first time, I saw my first Infantry Regimental area, which belonged to the 505th.

First you came upon 2 Panther headquarters, with a row of barracks lined up behind it. There were four three-story buildings for each company individually. Rows of pull-up bars and large thirty-foot wooden structures with ropes to climb were set up all the way down the battalion's row of buildings. Next to that was a large, open field called Lindsey Field, which I would use pretty much my entire time in the 82nd. The other side of it belonged to the 3rd Battalion, known as 3-505, or 3 Panther. This and every other infantry battalion for an approximately two-mile stretch down Ardennes Road followed almost exactly the same format. Looking at these unit areas for the first time was somewhat intimidating to me. I know most people reading this are like, *What's the big deal with pull-up bars and ropes?* Well, if you've been serving in support units for the past four years, you're not used to seeing unit areas as intimidating as this. It all resembled a Basic Training or Airborne School view. The direction I was walking in toward the PX, lined the units in the order of the 505th, the 325th, and the 504th. Each regiment had three battalions during this time.

The Airborne PX consisted of a small shopping center where you could purchase snacks, personal hygiene items, unit physical training (PT) shirts, tobacco, beer, and a small portion of some whiskeys. The nearest liquor store was down back past the Replacement Battalion known as the Reilly Road Class Six. It was rumored more alcohol was sold from this Class Six than any other party store in the entire country! After serving a year in Division, you would believe it in a heartbeat. The next nearest Class Six was on Yadkin Road, right before leaving post, and that place was pretty huge.

Okay, now that I have the important shit out of the way—where to get your booze—let me continue my tour of the rest of the Airborne PX. Next to the small shopping area was a food court, which consisted of a sub shop, an Anthony's Pizza, and a burger bar. Years later, when I was a platoon sergeant, that burger bar would turn into a Taco Bell. On the walls around the food court were old pictures of the 82nd during World War II, Korea, and Vietnam (remember, this was pre-Global War on Terrorism). Across from the food court was the Airborne Barber Shop, which if I remember correctly, was closed on Sundays, so we normally had to get our hair cut on Yadkin Road at one of the numerous barber shops on that strip. God forbid we showed up to PT formation Monday mornings needing a fresh, tight haircut. I believe there was a little AT&T phone center next to the barber shop for those paratroopers that wanted to get a phone in their barracks room.

Replacement Battalion was broken down into a few sections that were like the size of a small platoon, usually twenty-five or thirty soldiers. One section consisted of those newcomers just arriving in Division, like me. Another section were those soldiers shipping out or getting ready to ship out to their units. One section had physical fitness test (PFT) or height and weight failures, and one section of *legs* that were awaiting a date to attend Airborne School at Fort Benning. A *leg* is a soldier who is not Airborne qualified and pretty much looked down upon, not just in Division, but pretty much throughout the entire fucking installation. Trust me, in 1994, you did not want to be in the PT failure or leg section. It wasn't the assigned cadre they had to worry about; it was the Junior NCOs that were also replacements themselves. In those days, no soldier could be assigned to any unit in Division, combat arms, or support without being parachute qualified. I believe the PT failures could eventually ship to a unit, but God forbid you showed up to any unit with a failed PT test in Replacement on your record when you arrived at your company.

E-5 sergeants and below were required to be in all formations in Replacement. E-6 staff sergeants had to be at all appointed in-processing timelines, but they did not have to march or be in the formations. E-7s and above could in-process themselves.

Fast forwarding some years later when I in-processed in Division for the third time in my career, I was an E-6 promotable, coming off the "Trail" (two years of drill sergeant duty). I told the cadre at Replacement to hand me the checklist and have a good day. That was a good feeling. Hell, by then, I was an 82nd veteran and jumpmaster qualified. I knew every drop zone, qualification, and live-fire range on Fort Bragg like the back of my hand. I'd be damned if a Replacement NCO was going to tell me my shit. But back then, I was the new guy just coming in.

Those sergeant E-5s within the ranks were not to be fucked with. They were like miniature drill sergeants, all over the junior enlisted soldiers, smoking them in formation at the drop of a dime. Do you think for a second they gave a fuck that I was an E4 promotable? Hell no. My face was in the front leaning rest position (push-up position) too.

These were young Infantry NCOs that had all these high-speed badges sewn on their battle dress uniforms (BDUs). Half of them had Ranger tabs sewn above their Airborne tabs as part of the 82nd unit insignia.

I was freaking out, having come from "71L Land" my first few years in the Army. I had never interacted with or seen infantry leaders in action other than my nine weeks of basic training as a private at Fort Leonard Wood, Missouri. I remember telling myself, *I will be one of these guys someday soon.* The only reason I wasn't already was that I had failed the color vision test during my initial physical trying to get into the Army. If a recruiting prospect failed the color vision test with the numbers identification key, they were automatically exempt from combat arms positions, which is why I initially came in as an administrative guy. When I took the physical to reclassify into an Infantry MOS (military occupation code), I only had to identify what color was green and what color was red. The test was conducted on a computer screen where all the soldier had to identify was "green on the left; red is on the right," or however the colors were arranged. That was it. The original test I had failed had been the old pseudoisochromatic plates test where you had to identify numbers within circular shades of different colors on metallic plates, which had been more difficult.

In-processing into the Division is the primary function of the Replacement Battalion. It follows a concise methodology, taking approximately a week before they ship you off to your unit. Twenty-five years ago, these were the stations you had to in-process before they sent you off. I can't imagine it's much different these days. Each Replacement soldier had to not only take and pass the Army PT test and weigh-in, but also go through finance, where we were excited to process our $110 additional monthly parachute pay. The issue of all field equipment at the post's clothing issue facility was usually a half-day event, not just at Fort Bragg, but throughout any other military installation. They marched us to the Hall of Heroes, where the division commander and command sergeant major briefed us on the honor and respect of being a paratrooper in Division. They also included the do's and don'ts of Fayetteville night life. It was the first time we had heard that the city of Fayetteville, which surrounds Fort Bragg, has easy access to illegal drugs. This is primarily due to the city being on Interstate 95, and also because it lies directly at the halfway point between Miami and New York City.

The Hall of Heroes was also medical in-processing and the place to turn in your official records. Back in those days, this was your 201 file. We also got to experience the 82nd Airborne Division Choir, who were, and I guarantee still are, impressive. They got on the stage and sang a couple of classic Airborne songs, such as "Blood on the Risers." This small group of paratroopers come from all units and all military occupational skills (MOSs) throughout the entire division. The choir is displayed every single morning during PT timeline on loudspeakers that cover the majority of Ardennes Road, all through the entire division area. Their singing echoes as thousands of paratroopers run up and down Ardennes Road every morning, Monday through Friday. Witnessing Ardennes Road during PT hours is an experience in and of itself.

Everyone in-processing also had to visit the Airborne Museum, which was pretty cool, especially if it was your first time at Fort Bragg. Equipment used in the past such as aircraft, anti-air weaponry, and artillery guns is on display outside the building. Inside are showcases of memorabilia of every war the 82nd has been involved in throughout history. It also has a small shop of 82nd merchandise and a small movie theater, where it shows a film of the division's history. The film was always my favorite part of the museum.

The final day of in-processing consists of an all-day airborne refresher course at the 82nd Advanced Airborne, or Jumpmaster School, which was and still is located on the corner of Ardennes Road and Long Street. The new paratroopers get a crash course of rigging their equipment to jump, receive prejump or sustained airborne training, actions in the aircraft or mock door training, and exiting out of the thirty-four-foot tower. Once all these in-processing requirements are complete for the week, the paratroopers are then sent to their units.

In my day, the "cattle trucks" lined up on Ardennes in front of Replacement headquarters and took us to our respective brigade headquarters. We were dropped off with our bags in front of the building, where we were required to in-process the brigade and receive our battalion assignments. I was assigned to the 505th (3rd Brigade) but did not receive a battalion assignment because I was still awaiting Infantry Training at Fort Benning. Until my departure to Benning, I was kept at Brigade Headquarters and placed in the S-2 Shop (managing security and safety) for a few months, where I got to attend the Primary Leadership Development Course (PLDC) and got a couple of "cherry jumps" out of the way. These included my first jump, which was out of a CH-47 Chinook helicopter. That daylight jump at three thousand feet had my ass puckered tight.

Little did I know at the time, that would be my first permanent change of station (PCS) out of three separate times getting assigned to not only Airborne Division, but the 505th within the next twelve years. I look back on that twenty-five years later, and I wouldn't want it any other way.

CHAPTER 2

BEING ASSIGNED TO MY FIRST INFANTRY COMPANY

THE DIVISION, LED by the 505th Parachute Infantry Regiment, had just came back from Green Ramp at Pope Air Force Base a few months prior, actually as soon as I had arrived at the brigade the past September. Green Ramp is the area of the airfield where all paratroopers from Bragg prepare and board the aircraft to jump. The invasion of Haiti (also known as Operation Uphold Democracy) was underway. If you remember, a small coup with resistance fighters took over the government of the Caribbean island nation and President Clinton was prepared to send the entire 82nd Airborne Division into combat to restore the original government to power. Former President Carter was negotiating with the resistance and warned that the 82nd was en route. Soon after they found out there was going to be a full-out parachute assault, they stood down. The first wave led by us (3rd Brigade) was already in the air heading south. The aircraft were ordered to turn around and headed back to Pope. Although assigned to the brigade S-2 at the time, I, along with another E-4 from the shop, our NCOIC (noncommissioned officer in charge) and the S-2 himself were on board one of the aircraft. Again, my ass was puckered as tight as anyone could imagine. It was going to be the largest airborne invasion since World War II. But it didn't end up happening.

My infantry training at Fort Benning was a piece of cake, almost a check-the-box-type deal. Infantry basic training at Benning is thirteen weeks long. After week nine, the trainees begin their MOS portion: 11Bs do their Light Infantry, 11Cs go do mortar training, 11Ds are TOW Gunners mounted, and 11Ms are Bradley Fighting Vehicle Operators. So they started me and three other guys who were reclassifying as well at the beginning of week nine or ten.

The drill sergeants were cool with us. Actually, it got to the point where I think they were taking advantage of us. They had us demonstrating all the training, to include the confidence course, obstacle course, and so on. Years later, when I became a drill sergeant, I looked back at this time and said to myself, "Those motherfuckers had us doing their jobs."

It was all good. Hell, I don't blame them. At the end of the day, we just wanted our blue cords and blue disks for our Class A uniforms and to be on our way, just like they did. They didn't even make us stick around for graduation unless we wanted to. Hell no! We all jumped in our vehicles or taxis and got the hell out of Fort Benning.

When I got back to Bragg, I was given the choice of what unit I wanted to go to as long as it was within the regiment. I chose 3rd Battalion primarily because the barracks I was already living in was in the same row of buildings, so I wouldn't have to move my shit as far. Makes sense, right? Anyway, the mentality was, and probably still is, that every battalion on the street is the same in the "Airplane Game." The only differences are that you wear a different PT shirt and a different flash on your beret.

One thing I need to point out before we get any further is that I will not be mentioning specific companies or platoons that I've been assigned to. I will not be mentioning specific names of people either. Instead, I'll use some form of generic nickname. This is obviously for privacy reasons. However, I will call certain individuals by the nicknames they went by during that time. Trust me, if you served with me or in the same company during these periods, you'll know exactly who I'm referring to and I hope it puts a smile on your face.

I walked into my new company and went straight to the orderly room, where in-processing and all administrative work is conducted. I turned in my packet and waited for the clerk to go notify the first sergeant. I was kind of nervous, but not as much as a new private just coming out of airborne school and going into their first company ever. After all, I kept in the back of my head that I was a specialist with some experience in the Army under my belt.

As I said, all these companies were set up as three-story buildings with the barracks combined. First floor consisted of company leadership offices, a day room, and 1st Platoon rooms. Second floor was living and working areas of 2nd and 3rd Platoons. HQ Platoon personnel were spread throughout the two floors. Third floors throughout all four buildings were reserved battalion HQ sections, such as mortars, medics, scouts, cooks, and the five S shops. Each bedroom was usually designed to accommodate two paratroopers. Also, each floor had one large latrine with open showers and one washer and dryer. There were about three larger single rooms for the NCOs who lived in the barracks, and they each had their own latrine. Past the CQ desk, around the corner, was the orderly room, which was connected through a small hallway to the first sergeant's office, which was also connected to the company commander's (CO's) office.

The orderly room clerk went to let the first sergeant know I was there. The clerk is usually an 11B as well, but normally is *broke* or a *shitbag*. A *broke* soldier is injured to the point they cannot perform their duties; the term *shitbag* is more derogatory. A shitbag is a trooper that does not or cannot conform to infantry standards, mainly a PT failure or someone who falls out of foot-marches, is late to formations, has a barracks room that's all fucked-up, doesn't give a shit about anything, you know—pretty much a shitbag. You get the picture now.

The clerk told me to go see the first sergeant, so I walked out of the orderly room and walked about five feet down the hallway until I was in front of his door. I started sweating a little bit as I heard hollering down the hallway toward the 1st Platoon area. I knocked on his door and turned my head toward all the ruckus. There were two soldiers in the front leaning rest, with a young NCO over top of them hollering, "Push, you fucksticks!"

He looked up and noticed I was staring in their direction. "What the fuck you lookin' at?"

I said nothing and quickly turned my head and eyes toward the first sergeant, who was sitting behind his desk. "C'mon in, Airborne," he said to me. I walked in and stood at parade rest in front of his desk. He had my file in front of him. I looked down and saw him grab my PT card. I felt good because I had like a 298 score on it (300 being max). He told me to go ahead and take a seat and started asking me questions. "You're the one coming from Brigade that reclassified right?"

"Yes, First Sergeant," I replied.

"You're promotable, right?"

"Yes, First Sergeant."

"You been to PLDC yet?"

"Yes, First Sergeant."

He turned around in his chair and grabbed the receiver of his phone and called someone to let them know that he had a new soldier for them. I assumed it was my new platoon sergeant. He told me he was putting me in "such and such" platoon. (Remember I said I wasn't naming numbers for privacy. I'll give a hint, though: it was on the second floor).

The first sergeant leaned toward me and told me someone was coming down to take me up to my platoon. He then said not to get mixed up into the wrong crowd, that there were some bad apples within not only the platoon I was going into, but the company as a whole. The first sergeant walked over to a metal box on his wall, opened it up, and handed me a key to my barracks room. I don't remember whether or not I signed for it.

Another specialist knocked on his door and the first sergeant told him to take me upstairs to Staff Sergeant So-and-so and to get me squared away. I said to myself, *Okay, first step is out of the way—piece of cake so far.*

I had heard rumors of the "E-4 Mafia" that existed within these infantry platoons throughout the division. They were the specialists within the platoons that would annihilate the new privates or "cherries" just coming in from Fort Benning Basic Training and Airborne School. Anyone that served in Division knows what I mean by *annihilate:* virtually smoke them from sunup to sundown, on and off duty. *Smoking* was another term for exercise to the extreme as a punishment. I heard about occasional ass-whoopings at the drop of a dime as well, almost as if it were a gang initiation. The rules were clear—what happens in the barracks stays in the barracks. What happens within the platoons stays within the platoons. I was prepared to defend myself at all costs.

The specialist dropped me off at the platoon command post, which was a large office area located in the center of the floor. Normally it was set up with the platoon sergeant and platoon leader of each of the two platoons that were on that floor. There were a few wall lockers located in the center of the room that separated the two command posts. Each platoon sergeant and platoon leader had a desk with a few chairs for their squad leaders. Most of the NCOs in these companies were married and either lived in government quarters on post or had a place out in town. Only a small percentage were single and lived in the barracks. If they lived in the barracks, it went two ways. Either they were studs, getting more ass than a toilet seat around Fayetteville, or they were so-called homebodies who couldn't get laid if they crawled up a chicken's ass. I was proudly in the first category. I retired more women in Fayetteville and Spring Lake than Social Security, not to mention in Raleigh, Durham, or Greensboro. Okay, let me shut up and get back to meeting my platoon leadership.

I stood in the doorway of the command post at parade rest until the staff sergeant sitting behind the desk told me to come in. He had three E-5s sitting around his desk, who, I quickly found out, were the three line squad leaders. A rifle platoon consists of three maneuver or assault squads and a support squad, known as the weapon's squad. The term *line* is slang for front line. It would be used in the text of "line company, line platoon, or line squad." Your average weapon's squad leader is usually the highest ranking or the most experienced squad leader within the platoon. The E-6 who told me to come in was actually the weapon's squad leader temporarily serving as the acting platoon sergeant, simply because the platoon didn't have one at the time. Throughout most of the 1990s, it was very difficult to get promoted to E-5 or E-6 because the cut-off scores for promotion were maxed out for 11Bs. Cut-off scores are how soldiers are promoted to E-5 and E-6. Each job in the Army has a certain score to get promoted depending on how many soldiers are in that particular occupational skill. So it was nothing in those days to see a platoon of mostly E-5 promotable squad leaders and E-4 promotable team leaders. Most of these E-4s were laterally promoted to corporal, which put them instantly in the NCO category. So the assigned original rank structures for these duty positions were team leader—E-5 sergeant; squad leader— E-6 staff sergeant; platoon sergeant—E-7 sergeant first class. It may sound confusing, especially if you have never served in the military, but it was and is the way these units are structured in the Army.

I stood in front of these NCOs at parade rest, head and eyes forward, with my heavy starched BDUs and spit-shined green jungle boots on, and a fresh high and tight haircut that I had just gotten the night before. So I was feeling pretty confident because I already knew that first impressions meant everything, especially in 82nd Airborne Division. The conversation from this point went somewhat like this.

"How do you pronounce that name, Specialist?"

I told him, "Aga-naga, Sergeant." "

Aga-naga??"

"What the fuck is that, Japanese?"

"No, Sergeant, it's Spanish."

One of the squad leaders asked me, "Where you comin' from?"

"Brigade, Sergeant."

"Brigade? What were you, a driver or something?"

"No, Sergeant, I reclassified to 11B and was assigned to Brigade until I went to Benning for training. I just got back a couple days ago."

The platoon sergeant asked me what my old MOS was, and I told him. I thought I was going to get crushed verbally, but they just nodded their heads and shrugged their shoulders, as if it simply made sense. All four of them were pretty much being cool with me. There was no yelling or sarcasm or anything.

"What's your PT score?"

"298, Sergeant."

"I want him!" two of them shouted simultaneously to the platoon sergeant.

It made me feel pretty good inside. Damn! I was being fought over, for Christ's sake.

"You promotable?" The platoon sergeant asked me.

"Roger that, Sergeant."

"Been to PLDC?"

"Roger, Sergeant."

It got real quiet all of a sudden and he just looked at the other three as they looked back at him. "Okay, that makes things a little different. Did the first sergeant give you a key?"

"Yes, Sergeant."

"Okay, go down to the right. Your new room is at the end of the hallway on the right. Go ahead and start unpacking. One of these guys will be down once we figure out what squad you're going in."

Being a promotable E-4 and a Primary Leadership Development Course graduate meant I was only waiting to make the cut-off score to what I had, and I was going to be automatically promoted to E-5. The only problem I had with that was that I didn't know shit yet. Damn sure not enough to immediately become a team leader.

As I walked to my room, the thought of them making me a team leader right off the bat kept going through my head. The more I thought about it, the more nervous I got. One thing I did notice was that the platoon area was completely empty and all the doors to everyone's rooms were closed. I went into my new room and noticed there was only one bed, no bunk system. I remember thinking that if I got a room to myself, that would be the shit. At this point, I didn't have anything with me to unpack because all my shit, to include a hand-me-down couch and TV, was still in my other barracks.

A little while went by, and here came my squad leader. I snapped to parade rest and he immediately told me to relax, which is a cool way of saying, "At ease." Yeah, he was cool, but he was pretty stern at the same time. He was a no-shit kind of NCO: when he told you something, he meant it. With that, he right away set my worries at ease—I was *not* going to be one of his team leaders right away. I needed to learn my job, learn the squad and platoon, and the lifestyle as a whole first and foremost. I just nodded in agreement, relieved.

Although he only had one team leader at the time, and this was the primary reason I got assigned to his squad, he told me another specialist was going to be the Bravo Team leader for the time being. I just kept nodding.

He looked around my room and noticed what I did, or maybe he already knew—I was without a roommate. "Okay you're by yourself, and I'll go ahead and keep it that way for now, but if I ever come in here, and I will daily, this room better not be fucked-up. You better keep this motherfucker clean every day. You keep it clean, and you'll never worry about having a roommate." He wasn't yelling at all either; he was just telling me the way it was going to be—period.

"Roger that, Sergeant."

"Where's all your shit?"

I replied that it was still over at the other barracks. I asked him where the rest of the platoon was at the time. He said they were all in Area J with the team leaders, taking a couple of classes. Area J was a small training area up on "the hill," across Gruber Road, behind division headquarters. I knew where it was and asked him if he wanted me to go link up with them. He told me not to worry about it because they were going to be done soon anyway. He told me to start bringing my shit over from the other barracks and that he'd see me at 0600 the next day, prior to PT formation.

I remember feeling calm, relieved, and really good about myself that I'd finally made it into an infantry company pretty smoothly. I also felt relieved my squad leader wasn't "tabbed," that is, Ranger qualified with a Ranger tab sewn on his left shoulder. That was a pretty big fucking deal in this place. As a matter of fact, years down the road, being tabbed would be the difference between whether or not I would serve as a platoon sergeant.

Years later, when I was a squad leader, I called him up. He was a platoon sergeant over at the O-4 and explained to me that he did eventually go to Ranger School and had gotten his tab. He said, in his thick Southern accent, that he had wanted to see what all the "hoop-law" was about, so he decided to find out. I remember thinking, *Bullshit! You were told to go, motherfucker!* He wasn't going to fool me.

Now that I'm on the subject, I'll get this out there now. There are only three things on your uniform that really count in the 82nd Airborne Division: a Ranger tab on your left shoulder, jump wings with a star above them, and a rifle badge above that. The last two I just described are the Senior Parachutist Badge (Master Parachutist Badge is a bonus), and the Expert Infantryman Badge (Combat Infantryman Badge, is a bonus). That's it in a nutshell. If you have those three items sewn on your BDUs, you're golden, wherever you go in Division. I'll go into more detail that supports this fact later. In this platoon, there were only about two or three tab wearers—one squad leader and a couple of team leaders. One of those team leaders was kind of "chewed up" too (not really a proficient leader) and his squad leader consistently ripped his ass at the drop of a dime.

The first couple of months went by pretty smoothly. I pretty much became friends with everybody in the platoon and throughout the company too. I have always been a social person with a pretty positive attitude—most of the time anyway. As partiers living in the barracks, we all pretty much stuck together. The barracks life was wild. I can't imagine college life being any wilder. No way! We'd get off duty and before we had our BDUs off and got into the shower, we already had at least a six-pack apiece gone. We'd get all dressed up and either head to the clubs down on Bragg Boulevard or go over someone's house or apartment off post and party all night.

Back in the mid-1990s, the CQs or battalion staff duty NCOs didn't really enforce the no-females-in-the-barracks policies too much, so it was nothing to see a few girls walking down the hallways or even walking out of the latrines. And there were some fine women in Fayetteville. North Carolina was a state full of good-looking girls. I'll give just these two funny-ass stories about the barracks when I was a "Joe" back twenty-five years ago. I still tell them to my civilian friends years after retirement.

One of my good buddies was quite the stud. The son of a bitch looked just like a young Sean Penn. And there was a "barracks whore" we used to see throughout the company all the time. "Sean Penn" had been with her a time or two in the past. But something had happened, and they could no longer stand each other. Every time they walked past each other in the hallway, they had something derogatory to say.

One night a group of us came back in the barracks drunk as hell and were walking down the hallway in our platoon area. She came out of a room with a little chihuahua in her arms. "Sean" looked at her and said, "I like your pig." With her strong Southern accent, she turned around and yelled back at him, "It's a dog, you asshole!" He said, "I was talkin' to the dog." Funniest shit I ever heard in my life.

Okay, one more quick, funny barracks story before I get back to company shit. It was early in the morning on a Saturday or Sunday. I woke up to take a piss, so I lit up a cigarette and walked down to the latrine in my boxers and flip-flops. On my way back to my room, the guy across the hall's door opened. Out came a very large woman. I stood in my doorway smoking my cigarette. I had caught him trying to sneak her out of his room before anybody woke up. He walked her out of his room, down the hallway to the double doors at the stairwell. As he came back to his room, I was looking at him with a big-ass smile on my face.

He said, "Hey, man, don't tell anybody about this."

I just kept on smiling at him, not saying a word.

He said, "C'mon, you have to admit that she was cute."

I replied, "Dude, a baby whale is cute, doesn't mean I'm gonna bring one home from the club though."

Like I said, the first couple of months went by pretty smoothly. We conducted about two nighttime jumps, PT every morning, a zero and qualification range with our weapons—pretty much standard living in Division. We were getting ready for Division Readiness Force 1 (DRF1), so we were in the middle of maintenance on our equipment, such as weapons and night vision, in preparation for our operational readiness survey (ORS). This is mandatory before any unit on the street takes over DRF1. This means you are the first battalion within the brigade that will be the first to deploy in an emergency situation, to include war. The brigade was already on DRB1 status, which meant we'd be the first brigade to deploy within Division. ORS is conducted by members of Division staff and is generally an inspection of a unit's readiness. Randomly, one platoon may get selected to conduct a PT test, one gets inspected on rigging equipment to jump, another will get a packing list and barracks inspection, and a team will go downstairs to the arms room and inspect weapons and other sensitive items as well. Once a unit passes ORS, that afternoon they will officially be on DRF1. I honestly never heard of a unit on the street failing ORS, but that doesn't mean it never happened. Wow, imagine those letters of reprimand to the chain of command.

DRF1 standard is a two-hour recall status for all paratroopers within the battalion. We were not allowed to leave more than a fifty-mile radius of Fort Bragg. Back in the day before cell phones, we had to call in or leave a location and number of where we would be with the company CQs. We were not allowed to have a blood alcohol content above .05—therefore, we were told we couldn't have *any* alcohol for two weeks while on DRF1. If we were caught on a recall formation, or really any formation on DRF1, smelling like booze and above .05 when they made you take a breathalyzer, the punishment was an automatic Field Grade Article 15. I won't get into the specifics of the Uniformed Code of Military Justice (UCMJ), but it meant they could reduce your rank and restrict you to the barracks for a few weeks to a month. NO ALCOHOL!

So what did we do in the barracks that night? We would have a "DRF1 Assumption Party" and get drunk as hell and nobody ever said shit . . . Supposedly, Geraldo Rivera did a small documentary a few years before I got there on a paratrooper's life in the 82nd Airborne Division. I have never seen it, but a lot of guys used to talk about it. Supposedly again, he spent a few days with a platoon in Division and did the night life in Fayetteville and PT with them the next morning where they ran three to five miles and did upper and lower body workouts. That is where the rumor I mentioned earlier on the Reilly Road Class Six selling more alcohol than any other party store in the country came from. He referred to the paratroopers as "the most physically fit alcoholics" in the world.

One morning for PT, we were doing a ruck march and were heading on our way back to garrison (main post). We began hearing sirens in the distance. The closer we got to Division HQ, the louder they got. We were all thinking there was a big fire or something up ahead. By the time we got back to the battalion area, the companies were all in their respected formation areas. The entire Division had been on lockdown. We were ordered to go upstairs and get our ID cards and ID tags and be back in formation in five minutes. We didn't know what the fuck was going on, but we knew it was serious and not some kind of drill. Apparently some disturbed bastard in the 2nd Brigade Combat Team known as the Falcons had gone on a shooting spree at Towle Stadium. The entire Brigade Task Force was formed up in the outdoor stadium either preparing for or just coming back from their DRB1 assumption run. The first brigade to be alerted for war within the division is the DRB1. The assumption run is where the whole brigade conducts a four-mile run at the beginning of this six week cycle. This disturbed individual apparently had an issue with his chain of command and decided he was going to wait in the wood line with a personally owned weapon and open fire when the unit formed up. He did just that. Some Special Forces personnel were going for a run nearby, heard the shots, maneuvered up on him in the woods, and beat the shit out of him. We heard they had broken his jaw. He wounded eighteen paratroopers and killed Falcon 2 (their brigade S-2).

A couple more months went by, and it was time for the 505th to deploy down to the Joint Readiness Training Center (JRTC) at Fort Polk, Louisiana. It was my first JRTC rotation and my first real field training exercise as a grunt. The entire brigade rotates down there as a whole, and usually one company from each battalion goes down a week earlier to conduct and be evaluated on some of the installation's live-fire-maneuver ranges. Our company from 3 Panther Battalion was chosen. The rest of the brigade goes through the eighteen-hour sequence, gets locked down at the personnel holding area right outside of Pope Air Force Base, and conducts a night parachute assault into the simulated war scenario at JRTC.

Our company went down a week early to practice at the live-fire ranges. Each platoon was selected for a certain range for that week. I'll never forget our platoon's. It's where reality slapped me in the face for the first time as a grunt. My squad leader put my ass in check for the first blank-fire certification. All live-fire-maneuver ranges in the Army require the element conducting the range to certify blank fire before anyone is cleared to shoot live. We were selected to do the bunker and trench live-fire-maneuver range. Our squad was the breach squad for the platoon. We set security up for the engineers while they moved up and emplaced the Bangalore torpedo to blow the concertina wire around the target so that the platoon could maneuver through and begin their assault on the trench system.

One key fact I forgot to mention earlier was that my squad leader also had reclassified to 11B. He used to be a 12B, combat engineer—hence why our squad was always the breach squad on these exercises. He selected me as the grappling hook thrower. He taught me to throw it to the left, just outside the wire, and slowly drag it back in order to check for trip wires or any other booby traps. As you dragged the hook back toward yourself, you ensured your head was down in case of a blast. Then you'd repeat by throwing it to the right and then in the middle. The fourth and final throw was into the wire, giving the rope three strong tugs to ensure the wire wasn't mined.

Well, my blank-fire certification didn't go very smoothly. I was a soup sandwich, and all ate up. Squad leader yelled, "Hurry the fuck up, Augi, get your ass up there with that fucking grappling hook!" The support by fire was rocking their two M-60s up on a ridge to our left, onto the objective (the trench). I couldn't get the rope untangled at first, so it was taking me a few seconds to get it unfucked.

"Hurry the fuck up, Augi! Get that motherfucker out and get throwing it, goddamn it!"

I threw it to the left, to the right, in the middle and the last throw, I threw it into the wire without the rope secured to my wrist like I was taught, so the grappling hook was in the wire without me having control of the rope to pull.

"What the fuck are you doing? Low-crawl your ass up there and get that fucking rope, asshole!"

I started crawling up but forgot one thing behind me—my M203.

"You fucking stupid ass, go back and get your fucking weapon!"

So I did. I got the rope, did my three tugs, and low-crawled back to the squad. The engineers then moved up. Oh yeah, did I mention it was a hundred degrees out and we had to wear the old Ranger body armor at this range?

We eventually finished the live-fire range for the day, and we were smoked. I was embarrassed the rest of the day and felt like shit. During the after-action review (AAR), the captain who was evaluating us tried to make me look more like an ass by asking me why it took me four throws to get the hook in the wire, as if I had been too weak to do it the first time.

My squad leader immediately broke in and said, "Because that is what I taught him, sir." That's our standard operating procedure." Then he went into explaining the procedure, according to the combat engineer standards in their technical manual.

The captain just nodded his head and said, "Okay, makes sense."

My squad leader proved to me that he had my back and that nobody was going to sharp-shoot me in front of him. I learned many lessons that day. Lo and behold, when we got back to the World War II barracks we were staying in, he had me outside practicing that damn grappling hook until dinner chow.

I made up for my embarrassment at the live-fire range during the two-week field exercise. They had us spread out all over the drop zone waiting for the brigade to jump in. The night sky was lit up with a full moon. After a while we could hear the birds (aircraft) coming in from the distance and see their red blinking lights on the wings. Most were C-141 Starlifters, which carried about 120 paratroopers each. Soon the sky was full of canopies. I mean *full*. Up until this point in Division, I had never seen anything this awesome and intimidating from the ground.

Once the first wave landed, we were able to move and assemble at our company Steiner aid (a nylon cloth used to designate landing areas) as if we had jumped too. Most of us in these days did not have night vision goggles yet, so the Steiner aides were lit up with regular chem lights so we could all find our assembly area. Once the platoon sergeants and first sergeant had accounted for everyone, we moved out for a long and tiresome two weeks fighting the opposing force (OPFOR).

I won't get into the simulated battles during the next two weeks, but I will highlight one major movement we made that has stuck in my head to this day. We were conducting a company movement through some of the thickest shit I had ever walked through in my time in the Army. Anybody reading this that has been in JRTC knows what I'm talking about. Each of us was carrying at least eighty to a hundred pounds of equipment with our ALICE (all-purpose, lightweight, individual carrying equipment) packs (also know as rucksacks) and LCE (load carrying equipment) vests. Some had more with the AT-4s (shoulder-fired anti-tank weapons), and those poor bastards from the mortar platoon that carried the mortar gun base plates strapped to the back of their rucks. We took turns carrying the two M-60s throughout the platoon. We were moving in a line formation (a single-file line), one paratrooper behind the other. Did I mention how thick and hot it was? Yes, I did, just wanted to make sure you didn't forget.

Our group of friends back in the barracks at Bragg were spread out throughout the company, except for my little buddy nicknamed "Run" who was a few guys ahead of me, but still in my line of sight. He was a little dude. Hell, he was probably carrying the same amount of weight that he weighed himself. I don't know why they called him "Run," it was before my time. He was a mortarman and carrying one of those base plates. This movement looked like a Vietnam movie to me and all I could think about was how much farther we had to go. There was a big log up ahead that everyone had to walk over. Not such an easy task when you are smoked and carrying a hundred pounds.

Run stepped up on the log, and when he came down, his leg snapped like a twig. He went down and began screaming to the top of his lungs. The movement halted, everybody got down and faced out for security. His section sergeant was behind him, and the medic went straight to him too. Next the first sergeant showed up and eventually the commander did too. I remember asking myself how the fuck were they going to get him out of there. The JRTC cadre called in a real-world medical evacuation (MEDEVAC).

Apparently, there must have been a firebreak not too far away. They carried Run out of the bush, and we didn't see him again until we were back at Bragg in the barracks a few weeks later. Needless to say, he was broke (literally) for quite some time after.

After the exercise, back in those run-down barracks, it was recovery phase for everyone. Cleaning and turn-in of issued equipment from the facility was priority. On downtime, we were not allowed to leave post, but we could drink beer and play cards. Phone booths were lined up outside for those that wanted to call home. The 101st Brigade coming in from Fort Campbell was next in the rotation and I remember our brigade commander ordering to keep us separated and that we were not to engage with them what-so-*ever*.

I believe two of us from each platoon were selected to be awarded an impact Army Commendation Medal (ARCOM) for excellent performance during the rotation. I was one of them. I never forgot that. I was looked at from the eyes of the leadership within my platoon as worthy enough to be awarded an ARCOM. An E-4 back in those days really only received ARCOMs as PCS awards, given when you were leaving your unit. I was so proud, not because I had gotten a medal, but because I meant something to this unit. I finally could say that I "broke my cherry" as a grunt in the 82nd Airborne Division.

CHAPTER 3

FIRE TEAM LEADER

ABOUT TEN MONTHS into 3rd Battalion, I made the cut-off score for E-5 (sergeant). I couldn't wait to finally pin on the rank of sergeant and become a team leader. After all, I had over five years' time in service. Like I said, the cut-off scores had been maxed out for some time during the early- and mid-1990s. I considered myself lucky that they dropped enough for me to make it without a tab. Junior enlisted that are Ranger qualified are automatically promoted to sergeant after they complete the process of a promotion board and graduate Primary Leadership Development Course—and rightfully so. I was going, there was no doubt, and my mind was already made up. Expert Infantryman Badge (EIB) testing was right around the corner and then after that, I would be off to the 82nd Pre-Ranger Course. It was mandatory in Division that all paratroopers volunteering for US Army Ranger School must graduate from the 82nd Pre-Ranger Course first. This was to ensure that the individual is totally and completely prepared for the grueling full Ranger course down at Fort Benning. Actually the 82nd had, and probably still has, one of the highest graduation rates of Ranger School in the whole Army.

The problem with making E-5 in our battalion was the command sergeant major's policy that the new NCO had to move companies.

Actually, the policy allowed tabbed individuals to stay, but if you weren't tabbed, you had to move. I never agreed with this, because the original concept is that once you get promoted to an NCO rank, you can no longer remain buddies with friends you "grew up with in the unit." If one day you're drinking buddies and the next you are in charge of them, there was potential for favoritism. I got it. It made sense, but the rule didn't apply to the Rangers that were newly promoted also. It was one of those situations that you just sucked it up and told yourself, it is what it is.

I said goodbye to my buddies, but not really goodbye. My squad leader had finally gotten promoted to E-6. We shook hands and he wished me luck. It wasn't really that sad of a moment because I was only going two buildings down the sidewalk. I didn't even have to move any stuff because me and a buddy of mine from the company mortars were already living off post. He and I were renting rooms in a civilian couple's house in Fayetteville. They were a cool, young couple who liked to party, so after a few months of hanging out with them, they asked us if we wanted to move into their house and pay them $100 per month for each of our rooms. It was a party every night with a lot of young single women constantly over. Enough of that subject—that's another book by itself, and I'm not even bullshitting.

I was in the Battalion S-1 Shop awaiting my transfer orders to go to my new company. Here came two NCOs from that company to pick me up, squad leaders from the platoon I was going to. They both kept staring at me and looking at my chest. I knew what they were looking at and what they were wondering. *Why does this guy only have "bald-headed" jump wings and no EIB?* I got a "Tab check" on my left shoulder from both of them, too, even though only one of them had a Tab. They said hello, told me what platoon I was going to, and that when I was done with the S-1, I should go over to the company. I guarantee they weren't there to "pick me up," but to size me up. That's the shit that used to piss me off about that place sometimes. But, it is what it is, right?

I dropped my packet off at the orderly room and walked straight to the platoon command post. I didn't even bother waiting to see the first sergeant. All I wanted to do was meet my new squad leader, leave Fort Bragg, go home, and crack a beer. I didn't even want to meet my new soldiers yet. *I'll meet them first thing tomorrow,* I thought. It's not like I needed to know what time to be in the next morning. The timeline didn't change from company to company: be in at 0600 and be standing on the rocks by 0620 waiting for PT formation.

So my new squad leader was an E-6, tabbed, and had a CIB above his jump wings. He wasn't jumpmaster qualified and seemed kind of out of shape (that's me being polite). He had longer hair than most people on the street. Hell, he had his hair feathered for Christ's sake—very unusual to see in Division. Honestly, though, he was a great guy. I mean he was one of the politest NCOs I ever met in Division; fuck it, I'll go as far as saying throughout my entire time in the Army thus far.

I found out the next morning at PT that he was on permanent profile (exempt from full duty), pretty much for everything except for breathing. He had some kind of digestive disease they had discovered in him about six months prior, and I believe he was waiting out his time to retire because he had like nineteen years in or something like that. He probably had gotten into trouble in the past if he was a Ranger-qualified E-6 that could never make E-7. Of course, I didn't ask. I never understood why they didn't remove the poor bastard from the line and put him in HQ Company in one of the S shops until he retired. That would open a slot for another squad leader to come in.

He told me I was the Bravo Team leader and brought in the Alpha Team leader in the command post to introduce us to each other. At first, I was like, *Here we go again.* He was about my age and had all the bells and whistles on his uniform. At first I thought he was going to be sizing me up like the other guys had earlier, but he didn't. He actually was a really good guy who immediately took me under his wing. A good-looking young man with blond hair and blue eyes, I remember thinking that this guy must be getting all the ass in town, until he opened his mouth. He had a big old dip of Copenhagen in *and* all over his mouth. That shit was all in his teeth and all over his lips. I dipped too—hell, the whole division dipped and smoked cigarettes—but my mouth didn't look like his. I mean—Damn . . .

All teasing aside, he was a good guy. Overall, during the next couple of days, I came to realize that everybody in this company turned out to be good people. It was a tight company, and everybody seemed to have everybody's back. Even the two squad leaders I initially met in the S-1 Shop turned out to be cool. As a matter of fact, a couple of months down the road, I became a team leader for one of them.

"Mr. Copenhagen" introduced me to the squad and to my guys in particular. He told me that he didn't look at the squad as A- or B-team because the reality was that our squad leader really couldn't do much, which pretty much meant that he and I, as the team leaders, would be running it together. He was happy that he finally had some help. So he and I hit it off pretty well. For the next couple of weeks, we were always taking the squad outside and doing some kind of tactical training. Either across the street in Area J, or simply in the battalion area. If anything, we would take white engineer tape and stake off four corners on the ground and run them through room-clearing drills all afternoon. If we weren't training them on something, we'd have them get into PT uniform and take them on a run through the firebreaks behind Division Headquarters until close of business, or, in civilian terms, the end of the work day.

It was EIB time! My first time training and testing for the coveted badge that signifies excellence within any infantry unit across the Army as a whole. Mr. Copenhagen didn't have to be a lane grader or even take the squad through the process because he was already slated to attend the next jumpmaster course, which would start in a couple of days. He did tell me something before we started the EIB training that I always kept with me and would tell my soldiers in the future: "If you care enough and want the EIB, you'll get it. Just like taking any other test, you have to study. So do not leave a station until you practice a test and pass it according to the way the lane grader taught you—and make sure he knows your face. Make him sick of seeing you and you'll pass on test day." He was absolutely right on.

We all had to assemble on the hill behind Division HQ. The EIB Tactical Operation Center (TOC) was a large tent with a set of bleachers next to it. EIB testing was a brigade-run function back in the day. It consisted of a full week of training, including the weekend and one week of testing on approximately thirty or so hands-on tasks, starting with a PT test and finishing with a grueling twelve- mile foot march conducted within three hours. Each regiment in Division attempted to conduct an EIB test at least once a year. There was one man who was in charge and was the overseer of the next two weeks of our lives—the brigade command sergeant major.

Okay, here it comes. I've been waiting to introduce this man to everyone reading this. We'll call him Command Sergeant Major "X," but if you served anytime in Division from 1994 to 2005, you'll know exactly who I'm talking about. He was a short Black man with the loudest, raspiest, deepest voice I ever heard. Command Sergeant Major X was actually a legend within Division. I believe he spent all thirty-three years of service, except two years on the trail and maybe one or two tours in Korea, right on Ardennes Street.

He walked out of the tent and started his introduction for the next two weeks. "Welcome to the Regimental EIB testing, Airborne! Let's get this shit straight! This ain't the goddamn *FREE* IB, it's the goddamn *E*IB, and none y'all walkin' outta here with a free pass, Airborne!

"Now listen up, on Lindsey Field, there's gonna be two formations. There's gonna be a receiving formation and there's gonna be a spectator formation! I'll betcha two fat babies and a jelly doughnut that most y'all is gonna be standin' in my goddamn spectator formation! And surprise! I got somethin' for y'all that think you just gonna fail out on day one and go sit yo' lazy asses back in the barracks! Y'all *belong* to Brigade for the next two weeks; therefore, I got plenty of landscapin' you'll be doin' around my EIB site, Airborne! I got plenty of rakin' and sandbaggin' for yo' asses in order to keep my lanes lookin' beautiful, Airborne! Don't get in any goddamn pissin' contests with any of my graders either, Airborne! If you gotta problem with the grader's decision, you don't say shit to 'em! He'll call me or my NCOIC to come down and dispute yo' goddamn problem, Airborne! And I'll tell ya this: I'm not gonna even try to bullshit ya. Nine times outta ten, I'm gonna take the grader's side, Airborne, and you gonna lose! Good luck and have yo' selves an Airborne day!"

That was my first EIB briefing. He then turned it over to the brigade S-3 NCOIC and went back into the tent. Reading this, one might think it is a little exaggerated. I assure you, it is not. That is how the legendary Command Sergeant Major X used to convey his point to all subordinate paratroopers. I'll have some other memorable snippets from him later on.

Training for the whole week went from sunup to sundown. I got to know the lanes like the back of my hand. I felt real comfortable and confident. I was actually excited because I could just about guarantee that I was going to be sewing an EIB above my wings the next week.

I was wrong. I failed my first EIB testing.

The first two days went perfect. I passed the PT test, day and night land navigation, and the entire second day of hands-on tasks. Day three, I had hand grenades and failed twice (double no-go) on the twenty-meter throw into an enemy fighting position. The lane grader handed me my score sheet with a big old *no-go* on it and I was instructed to go turn it into the TOC. If you double no-go any station, you are dismissed from the test and must leave the site. Now, each EIB candidate has the right to appeal any no-go during the testing, but the grader must call down the S-3 NCOIC or the brigade command sergeant major and they will determine whether a retest is valid or not. Since Command Sergeant Major X would have been the one to do that, it wouldn't be pretty.

I did not appeal because, after all, I had failed a task that was black and white: you either got the grenade in the hole or you didn't. *Almost* doesn't count on this one. I walked up the hill, turned in my score sheet, and did the famous "EIB walk of shame" back to my battalion. I got into the barracks, and everybody was gone except a couple of NCOs that were fucking off. So I got into my Chevy S-10 pickup and drove home for the rest of the day. It is what it is, right?

The next few months went by, and we were into the fall season. What a busy summer. Of course, it's busy in Division twenty-four-seven, 365 days a year. We went from EIB right into All-American Week, an annual celebration of the Division from past to present. I always thought it was a good week of competition and fun. You kind of were allowed to let your hair down a little and have a good time until the Division Review, which is the last hurrah of the week. The week always (I'm sure still does) started with a formation at the parade field across from Jumpmaster School. The entire division conducted a four mile run and, when it was over, received a speech of motivation from the division commander, and the week began.

The competitions consisted of almost everything from volleyball to tug of war to boxing. I always volunteered to do the UH-60 jump competition on Sicily Drop Zone (DZ). We'd go up in the bird and they'd drop us a few thousand feet above ground level. The goal of this competition was to land on or as close to the point of impact that was marked out on the drop zone. I can't really remember, but I think the spots were marked out in engineer tape with colored smoke or something. Didn't matter. Realistically, there's no controlling a T-10C or T-10D parachute anyway.

Back in the day, the World War II veterans would always visit during All-American Week. In the nineties, there were still a good number of them that would come in from all over the country, and we *did* respect the shit out of them.

I talked to one old-timer from World War II at a cookout outside of 3rd Brigade Headquarters. He asked me, "How many jumps do you have young man?" I remember answering, "Oh, not too many, only about twenty, sir."

He said, "Twenty? Hell, that's a shitload! I only have five. And four of them were COMBAT!"

Wow. I remember feeling very humbled talking to these real world heroes. Four combat jumps? That shit is unheard of. Can you imagine having four "mustard stains" on your jump wings? A mustard stain was slang for the gold combat star sewn into the parachute badge. Our brigade commander had two on his. He had jumped into Grenada and Panama, a decade earlier. He was old-school, with the old Airborne Ranger on the 75th scroll he wore on his right shoulder.

There were other events during All-American Week, such as a nighttime mass-tactical (mass-tac) airborne assault put on as a show at Sicily DZ. Most of the visitors for the week would go to see it. VIPs would come in from around the base, Fayetteville, and maybe even the state to sit on the bleachers and watch the massive jump and simulated assault on the ground afterward.

The final event for the week was the dreaded Division review. It was a massive parade of every unit in Division. Every "swinging dick" on Ardennes was part of it. It was on Pike Field, at the end of Gruber Road, across the street from the confidence course. It was a two-day event, with one full day of practice and the next day with the actual parade itself. The uniform was LCE with everything stripped off except for one canteen and a bayonet on one side. Clean, new, starched BDUs, and highly spit-shined jump boots. But the spit shine on the jump boots seemed irrelevant because by the time we got to Pike Field on the morning of the actual parade, they were already fucked-up and dusty. Everybody within the ranks carried an M16A2, no matter what their assigned weapon was. There was the first rank of each infantry battalion that would carry M60s and the rank behind them carried M249s—squad automatic weapons, or simply SAWs. Oh yeah, everybody had to have a fresh haircut too. We all called it the biggest "dog and pony show" of the year.

Getting your LCE ready for it was a pain in the ass. We had to cut all the tie-down off, strip our ammo pouches, first aid kit, compass, canteens, extra ammo pouches, buttpacks, knives, D-Rings, and anything else we could tape on or tie off to it. After one All-American Week, you learned to go to buy yourself a "parade LCE" and put that shit away in your wall locker.

The practice day was hot, long, and drawn-out. We had to go through rehearsal two or three times until the division command sergeant major was satisfied. The day of the parade itself was no joke either. We actually had to stand at parade rest longer while all the VIP speeches were given. Troopers would fall out within the ranks and would have to get pulled to the back of the formations. "Don't lock your fucking knees," was said throughout the ranks. The best part was actually marching and the review itself, because you got to move your legs after an hour or so. When the words "pass and review" were given over the loudspeakers at the end of all the speeches, you could hear a loud sigh within the ranks of every battalion standing on Pike Field. One thing in Division that you can bet your ass on is that unless your unit is deployed, you ain't getting out of Division Review. Every May you can count on it.

After All-American Week, our battalion was getting ready to do two long weeks in the field for the Intensive Training Cycle. ITC is a series of team-, squad-, and platoon-size live-fire maneuver ranges. It can and normally did get pretty intense because it's sunup to sunup. That's right, day and night live-fire certifications, and every team in the company must complete both before the company can move to the next range. Then you repeat with squad live-fires on another range, then platoon. My years in Division, most field training exercises would culminate with a good old-fashioned twenty-kilometer foot march back to the battalion area.

Just prior to the cycle, I told the platoon sergeant I was ready to go to Pre-Ranger Course and start the Ranger School process. He was cool about it, as he wasn't tabbed either. He said, "I want you to wait until after we're done with ITC, then you can go. Hell, you and I can go together." I knew better than that because E-7s didn't have to attend Pre-Ranger Course, they could just walk right into Ranger School itself. "Okay, roger, Sergeant." I understood the importance of getting our squads and platoons through ITC. After all, that's what we were there for; that's what you do in peace time—train for war. Too easy.

When we got back a couple of weeks later, we had a week of downtime, cleaning, and conducting maintenance on our equipment—pretty typical after coming out of the field. One afternoon I was walking down the hallway, and I heard the first sergeant holler, "Sergeant Augi!" I turned around and went back toward his office.

"Yes, First Sergeant!"

"Come on in. I got a Levy Notice on you." Being put on Levy, was a nice way of saying you had been drafted to PCS somewhere.

"Where to, First Sergeant?"

"Korea."

"What, Korea? Fuck that, First Sergeant. I can't go to Korea. I already started packing for PRC!"

He apologized and gave me the estimated report time, which was still a few months away. I asked if he or someone in Division could get me out of it, but he couldn't. Division would not pay for a soldier to attend Ranger School if they knew you were leaving for another installation. Once a soldier becomes Ranger qualified, that unit gets to keep him assigned to them for a year minimum. Now, if a soldier is actually in Ranger School at the time they come down on Levy back at their unit, the unit can get his orders deleted. That's just how the system works.

Fucking Korea. Give me a break.

It is what it is, right?

CHAPTER 4

OUR THIRTY-DAY DEPLOYMENT TO PANAMA

I WASN'T DUE to head to Korea for a few months. In the meantime, the platoon sergeant was making some leadership changes within the platoon. Our sick squad leader was finally moved out of the company and went to HQ's company. Mr. Copenhagen moved into the squad leader slot, I went to another line squad, and an E-4 moved into my spot. The platoon was thinning out, with people PCSing or moving companies, like I would soon do. Plus there were always a few shitbags and some who were broke. Hell, it got to where each line squad had a squad leader and one team leader. It was an easy move, like I said. Everybody pretty much got along well with each other.

Another ORS and DRF1 Cycle came and went. One thing about Division, every event rotates around and back again. On my last DRF1 Cycle before my PCS came up, things went a little different. We actually got an alert call out at 0400 one morning. I drove in wearing BDUs. All my equipment was already in a locker in the basement of the company. The arms room was already opened, and soldiers were drawing their weapons and other sensitive items. We all formed up on the rocks and started getting accountability of our personnel. Our whole squad was there, except for the squad leader. He and the others were getting briefed by the platoon sergeant in the command post.

We all sat down on the rocks, leaned up against our ALICE packs and closed our eyes. I stayed awake and lit up a cigarette while waiting on the platoon leadership. They came out with the first sergeant behind them. I told our squad leader we were 100 percent with personnel and all equipment. He said, "Cool. Thanks and good job."

We were hoping and pretty much expecting the first sergeant to tell the company to stand down and put all equipment back in the arms room. We figured it was just another two-hour recall drill for accountability and maybe a piss test to go along with it. Nope! We couldn't get so lucky. If memory serves me correctly, we had to take our duffel bags and stack them on Lindsey Field. The chow hall was open, and we were told to go eat breakfast and get back on the rocks. While we ate, the word was already going around that this was going to be a training sequence for the next twenty-four to forty-eight hours, and it was. The eighteen-hour sequence had begun at 0400 when we got the call.

We loaded up on the cattle trucks that were already parked on Ardennes in front of Lindsey Field. It's remarkable how fast they got the shit moving in that place. We had our ALICE packs, Ballistic Helmets, LCEs, and weapons. We pretty much knew what was coming up: lockdown at the personnel holding area (PHA), followed by a good old-fashioned nighttime battalion mass-tactical jump into someplace. As we moved down Ardennes toward the PHA, I remember noticing it was still dark outside. We had done all this shit before the sun even came up and already felt worn out. We hadn't even gotten started with the real chaos yet.

The PHA was a series of old white World War II barracks just outside of Green Ramp. It was the unit holding area, which was fenced in because nobody was allowed to leave or come in except for the company chains of command or the first sergeant and supply sergeant in order to go back and forth to the battalion area to pick up mermite chow cans (these held our hot or cold food) and take back the empty containers. It was the final planning area of a unit's upcoming operations.

After a few hours of lying around, waiting on news from the leadership, the platoon leaders came in with the operations order. Our mission was to jump into Holland DZ and secure the small enemy complex on the northern edge. TOT, or time over target, when the jump begins over the drop zone, was like 0100 or 0200. Squad leaders had us rig our ALICE packs to jump and then go outside the barracks to begin room-clearing drills. After a while, we ate an MRE (meal ready to eat, which is prepackaged and not out of the mermite can) for lunch and did more room clearing.

One of the squad leaders said, "Okay, it's euchre time," and he broke out a deck of cards. We played euchre in the old barracks until dinner chow, which was mermite hot chow outside. Chili-mac over rice, washed down with red or orange warm Kool-Aid, was my favorite. If you got ice in the Kool-Aid, that was a bonus. Then I'd head to the coffee jug and fill up my canteen cup full, sit back, light up a Marlboro Red, and sip my coffee. If we were still hungry, we just waited for the magic words from the first sergeant: "First PLT, all your guys ate? Second? Third? HQs? Okay, go get seconds!"

It was nighttime and time to head down to Green Ramp. We all got out our camo sticks and started painting our faces, necks, backs of our necks, ears, and some on the backs of our hands. The rule on the street was if you went west on Gruber Road, you'd better have your ballistic helmet and your face painted. Everybody lined up in two single-file lines with their ALICE packs hanging over one shoulder and began the long walk across the open field to the big parking lot outside the hanger. Remember, this is before they built the new high-speed hanger buildings with the overhead mock door systems out front.

Once we arrived, we broke down into *chalks* (aircraft numbers). I believe this was only our battalion conducting this operation, since we were the DRF1 battalion, and this was generally our test of conducting everything to division standard. Each company had their own chalks, maybe two C-130s per. I believe we each had our own objectives on separate DZs. For example, we had Holland, another company or two had Sicily, with their Headquarters and Headquarters Company—their medics, mortars, and scouts—spread out within. The jumpmasters put us through sustained airborne training, practice parachute landing falls, mock door training, parachute issue and rigging, jumpmaster personnel inspection, and finally, loading the aircraft. The dominating smell of jet fuel filled the air around us. After we got packed in like sardines aboard the aircraft, it became nap time until we got the ten-minute warning in the air. Most jumps in Division out of a high-performance aircraft had a minimum of an hour flight time prior to exiting. That way the pilots got their flight hours in.

It was my first time being number one jumper, where I had to stand by in the doorway until the red light changed to green and I got the famous "Go!" from the jumpmaster. Normally I dropped at eight hundred feet above ground level. When I stepped out of the aircraft, the force was pretty powerful because the aircraft was moving pretty fast. Actually, upon nearing the drop zone, the aircraft would slow to approximately 120 knots, which equals around 138 miles per hour. I counted to four thousand. At the end of the four thousand count, if I felt no opening shock, I was to immediately activate my reserve parachute. But that never happened to me. After the opening shock of my canopy, it became quiet and peaceful as I floated down to the ground. I didn't waste any time, and untied my equipment tie-downs and lowered my equipment.

I'll give you the sustained airborne training or "prejump version" of landing in a parachute. At night, especially when it's chilly or cold, the ground would come up on you before you knew it. Pull your risers into your chest to slow yourself down as much as possible. Keep your feet and knees together, knees slightly bent. Keep your elbows tight into your side, with eyes open, and chin on chest. Make a parachute landing fall by hitting all five points of contact. They are the balls of the feet, the calf, the thigh, the buttocks, and the push-up muscle. Never make a standing landing. Back in reality, it's either a "crash" or a soft and easy landing, depending on the wind. Usually, it's feet, head, ass.

After linking up with the company on the drop zone, once we had 75 percent accountability of everyone, we moved out and began our assault on the small building complex. After our company cleared and secured the objective, all reporting went up to the battalion commander that the area was secured and the mission accomplished. The sun was coming up over the drop zone and as daylight was getting brighter, the CO called for the "end of exercise" (ENDEX). Years later, for some reason, it became unauthorized for leaders to call ENDEX; instead it changed to "change of mission." The cattle trucks lined up in the entry area of the drop zone. We walked over with our equipment, got onboard, and headed back to Ardennes Street. About twenty-seven hours after the call out the morning prior, it was over.

One company within 3 Panther was tasked to deploy to Panama and it just happened to be ours. We were to go down there for thirty days with the primary mission of being on quick reactionary force standby if needed for riot control. It was the sixth or seventh anniversary of the 1989 US invasion of Panama (also known as Operation Just Cause), where US forces had captured the dictator, Manuel Noriega, and removed him from power. There apparently had been demonstrations outside of Fort Sherman and Fort Amador within Panama throughout the years during the December anniversary of the invasion. By this time, both installations in Panama, which were strategically located on both ends of the Panama Canal, were dwindling down. The jungle operations training center (JOTC) was in the middle of closing down with Fort Sherman, and by 1999, both installations were turned over to the government of Panama.

Going to Panama in December was fine with me and pretty much everybody in the company. I had never been to Central America. Hell, up until that point, I had never been south of Florida. The only problem with this timeline was that it was going to be during Christmas and New Year's. I was fine with it anyway. It was going to be my last hurrah with this company and 3 Panther before I had to leave for Korea. It ended up being one of the best months in my time in the Army.

We arrived at Fort Sherman, Panama on or about December 1, 1996. Man, it was beautiful! Palm trees everywhere, white sand, and the temperature was a nice, breezy eighty-five degrees. You couldn't ask for a better deployment, and the best part was, we were thousands of miles *away from the flagpole,* away and out of sight of our headquarters, which was back at Bragg. It was just our company and our company alone. The barracks building they had us staying in was an open bay. I don't even think we had bunks to sleep on. Instead, they had sleeping cots stacked up, so we issued them out, and everybody set theirs up within the bay. There were weapons racks, so each platoon was responsible to lock up and guard their own weapons for the duration of the month. The platoon leader, platoon sergeant, squad leaders, and team leaders were all down on one end. Hell, we didn't even have wall lockers, so it was living out of our duffel bags—too easy.

I still folded and stacked my clothes underneath my cot, especially my civilian clothes. Oh yeah, and we did have a few sets of civilian clothes to wear. We knew it was going to be a good deployment when the packing list said unlimited amount of civilian clothes, as long as you could fit everything into one duffel bag and your rucksack. They pretty much gave us that first day off, so we found out where the chow hall was and, more importantly, the pool area.

None of us thought to pack a swimsuit, so fuck it, we wore civilian shorts. We all went swimming all day, laid out in the sun, and looked at all the fine women that were around us. Unfortunately, most if not all of them were dependents of soldiers, but sometimes that really didn't matter. Anyhow, it was something to look at. Even the CO, XO, and first sergeant joined us.

Oh yeah, I never did mention what the XO is: *executive officer,* usually the highest ranking lieutenant in the company, who generally had already completed their platoon leader time. Their primary duty is all logistic and training coordination, such as ranges, chow, ammunition, transportation, and to oversee supply functions. They work very closely with the supply sergeant and first sergeant. They are also second in command of the company. Anyway, it was a great first day at Fort Sherman.

The next couple of days weren't bad either. As a matter of fact, there wasn't really a bad day until we had to go train in the jungle toward the end of the trip (*la jungle in Spanish*, which we pronounced "*hoongla*"). They had the post military police (MPs) detachment give us classes on riot control and then had us conduct drills with shields and billy-clubs for the entire morning duration for the first week. Notice I said "mornings." After the training, we were set free to go fuck off again for the rest of the day as long as the platoon sergeants knew where we were generally located, which was either at the pool, PX, food court, or the little club they had over by the housing area. We were not allowed to leave post, so that wasn't a problem.

We couldn't drink during the day, only after dinner chow. But the CO and first sergeant made it abundantly clear to all paratroopers in the company right off the bat: if anybody gets drunk and into trouble, no more alcohol for the entire company for the remainder of the thirty days. So if "Joe" started getting stupid, we'd snatch his ass up, take him back to the barracks, and tell him his ass wasn't allowed to leave until the next morning. God forbid if he disobeyed us and attempted to sneak out. He'd spend the remainder in Panama in the front-leaning rest, or on his back, with his feet elevated six inches off the ground. There's nothing more dangerous in the infantry as a whole, than a pissed off team leader or squad leader, especially back in those days.

After the boring riot-control classes from the MPs, we got to do some cool water training. That's actually funny that we hated the riot control portion because that was our primary reason for even being down there, but we didn't give a fuck, it still sucked ass. Our company received a class on setting up and crossing a one-rope bridge over a body of water with our equipment. One of our platoon sergeants and one of his squad leaders gave the class and we spent most of the day learning it and going through it a couple of times. Every day was laid-back, without much of a timeline for anything. We'd get the class and then sit back, eat an MRE, and shoot the shit. It was definitely a break from Ardennes Street back home.

For a few days we got to go to the JOTC HQ, which still had a small cadre and a special forces detachment working there. I'm pretty sure JOTC at Fort Sherman was already slowing down rotating units through by this time, but some of the training areas were still open. So we were given the tour of their zoo, showing the wildlife we could expect to see in the "hoongla": different kinds of lizards, small snakes, monkeys, leopards, raccoons, badgers, caiman alligators, and sloths. It was the first time I had ever seen a live sloth before and it's true—they're some slow bastards. They're also ugly little motherfuckers too. The Special Forces "tour guide" strongly advised us *not* to fuck with them out in the hoongla. They may naturally move slower than paint dries, but if provoked, they would attack quickly, and the little bastards had nails that looked like Freddy Krueger's. Later on, one of my soldiers got to find out first hand. He started throwing rocks at one, moved up on it, and it swiped at him, very quickly. Stupid ass!

We then finished the tour off with one of the largest anacondas in captivity. They had a name for it, but I can't remember. I even tried to research the history of Fort Sherman zoo and couldn't find it. The snake had been in captivity there for twenty or so years and was over twenty feet long. The guide told us they would feed it a live goat as a meal and a monkey as a treat. There was an obstacle course behind the zoo, and of course, the first sergeant made us all go through it. I'll admit, it was a little bit of an ass-smoker. But it was all good; we were still at the pool by 1400.

The next day was the best day down there. We got to learn and do some high-speed shit. The Special Forces crew gave us a crash course on helocasting, and we got to jump out of the back of a CH-47

Chinook into the Chagres River. For those who do not know what helocasting is, it's a method of airborne insertion out of a helicopter into a body of water. You basically walk out the back of the aircraft, approximately thirty feet above the water and wait to be picked up and extracted by boat. This is a pretty common method of insertion for special operation and light infantry units.

The Special Forces crew put us through a little crash course training session that lasted about two hours. First they gave us all a small swim test in the body of water outside their facility. It wasn't a full-blown combat water survival test like Ranger School, but a simple twenty-meter down and back. Even though you had to wear a life preserver, you still had to be able to swim. I think our company only had about two or three nonswimmers. We then went through their mock door training a couple of times to ensure we knew exactly what to do in the aircraft and how to properly exit, which was obviously feet first. The drop was going to be a *thirty and thirty*: thirty feet in the air at the speed of thirty knots, or thirty-four miles per hour. We were instructed to exit with our arms crossed over our chests and our legs crossed. The instructor explained that crossing our legs would prevent our balls from going up into our throats as we impacted the water.

I remember flying for a while. I'm sure the pilots needed to get their flight time in. The door remained opened for the entire flight. The cast master was strapped into a harness to a d-ring on the floor. As we flew through the canyons and above the hoongla, we kept noticing he would disappear outside the aircraft and then pull himself back inside by the A7A cargo strap he was linked into. I'm quite sure that was a safety violation, but we thought it was kind of funny. It wouldn't have been too funny if the damn strap had frayed and ripped and sent this adrenaline junkie crashing into the canopy of trees below.

We were given the one-minute warning; everybody stood up and grabbed the static line cable that ran through the bird and started moving toward the rear. I don't remember the exact commands for helocasting, but he gave us the command "Go" individually about one or two seconds apart so that we landed at least a hundred meters apart from one another. It was a pretty rough slam into the water, but nothing was hurting. Our instructions were to tread water and wait for the zodiac boats to come pick us up. This is when my ass got puckered and this little high-speed exercise wasn't fun anymore.

This was my first time ever in saltwater. When I was four years old, my parents took me to see *Jaws* and I was instantly traumatized. After watching that movie, my parents could barely get me into the bath tub. Although I did learn how to swim at a young age, even in fresh water, I always had a fear of sharks—as most people do.

I remember telling myself, "Damn, this water really is salty as hell. Now I know why it's called 'saltwater,' right?" The guy up ahead of me hollered, "Hey, Sergeant Augi!" I said, "Yeah, what's up?"

"You want some trivia?"

"Sure, what do you got for me?"

He said, "This is where Jacques Cousteau's son got killed."

I replied, "Oh yeah, how?"

"He was eaten by hammerhead sharks! We happen to be in hammerhead shark-infested water!"

I almost passed out. I'm not shitting. As a matter of fact, if I had seen a dorsal fin, I damn sure would have. The boats picked us up and we got off the water.

The time down in Panama was getting near the end. What do you know? They had to put together a field exercise for us out in the hoongla. It was too good to be true. We just knew they weren't going to let us go through the entire month down there without a blank-fire force-on-force exercise. The CO and the platoon leaders had put together a lane and each platoon went through as the assault force with a squad of another platoon playing the OPFOR. The XO found us plenty of blank ammunition and pyrotechnics such as smoke, star clusters, and overhead flares.

The objective was pretty easy—it was a small shack with a three- or four-story tower next to it. It was in a little open area next to a firebreak. Of course, we don't use firebreaks, and guess who the lead squad was to navigate through the bullshit? Guess who was the point man? Oh yeah, did I tell you it was nighttime too? It wasn't bad, though, because we only had to move about five or six hundred meters. I had a set of the old PVS-7B night vision goggles on my head. They only really worked if there was some kind of illumination out. That's nonexistent in the hoongla. I stopped for a second, took them off, and kept them around my neck, along with the old head harness still underneath my ballistic helmet, for the duration of the small movement. These head harnesses for night vision were before the helmet mounts were created. Hell, this was before everybody even got a pair of night vision goggles. In those days, it was really only the leadership that had them.

Anyway, I got us close enough to the objective, and we went into a security halt. We didn't have rucks, just assault packs on our backs, so we didn't set up an objective rally point by the book. Instead, the platoon leader grabbed a few guys from the reserve squad and went out on reconnaissance (recon) to locate and check out the objective. He then dropped off the two security teams on each side of the objective, facing down the firebreaks.

I about shit my pants when I heard the first howler monkey above us sound off. I remember thinking, *Well, the enemy knows we're here now. Good luck having the element of surprise in this place.* Dudes in my platoon that have been here before for JOTC rotations said the howler monkeys used to shit in their hands and throw it down on the soldiers beneath them.

The platoon leader came back with one guy and then grabbed the weapons squad, took them up and pointed out where he wanted them to sit in the support-by-fire position. Then the rest of us moved up and prepositioned for the assault. The platoon was in place and prepared to go to work. The platoon leader popped an overhead illumination parachute flare that lit up the area, which invited the M-60s to open fire onto the objective.

After about a minute, I popped a star cluster for the initial shift fire and then moved up my team for the internal support. Once set in, I ordered my guys to start shooting at building one and over to building two, which was the tower. My squad leader shot another star cluster for the support by fire to lift fire. Once confirmed, I ordered lift fire on building one. He then led B Team to stack up outside to enter and clear the building. (It was simply a big, four-cornered room.)

We were still firing on building two. My squad leader had building one secured, so he popped a chem light and dropped it outside the entrance to mark it as cleared. The platoon sergeant and the medic then moved into it and marked it as the casualty collection point, using red chem lights in the shape of a cross and set outside the entrance as well. Simultaneously, I ordered lift fire on the tower, then the next squad moved up to begin clearing it. Once it was cleared, the platoon leader gave the reports to the CO, squad leaders consolidated and reorganized their troops for security around the objective, and we prepared to move off on command. Then the word was given. "ENDEX!" Too easy.

FM 7-8 is the field manual for the infantry squad and platoon (known as the Infantry Bible). This operation wasn't exactly step-by-step FM 7-8, but it was damn close to it, and we got it done with a short platoon of minimal personnel. Actually, I have to ask those reading this that have served in the infantry, was it really ever *exactly* 7-8 step-by-step?

We got our personnel and equipment checks completed, gave it to the platoon sergeant and then we moved off the objective. We walked down the firebreak to an open area with two five-ton trucks parked at it and began an after-action review with the CO and first sergeant. We did pretty good overall, but we could have used more smoke on the objective for concealment, and we were told to slow it down a bit. First Sergeant said, "Hey guys, if you have the equipment, use it. It may save lives." As we all looked at each other, we realized some of us NCOs still had unused smoke grenades on our LCEs. "Dammit," we muttered—but at least we had the shift and lift signals down to a science. Being told to slow down a bit is always better than, "form up and run through it again."

We then got on the trucks and moved back to main post and the barracks, where we cleaned our weapons, showered, and went to bed. It was a good training mission and a damn good thirty-day deployment. Anyway, no riot ever broke out near or on Fort Sherman from the Panamanian civilian population.

CHAPTER 5

THE TOUGHEST PLATOON SERGEANT I EVER HAD

A LITTLE OVER a year later, I was driving down Interstate 77 from Michigan, my home state, just coming off PCS leave after my time in Korea. I was on my way back to Fayetteville, North Carolina and my second PCS to Fort Bragg and the 82nd Airborne Division. I really did miss it, and it felt good driving through all the scenery of the Virginias, knowing I was heading back to Fayetteville.

I was excited for a few reasons. First, I wondered what brigade they were going to put me back into. Second, I wondered if I was going to be assigned as a squad leader, since I'd made it out of Korea as an E-5 promotable. Third, I was excited that I'd get to visit old friends that I'm sure were mostly still there in the 505th and particularly 3 Panther. My plan was to go visit and maybe stay with my old civilian roommates I had rented from before. I knew they had moved from the house we lived in to another neighborhood. They had said on the phone that it was cheaper for them, so they had to move. I figured it was because they weren't getting any more money from me and my buddy, who had gotten out of the Army and went back home before I left for Korea. Anyway, I was excited to get back.

I hadn't realized until I got there that Korea would be pretty much an entire year of being in the field training with some time off here and there. Literally, if you were in one of the two light infantry battalions, you lived in the field. One thing was for sure, you definitely left that place more technically and tactically proficient. I got to do the entire year as a line squad leader and thought I did a pretty good job at it too. At least all the first sergeants and command sergeant major of the battalion thought I did. When I went to the E-5 Promotion Board at battalion headquarters, I wasn't asked one single question. The command sergeant major asked if any of the board members had any questions for me and they said no. He told me I was maxed out on board points, with no questions, and then said, "Have a nice day."

I stood up, went to the position of attention, rendered a hand salute and shouted, "Stands Alone, Sergeant Major!" He replied, "Currahee!" *Stands Alone* is the motto for the 506th Parachute Infantry Regiment. "Currahee," which means "stands alone" in Cherokee, is the response. I did a right face and walked out. If I could have, I would have done back flips all the way out of the auditorium where it was held. All I needed now was to attend and graduate Basic Noncommissioned Officer Course back at Fort Benning, make the cut-off score, and a staff sergeant I would be. That would have to be coordinated when I got back to Bragg.

One of the most memorable moments I and everybody else in our company at the time had was when the battalion commander fired our first sergeant after a training exercise. He was the toughest, most no-shit, most down-to-business battalion commander I ever met or served with in the Army. No offense to any of my other former commanders reading this. We conducted a nighttime battalion air-assault mission with a good old-fashioned "movement to daylight," culminating with a massive attack on a complex. It was January and very cold outside, especially when the sun was just coming up. Prior to hitting our company portion of the objective, we got an injured mortar guy. Another mortar guy with an injured leg from carrying the extra weight like back during my first JRTC rotation that I discussed in an earlier chapter, but not as gruesome. First Sergeant left two or three guys with him from the mortar section, the company forward observer (FO) with his radio, and the rest of the company continued on the mission. We weren't that far from the objective anyway.

After the mission was complete, the first sergeant formed us up, took accountability from each platoon, and told us to get on the trucks to head back to base. The headquarter's platoon sergeant reminded him that he still had some soldiers back there with the wounded guy. The first sergeant told him to get his guys on the truck and that he'd go get them and take them back to base in his vehicle.

Well, he must have got sidetracked by something because he forgot them, and they remained out in the woods in freezing temperatures. A couple hours went by, and we were all back in the company area cleaning weapons. I just happened to be in the company HQ making copies of 2404s (maintenance record forms) for my squad and lo and behold, here came the battalion commander and command sergeant major with the few soldiers that were left behind during the mission. As I looked out the window, I said to myself, *Oh shit, this ain't gonna be good. Here comes Currahee 6 and he looks pissed.*

They both stormed in, and I shouted, "Company, attention!" The command sergeant major looked at me and said, "Get out of here, Currahee!" The leadership referred to subordinates as "Currahee." Apparently, the FO had been trying to call anyone on the radio to help them. The battalion commander's vehicle had luckily picked them up, found their location, and brought them the hour's drive back to our company. They could have frozen to death.

The first sergeant had already been in the company commander's office. The battalion commander and command sergeant major were heading that way and fast. I squatted down next to the copier machine. I wasn't missing this. *I'll take my chances.*

I guess the first sergeant was trying to walk out because then I heard the battalion commander shout, "Get your fuckin' ass back in there you stupid fuck!" He then slammed the CO's door, and all hell broke loose. I'll just leave it at that, but I will say in my twenty years' time in service, I never heard or ever received an ass-chewing like I heard that morning. It was the first time I had ever witnessed a senior ranked person get shitcanned. He gave the first sergeant like three hours to get his shit packed and be at the battalion headquarters, where he got his orders and was sent to 2nd Infantry Division Headquarters down south, never to be seen in Currahee land again.

This battalion commander went to the top. I mean the very top. Twenty-two years later, as I am typing this, he recently retired from the US Army. He was the chairman of the Joint Chiefs of Staff. Now you may get an idea of who I'm talking about. That was one tough dude, not to be messed with. Unfortunately, however, his reputation today makes him more of a politician. His reputation has declined since the messy Afghanistan withdrawal a couple of years ago.

Anyway, I served a year in Korea on the DMZ. Now it was time to go "home" to Fort Bragg.

I arrived in Fayetteville pretty late at night. I stopped at a gas station in the vicinity of where my old roommates lived to get directions on what exact street and house was theirs. I grabbed a twelve-pack of beer, thinking we would celebrate a little, since I hadn't seen them in over a year. I remember pulling up to their house they were living in and noticing it was definitely kind of run down. I knocked on their front door and I heard, "Come on in." I walked in and they were both sitting on the couch staring at me. I said, "Hey! How are you two? I miss you guys; it's been a long time." They were both real skinny and pale looking.

They both stared at me with a blank look and the girl said, "Hey, what's up?" with no excitement or emotion in her voice. The guy was just staring off into space, not even at me, but in my direction. They were definitely on something and something very strong. It only took me about two more seconds to realize they had become heroin addicts during the time I was gone. I could tell they must have just shot up prior to me getting there because they were higher than a kite.

I left, drove onto Fort Bragg and signed into one of the lodges, where I stayed for a few days during my in-processing. I remember drinking the beer I had bought, feeling so sad, and wondering how they had allowed themselves to get hooked up with that garbage. I realized they were adults that chose to go down the darkest path in Fayetteville. Like Forrest Gump said, "That's all I have to say about that."

The next morning, I signed into Replacement and began the in-processing procedures for the second time in the 82nd Airborne Division. I asked if I needed to be in their formations and march from point A to point B with them like I did before. Of course I got the answer I already knew, which was yes. The difference was, when we were done for the day, I could drive off and go do my own thing. The only thing I got to get out of this time was that I didn't have to go through the museum tour. I tried to get out of the airborne refresher course, but that wasn't going to happen. It was a good thing for me to go through it again anyway, just in case there was something new from a year ago, and there was. I cannot remember exactly what it was, but there was a new version of an air item.

I received my orders, and it was back to the 505th. Once I got to the Brigade S-1 shop, I asked if there was any chance I could go back to 3 Panther. No, this time it was 1st Battalion. Okay, no problem. They told me the brigade was getting ready for another JRTC Rotation in a little over a month. I remember jokingly asking if I could go back to Replacement and get assigned to the Falcons or the Devils.

When they gave me my orders, I got into my truck, drove across the street to their S-1 and signed in. Once I got my new company assignment, I walked down the sidewalk, into the company, and straight to the orderly room. The first sergeant was in there shooting the shit with an E-7. He looked at me and asked, "What do you need, Sergeant?"

I said, "I'm here to sign in, First Sergeant."

He and the E-7 just looked at me and began the stare-at-the-uniform-and-the-left-shoulder-Tab-check thing right away. "You married?" the first sergeant asked.

"No, I'm single, First Sergeant."

"All right, so you're gonna need a room, right?"

"Roger, First Sergeant."

The E-7 just kept staring at me with the most serious look on his face. He was intimidating as shit. I'd glance at him as he still stared at me, and then I'd calmly look away.

The first sergeant called me into his office through the little hallway from the orderly room. He had me sign for my room key. He said, "You're right across from the CQ desk out front."

"Roger, First Sergeant." I turned around and the E-7 was right behind me. He had followed us into the first sergeant's office.

He asked me, "You promotable?"

"Roger, Sergeant."

"Okay, you're comin' to my platoon as a squad leader." He didn't even wait for the first sergeant to assign me, he just up and did it himself. I remember feeling good that I was going to get to continue being a squad leader. After all, I was promotable. He then told me to go check out my room and meet him down at the platoon command post. I said, "Yes, Sergeant."

Then I started walking off and he yelled out, "Yeah, you're my new squad leader, for the time being . . ." I never forgot those words. Before I get any further in this chapter, I have to officially introduce you to the toughest, meanest, most serious, obsessive-compulsive, down-to-earth, and funniest platoon sergeant during my total nine years in the 82nd Airborne Division and my entire time in the United States Army. He was the best of the best. He had grown up in Division as a private, as most of these guys did. He had all the infantry bells and whistles on his uniform, including a drill sergeant badge to boot. He even had a combat jump "mustard stain" on his master parachute badge from jumping into Panama back when he was a squad leader in the 504th. He already had a year of platoon sergeant time in this company. He had come from Benning, where he spent four years straight: two years as a drill sergeant and two years as a Ranger instructor (RI), so he was also pretty networked within the infantry as a whole. He knew every Army regulation and field manual by hand, so nobody could tell him shit, not even the first sergeant. He was a good-looking guy too. A pretty built, light-skinned Black guy with piercing, intimidating eyes. You always felt you were in trouble when he talked to you. Anyway, I hold him, along with a future battalion command sergeant major (which I'll talk about later on), fully responsible for pushing me toward my success in Division and throughout my time in the Army. I will refer to him as Sergeant First Class "P."

I locked up my new NCO barracks room and headed down to the command post to talk to my new platoon sergeant for the first time. I knocked on the door and stood at parade rest.

"C'mon in."

I stood in front of his desk at parade rest. He was on his computer typing up something. This was still early 1998, before laptops, so it was a larger desktop computer. I looked around the office, which was pretty standard for a command post in Division. He had a small, Army- issued, dayroom couch in front of his desk, which happened to be a real nice oak desk, not the metal ones you commonly see in the Army. That told me it was his personal desk. There were two wall lockers behind the couch and on the other side was the other platoon's command post. I remember only his desk and not one for the platoon leader. I thought maybe we didn't have one at the time. Oh, but we did. He had a small filing cabinet to sit at in the corner.

I remember thinking this guy had more power than I thought. The damn lieutenant didn't even get to have a fucking desk—Damn! I thought to myself, *Well, maybe they share the same desk.* Then I looked down and saw the name plate with Sergeant First Class P's name on it. It was really nice, with a master parachute and pathfinder badge on both sides of his name with two gold ink pens on the ends as well.

Reading this, one would probably ask how I could remember in such detail someone's name plate on their desk. Trust me, there's a reason. Months later, I went to go grab one of them to sign something and he said to me, "Whoa, whoa, whoa, whoa . . . What the fuck you think you're doin'?" I said, "Oh shit, my bad, Sergeant," as I slid the pen back into the holder. He said, "You better have your own fuckin' pen on you." He looked at the other squad leaders that were sitting in there at the time and were laughing. He said to them, "This motherfucka must have lost his damn mind." Funny shit.

As he continued to type, I kept looking around. I noticed he had his plaques on the wall from his time before in Division and at Benning. He had a bookshelf against one of the walls with all kinds of Army regulations and field manuals. He had every one of them stenciled on the sides with their proper nomenclature. Pretty OCD of him, really.

"Have a seat," he told me as he reached over to his printer to grab the papers he'd just finished typing. They happened to be my initial counseling statement and a blank NCOER (NCO Evaluation Report) used as a working copy—pretty common documents. "How do you pronounce your name?"

I said, "Aga-naga, Sergeant. But I go by Sergeant Augi because Aguinaga has too many syllables in it, and most people end up screwing it up anyway," I chuckled. He just sat there with no emotion on his face and stared at me, then gave my full name a sarcastic emphasis. "Yeah, whatever, Sergeant *Aga-naga*. Where you comin' from?"

"Korea, Sergeant."

He just shook his head. "Well let me tell you something, Sergeant Aga-naga, this ain't Korea. Around here, you gonna go to schools. You ain't in Korea no more, this is the 82nd Airborne Division." He was talking down about Korea as if the units were beneath this place. That was one of the toughest infantry battalions I'd ever served in, and this guy was talkin' shit.

I said, "I know, Sergeant, I've been here before."

"You have? Where?" he demanded. I told him I had spent three years across the street in 3 Panther before Korea.

He about lost it. "Whoa, whoa, whoa, whoa! You mean to tell me you spent three years here before and you don't even have your fuckin' EIB? What the fuck you been doin'? Tell me you're at least jumpmaster qualified?"

I shook my head and replied softly, "No, Sergeant."

"So how come you ain't got your EIB anyway?"

"I failed hand grenades in 3 Panther and also in Korea as well, Sergeant." Oh yeah, did I mention that I had failed EIB when I was in Korea too? Same lane, same double no-go—the twenty-meter hand grenade throw into an enemy foxhole.

He looked at me with a real screwed-up face and said, "Grenades . . . Let me tell ya somethin', we got EIB coming up in a few months. If you fail it again, you're probably not gonna be in this platoon any longer. I'm gonna tell ya that right goddamn now. You got it?" "Roger, Sergeant," I replied. He then had me read and sign my initial counseling statement, which was the normal standard of a unit. I'd be responsible to lead my squad and would be accountable for everything my soldiers did or failed to do. And I would have to pass the APFT (Army physical fitness test) and height and weight standards, etc., etc.

He asked me for a copy of my last NCOER from Korea. I had it in my room and asked if I could go get it for him. He said to get it after we were done, and we almost were. He lifted up the blank, working NCOER he had started on me, and explained that all my accomplishments or failures were going to be the bullets and remarks that were eventually going to be typed onto it.

I told him I understood.

"You write your own evaluations as a leader in the Army," he said to me. I nodded. He meant *Your performances write themselves.* "Now, remember, around here you're gonna go to school. You ain't just gonna sit around and collect a paycheck for nothin'."

"Roger, Sergeant." What he really meant was *You're going to be Ranger and jumpmaster qualified, with an EIB.*

He reached into his desk and handed me a hard-covered green notebook and told me he wanted my name stenciled on the front of it and to have with me whenever he called me and the other squad leaders into his office. He then got up, walked over to his wall locker and pulled out a brand-new FM 7-8 (The Infantry platoon and squad regulation guide) and an 82nd Advanced Airborne School (Jumpmaster School) study guide. He told me to stencil my name on both of them as well.

He got a knock on his door from a young sergeant. He changed his tone from stern with me, to surprised and pleasant to this kid. "Hey, Sergeant So-and-so, get in here! Well, did you pass?"

The young man replied, "Roger, Sergeant."

Sergeant First Class P introduced us. "Sergeant So-and-so, this is your new squad leader, Sergeant Aga-naga. Sergeant Aga-naga, this is your A Team leader." We shook hands. This kid was an "82nd Golden Child," one of the young kids who came in, went straight to Pre-Ranger Course and Ranger School, got their EIB right off the bat, graduated PLDC, and were basically the rank of sergeant right at two years' time in service. Trust me, this kid could do no wrong whatsoever in the platoon sergeant or first sergeant's eyes. It was well deserved too. Make no mistake, I wasn't bitter. But to be honest, I was maybe a little jealous.

Sergeant First Class P told him to take me upstairs and introduce me to the B Team leader and the rest of the squad. I asked him if he wanted me to go get my last NCOER first and he said not to worry about it but to bring it back in the morning for our meeting before PT.

"Roger that, Sergeant, I replied."

On our way upstairs I asked the Golden Child what he'd just passed. He said, "The jumpmaster pretest, Sergeant."

I asked him when he thought he'd be taking off for that and he didn't know. I told him I'd find out and let him know. He took me to his room and then he went to go get the rest of the squad so I could give them my introduction and expectations. I stood in the hallway and looked down the platoon area. I couldn't believe how it looked. It was phenomenal! The floor looked like glass and the walls were painted infantry blue. The normal color and standards for all these barracks walls had always been a light tan color. Apparently, Sergeant First Class P didn't give a shit. He did his own thing, and apparently nobody was going to say anything to him either. He had had someone paint very cool murals on the walls as well of the 82nd insignia, a 75th Ranger Regiment scroll, a C-130 dropping parachutes out, and a special operations operator facing you with a weapon aimed toward the observers. This was all the way at the end of the hallway. I came to find out it was some guys within the platoon who were clearly artists.

What the hell was on the floor? That was not ordinary Army-issued floor wax. There were no streaks where the buffer would have gone back and forth. It was just all glass looking. I soon learned the platoon "floor man" was a kid in my squad. So when I asked him how the fucking floor ends up looking so shiny, he broke it down to me.

Sergeant First Class P would give him money out of his own pocket to go buy the kind of turtle wax you put on cars. Then one guy would apply it with a rag by hand on their hands and knees, all the way down the hallway. They'd let it sit until completely dry and then go over it two or three times with the buffer. The shit looked like a hospital floor.

Another squad member told me that Sergeant First Class P didn't tolerate any messes in the common areas. I said, "No shit!" My B Team leader had told me that about a month before there was a beer bottle with a couple of cigarette butts in it on the pay phone shelf. Sergeant First Class P happened to be walking through the platoon on a Saturday night, saw the empty beer bottle, and called the entire platoon in off the alert roster just to chew their asses about keeping the common areas squared away at all times. I'm sure the married guys and others who lived off post were pleased.

I lay in my bed that night, looking at the light outside on Gela Street while taps played over the loudspeakers on Ardennes Street. I was tossing and turning all night, thinking that I had come to the wrong place at the wrong time. One thing I did realize was that Sergeant First Class P had chosen me to be the squad leader when my new A Team leader had all the bells and whistles. *Why didn't he make him the squad leader and just use me for another platoon?* That's when I realized he valued time in service and experience over badges on a uniform. Even though he may not have wanted to, it was the right thing to do. I respected that after I thought about it for a minute. I didn't know what the near future had in store for me, whether I was going to be successful or be fired. I told myself to do the best I knew how to do and that I knew I could succeed with this guy or any other in this place. I sucked it up and drove on.

The next morning around 0530, I opened my door and left it open as people started coming into the company. I actually had been awake since 0430 because I couldn't sleep. I had made a pot of coffee, of which I was already on like my third cup. I had gone to the main PX the evening before after I talked to the squad, bought some stuff for my room like a pillow, sheets, a comforter, and a coffee pot. I needed to go to transportation on main post and have a delivery date set up for my stuff coming in from Korea, which wasn't a whole lot. Basically, it was all my electronics such as my TV, VCR, stereo, and big-ass Bose Speakers. The rooms already came with a small refrigerator and a microwave. I walked upstairs with my cup of coffee and made sure my guys were up and moving around. I then grabbed my new green book and a pen and walked down the hallway toward the command post. I looked inside and nobody was there yet.

The NCO room was opened directly across the hall from it and the guy inside said, "Hey, you the new squad leader for Second Platoon?"

"Yeah," I said to him. He told me to come in. He was one of the other squad leaders and there was another guy on his couch, who sat smoking a cigarette and drinking a cup of coffee. We did all the hellos and introductions. The guy on the couch stood up and asked, "Where you comin' from?"

"Korea."

He took a drag from his smoke and as he blew the smoke out said, "Yeap, been there, done that, dude."

I was trying to make conversation, so I asked where he was at over there. He told me LRRSD (long-range reconnaissance and surveillance detachment).

I told him I was in the 1/506th and he replied with, "Oh, you were one of those Stands Alone guys, huh?" He had a slight cockiness about him, as if you weren't going to tell him shit that he already didn't know. We were in PTs (our physical training clothes), so I really couldn't tell rank or anything else about these guys, but I just knew he was tabbed because of his attitude, plus the fact that he had been assigned to a reconnaissance detachment.

Later on that morning I found out I was wrong. The guy whose room it was was a little dorky but a great guy who would do anything for you. He was an E-5 promotable also and he was Ranger and jumpmaster qualified. The guy smoking was another squad leader in the platoon and was an E-6. He had come in about a month earlier from Fort Jackson, South Carolina, where he'd just gotten off the trail as a drill sergeant and had no Tab and wasn't jumpmaster qualified either, which made me feel better because that meant I wouldn't be alone in that regard.

"You met him already, I assume?" the smoker asked me, referring to Sergeant First Class P, who had just walked into the room.

"Oh yeah, yesterday when I signed in."

He looked at me and said, "Don't worry, dude, he'll lighten up on you once he gets to know ya."

Little did I know at the time, but this guy was going to be my best friend in the next couple of months. His nickname was "Shaky." I'll explain why a little later.

"What time is it?" Sergeant First Class P asked.

The other E-5, I'll call him "Sergeant E," replied with, "0600, Sergeant."

"I got fuckin' 0603 on my watch. Let me tell y'all motherfuckas somethin': when I say 0600, I don't mean 0603 or 0605."

We all replied together in a real low tone, "Roger, Sergeant."

He looked at me and asked me if I had that NCOER he had told me to bring in yesterday afternoon.

"Oh shit, Sergeant, it's in my room, I'll go it."

"Sit yo' fuckin' ass down. Let me tell you somethin': you're already fuckin' up around here." Then he continued to attack me in front of the other three. Oh yeah, the other squad leader was there already sleeping on the couch, waiting for the meeting before Sergeant First Class P had come in from the first sergeant's office. "Whatsamatter, you don't want me to see how fucked-up your performance was at your last duty station, motherfucka?"

"No, I just forgot it in my room, Sergeant." He looked at me with a disgusted look on his face and said, "Korea . . ."

The company was getting ready to go into the field for a few days the next week. It wasn't going to be a formal Intensive Training Cycle or anything like that with live-fires day and night, but something simpler, such as going over battle drills with our squads. The company, battalion, and brigade was preparing for a JRTC rotation coming up in about a month.

"Okay, today after PT and chow, keep getting your guys packed up for the field next week. Make sure you go off the packing list and you two"—he pointed at me and Shaky—"make sure you pack your jumpmaster study guides too. There's another pretest down there next week before the next class starts and I'm gonna try to get you guys out of the field to come back and take it."

He looked at me and told me to tell my A Team leader that he was getting one of the company slots for that next jumpmaster class and that he was going to be exempt from going to JRTC. I said, "Roger that, Sergeant, I'll let him know." Then I added, "Hey, Sergeant, can I get a copy of that packing list?"

He looked at me with death in his eyes and said, "No fuckin' shit you need a copy." He grabbed a copy off his desk and handed it to me.

I took it and sat back down. I looked up and he was still staring at me with the room filled with silence.

"You need anything from me?" he asked sarcastically.

"No, I'm good, Sergeant."

"Can I fuckin' go on now Sergeant Aga-naga??"

"Roger, Sergeant."

He still stared at me for about another five seconds and then went on to tell the other squad leaders what he needed from one or two of their guys.

As we left his office, and I was heading back to my room to put my book up, I thought to myself, *Fuck, this guy truly hates me.* As I walked outside the barracks headed for the rocks, I didn't think I would make it in this place by the weekend, let alone next week during the field with this guy.

When I was on the rocks, I looked over across the street to 3 Panther and my old company I had started out in a few years prior as they were forming up and remembered thinking about those good old days when everyone seemed more relaxed. Then I got accountability of my squad and reported to Sergeant First Class P. He gave the platoon report to the first sergeant, turned around, put up a hand salute and said, "Squad leaders, take charge of your squads and conduct PT."

The four of us returned the salute and said, "Roger, Sergeant."

I marched the squad off the rocks and over to the grass to start stretching them out. It was still dark outside but the company and street lights on Ardennes illuminated everything enough. The 82nd Choir recording began and echoed down everywhere. Of course, as I was stretching my squad out, Sergeant First Class P was roaming around behind me, checking me out. I could feel his eyes burning through the back of my head. He didn't say anything to me, so I must have been doing a decent job. I took the squad on a four- mile run that first morning, came back, stretched them again, and dismissed them until 0900 formation in BDUs.

I went in and took a shower, and me and my two new buddies went to breakfast chow together at the Battalion Mess Hall. The other squad leader was married and lived in housing down the street, so he usually went home after PT. Actually, Shaky was married too, but his wife was still down in an apartment outside of Fort Jackson, while his two kids finished up the school year down there. So he also had a room, and it was upstairs next to my A Team leader's. They were good guys, and I knew we were going to be pretty good friends. The way I looked at it, we had to stick together in order to make it through day to day with this platoon sergeant. Maybe I was just spun up because I had just gotten there and met this guy. The other two seemed somewhat numb about him and I'm sure that was because they had been there for a little while and were used to it, especially Sergeant E.

That weekend they took me out and we went bar hopping around Fayetteville. Sunday we finished packing for the few days in the field and me and Shaky did some studying out of the jumpmaster guide.

That next week in the field I got my first tactical debut with Sergeant First Class P. I had my entire squad out in the field with me too. It had been rare up until now to have a full nine-man line squad. In the year I had been gone, the equipment had changed. There were no more M16s, as all rifles had been changed to the new M4 Carbines. The M60s were gone too. They'd switched them out to the new M240B machine guns, which were three inches longer and three pounds heavier than the old M60s.

Plus everybody had their own sets of night vision goggles with the new helmet mounts. Squad leaders and team leaders were issued PAQ4-C, which were small infrared laser mounts for our M4s. This was before the rail system on the weapons, so there was a small metal attachment that went over the front sight post and got screwed in. Then the PAQ4-C screwed into that. Then you'd wrap the whole thing a few times with 100mph tape (known to civilians as duct tape) to ensure it was secured to the weapon. NODs (night optical devices) were tied off with 550 cord around the lapels of our collars on our

BDU tops. So during the year I was gone, the equipment had stepped up quite a bit, and it continued to do so from that point on. It seemed from 1998 to 2005 that every other month there was always some new type of equipment we had to learn and master.

The first day of training he had each line squad go through Battle Drill 2A out of the 7-8, which was Squad React to Contact. We did everything platoon-internal. Each squad would go through the lane while weapons squad, which Shaky led, would provide some guys to play OPFOR. Of course, we were the first squad to go through, as I expected. Too easy.

Sergeant First Class P and the platoon leader were off to the side with clipboards in hand. I remember thinking, *Damn, they're gonna do some real evaluation shit.* We had like a two-hundred-meter movement, so I had us in a spread out, wedge formation, moving in the direction of the objective. *Pop, pop, pop,* the blank fire went off from the OPFOR. We all got down and began the drill, and I made sure I didn't rush it. I set the lead fire team in support, then went back and grabbed the other team and led them around and through the woods, until I found a good assault staging area.

I blew my whistle for the support team to shift their fire. The A Team leader returned with two whistle blasts to confirm. Back in those days we didn't have internal squad radios, so we had to use whistles, or VS-17 panels (different colored nylon rectangles) during the day, and pyrotechnics or chem lights to communicate nighttime lift- and shift-fire signals.

I ordered the assault element to move forward by utilizing three-to-five-second rushes *(I'm up; he sees me; I'm down)*. I gave the lift-fire signal, they confirmed, and we assaulted the objective by fighting through until we were on the opposite side of it. I called "LOA!" (limit of advance).

The support team came up, passed through the objective themselves, and got down for security, so that the whole squad was in an L shape. I then called out for the enemy prisoner of war and search team to go back onto the objective and search the dead enemy for intelligence materials. Once complete, I sent up the report to the platoon leader and we consolidated and reorganized the squad.

Sergeant First Class P came up and called us in and he and the platoon leader started the after-action review. We got accountability of equipment, and I told Sergeant First Class P we were up.

"Roger," he said.

We broke out our canteens and took off our helmets. He asked how I thought we did.

I replied that I thought it was pretty standard and that we did pretty good. He told me to break out my 7-8, which I had in my buttpack inside a ziplock bag. I think he was testing me to see if I had it on me and God help me if I didn't. He went down step-by-step of Battle Drill 2A and I followed through mine. We'd pretty much executed everything, except I didn't send out an aid and litter team onto the objective. He asked why I hadn't.

My answer was simple. I replied, "Nobody was wounded, and I wanted to get off the objective as quickly as possible, Sergeant."

"Why?"

"Before more enemy troops might arrive, or they started laying indirect fire on us, Sergeant."

He nodded his head in agreement. He then told us to go back to the platoon area and eat chow. As we walked off, he shouted out, "Hey, Sergeant Aga-naga."

"Yes, Sergeant."

"That was an average performance," he replied sarcastically.

I looked at him and said in a low tone, "Hooha . . ." and walked off.

When I got back to the platoon area, I told the team leaders to have the guys break out an MRE and eat lunch. I went over to Shaky and Sergeant E, a fellow squad leader in our platton, and sat down.

"Well, how'd ya do?"

I said, "Uhhh, he said I did average."

Sergeant E said, "Hey, did he tell you to improve on anything?"

"Not really."

"Then you guys did good, because if you didn't, you know by now he'd damn sure let you know. Plus he'd have you start over and do the whole thing over again—trust me." So then I felt better, pulled out my number 11 MRE out of my rucksack and started eating (Number 11, chicken and rice, was always my favorite).

The next evening after dinner chow, Sergeant First Class P called me and Shaky over to his location within our platoon area—Oh yeah, I never did explain how Shaky got his nickname. In the field, he would have a little twitch in one of his hands (not like in *Saving Private Ryan* or anything). Anyway, he used to make fun of himself and say he twitched when he was in the field because he was sober. He was only kidding and was always joking. I think the guy, like me, drank way too much coffee those mornings in the field.

Anyway, Sergeant First Class P told us we were going in first thing in the morning with the XO and first sergeant back to the battalion area. They were leaving at 0500 to go pick up morning chow, and Shaky and I were to be at the Advanced Airborne School to take the jumpmaster pretest at 0900. That gave us enough time to get back to our barracks rooms, take showers, put fresh BDUs on, eat breakfast, and be at the school with our ALICE packs and air items.

"Roger that, Sergeant."

We started walking off, and then he called me back over to him. I took a knee next to him and said, "What's up, Sergeant?"

"Let me tell ya somethin,' if you fail that pretest tomorrow morning, I'm gonna fire your ass. You hear me?"

"Roger, Sergeant."

No monkey on my back or anything. I went back to my hooch, crawled under my poncho, turned on my red lens flashlight, and started studying the nomenclature out of my jumpmaster study guide.

We arrived at the schoolhouse around 0830. A bunch of soldiers were outside, sitting down on their rucks studying. The standard was you had to pass the nomenclature test, which was memorizing about forty different items of equipment. These included all components of the main and reserve parachutes, and all air items, including every portion of the ballistic helmet. The test consisted of the black hat instructors presenting twenty-five air items, and you had to get eighteen correct to pass. Then you went outside to the sawdust pit and rig your ALICE pack and M1950 weapons case to lower. The candidates had ten minutes to complete this task. At the end of the ten minutes, everyone was to leave the pit and the instructors would go through the equipment, inspect it, and pull it out if it didn't meet the standard. If you passed both tests, they would issue you a piece of paper that indicated you passed and that you had ninety days to make the next jumpmaster class. If your ninety days expired, you had to take the pretest all over again.

Shaky passed both sections and I passed the nomenclature exam but failed the time standard of rigging. On the way back to the barracks, I told Shaky I was going to be fired and was wondering where I was going to go. I didn't know if I would even remain in the company or not. He assured me that Sergeant First Class P wasn't going to fire me, but probably he would give me a good ass-chewing.

No shit! I thought.

I got back to the field, went straight to him and told him I had failed the pretest. He looked at me and said with a grin on his face, "I know you did."

"How did you know, Sergeant?"

"Because it was your first fuckin' time, right?"

"Roger."

"Okay, now that you know what to expect, you better pass it the second goddamn time I send your ass, you hear me?"

"Roger that, Sergeant!" I was so happy that I didn't get fired and furthermore, I began to think I was starting to figure this guy out.

JRTC was just around the corner. We had about three weeks before the rotation and we were expecting the usual of jumping in at night and going through two weeks force-on-force in all that thick, wet, nasty terrain down there. We got a pleasant surprise though. Sergeant First Class P called us squad leaders down to the command post. We all sat down in front of his desk with our green note books.

"Okay, I got a surprise and good news for you motherfuckas. When we go to JRTC in a couple of weeks, we're gonna be the brigade tactical operations center security platoon." We all just sat there looking at him. Nobody said anything.

"Well don't you motherfuckas all thank me at once," he said, in a surprised tone.

We still all looked at him, silent. I spoke up and asked, "So what's that mean? We're gonna set up a defensive perimeter around the brigade TOC?"

"That's right, motherfucka. We're gonna set up a perimeter, pull security on the fuckin' TOC, and that's it!"

Then Sergeant E spoke up, "Wait a minute, Sergeant. That's it for the whole field problem down there?"

Field problem was our slang term for field exercises or maneuvers. Then we all went, "Ooohhh shit, that's *it*?"

Sergeant First Class P had a big old smile on his face, leaned back in his chair and said, "Oh, *now* you motherfuckas get it, huh? There ain't gonna be no humpin' around all that bullshit for two weeks. Plus, guess what they get to eat at the brigade TOC at least twice a day? That's right, hot motherfuckin' chow!"

We were all like, "Hell yeah Sergeant, that's what I'm talkin' about."

Then we got even more great news. He had worked it out with his "brigade headquarters connection" that we were going to get to go down with the brigade ADVON team (advanced echelon), which meant we didn't have to jump in either. "Aaahhh man, Hell yes!"

Then he got even more cocky. "Unless you motherfuckas want me to go back to Brigade and tell them to never mind?"

"Fuck no, we're good, Sergeant!" We were like little kids in a candy factory. For once, we were excited about going to JRTC because we were going to be chillin' for the most part. Yeah, we had to go down a week early with the advanced party, but we didn't have to ride in a C141 packed in like sardines for a two-and-a-half-hour flight, jump in, and hump through all that shit for two weeks straight.

I remember the other platoon sergeant from the other side came over and asked Sergeant First Class P, "How the fuck did you pull that off?"

Sergeant First Class P replied to him with one of his famous sayings, "You gotta learn how to *network* around here."

Now that I think about it as I'm writing this twenty-one years later, he pulled that off going above the first sergeant. He coordinated it all on his own before the company knew about it. I'll be damned—I just realized that. What a smooth dude he was.

The next week we had another small field exercise and this time it was a practice run for the upcoming JRTC. It was a brigade mass-tac nighttime jump into a couple of drop zones. Our platoon jumped in with the brigade HQ's company on Rhine-Luzon DZ at Camp McKall. Our battalion conducted an airfield seizure right there on Rhine-Luzon, and the other two battalions jumped in back at Bragg on another DZ, probably Sicily or Holland, with their own objectives. Camp McKall was a training installation about twenty miles south of Fort Bragg, and over by a town called Southern Pines. I remember Sergeant First Class P was the primary jumpmaster on our C141 and our very own Sergeant E was his assistant jumpmaster. It was going to be his first nighttime jump as an assistant jumpmaster, which was going to earn him his star above his jump wings (senior parachutist badge).

While we were preparing for the field back at the company prior to the airborne timeline, Sergeant First Class P handed each of us squad leaders two Motorola radios he had bought with his own money. They were for extra means of communication between the squad leaders and team leaders during this training exercise and JRTC coming up so we could talk without the chain of command hearing us. During these days only the squad leaders, platoon sergeants, and platoon leaders had radios.

After the jump, we broke off from the company and tactically moved into the woods a few hundred meters and set up a platoon triangle perimeter. After the sun came up, Sergeant First Class P linked up with the brigade TOC NCOIC. The brigade HQ's company started going to work setting up the general purpose large tent with all the smaller tents for the commander, command sergeant major, XO, S-3, and so on. They set up the tactical operations center right on the edge of the drop zone. Sergeant First Class P and us squad leaders went to mark out where we were going to set up our positions around the outskirts of the TOC. We had the engineers dig us out fighting positions on each end of it, for a total of four positions. God bless those engineers with their backhoes.

The whole platoon filled up sand bags around each position, with overhead cover and sector stakes (left and right limit barriers for each weapon). Squad leaders filled out range cards, which showed the sectors of fire for each hole within the squad or platoon perimeter, accordingly. We completed the work before lunch. Then Sergeant First Class P got all the Brigade S-shop NCOICs and walked them around the perimeter of the TOC. Their TOC standard operating procedure was that if under attack, they were to send their soldiers out and fill in between our positions and fight. Guess who was walking around with Sergeant First Class P? Yup, Command Sergeant Major X. I don't remember him saying anything that memorable during this exercise or JRTC either.

Our platoon plan was pretty simple. We were set up about a hundred meters away from the TOC in the woods. One squad would rotate and man each hole with two soldiers per. Each hole would have one of Sergeant First Class P's Motorolas and their squad leader would have one. Another squad would send one fire team out at a time to patrol out in the woods. Once they came back, you'd send out another. One squad sat back in reserve as the quick reaction force, and we all rotated throughout the duration. Us squad leaders had it made as we sat back and oversaw everything. Every now and then, we'd go around and check on each position. I don't remember if there was any OPFOR for this training exercise or not; it was a pretty chill week. Once we got everything set up and began rotating, Sergeant First Class P pretty much was hands-off until we got to JRTC.

We got to Fort Polk and Sergeant First Class P wouldn't lighten up for anything. I don't know if he was nervous about being in the spotlight with the brigade HQ or not. I thought our exercise back at McKall had gone pretty smoothly, but that didn't mean somebody hadn't said something to him maybe after we were done. Who knows, but he definitely had a corn-cob up his ass down there.

Oh yeah, I wasn't the only NCO that he would go after and try to tear up. He ripped Shaky's ass one afternoon for damaging some piece of equipment issued by the JRTC OC (observer controller). Maybe that was what was different from McKall's training: we actually had eyes on us all the time now by having an OC with us and evaluating.

Anyway, we got issued our MILES gear (battery-operated sensors worn on the helmet and a harness over the LCE, with a laser mounted on the end of your weapons). This was common equipment used with force-on-force blank-fire training. There was also some kind of new laser system for the M240B machine guns. It had a thin cord that plugged into the laser and had a sensor by the trigger of the weapon, or something like that.

Anyway, one of Shaky's gunners broke the cord on his, and Shaky went to let Sergeant First Class P know he needed a new one. The OC made a major production out of it because apparently they had just gotten them in. Sergeant First Class P lost his mind. He went off on Shaky like he'd just committed murder. They were kind of going back and forth for some time and I believe Shaky ended up getting a counseling statement from him. That was it; Shaky was pissed the rest of the next three weeks during the rotation.

I was short a team leader. Sergeant So-and-so was back at Bragg going through Jumpmaster School. It was all good, my B Team leader, who was an E-4, stepped it up and besides, we were doing TOC security anyway. I made another E-4 from B Team the team leader. He used to be in the Navy and used tell everybody about the BUDS course(SEAL training) that he claimed he'd attended but hadn't made it through. We used to just laugh him off, and later on, he earned the nickname "Jack." I'll explain later.

During our preparations for the field, Sergeant First Class P made everybody in the platoon take off our suspenders from our LCEs. We had to replace them with the MILES harness. Sergeant E asked him why we couldn't just drape the harness over our LCE suspenders like pretty much every other unit did.

Of course Sergeant First Class P started yelling at him and the whole platoon. "Because one of you motherfuckas are going to forget to have it on during a firefight and we'll get penalized for it! Or you'll lose the motherfucka! Plus, we're all going to be in the same fuckin' uniform." He also made everybody have the metal box facing to the rear, which sucked because the front of it had a horizontal strap that would rub into your neck, and you were always pulling it down. So much for this being a laid-back JRTC.

What a miserable field problem. Sergeant First Class P made everybody in the platoon buddy up under one poncho to have minimum ponchos showing. So with our rucks, that tells you how much room we got. Even the squad leaders had to buddy up. Oh yeah, did I tell you it rained the entire two weeks, and it was cold as shit too? It was April, but it was cool with the constant rain. Here's the best part: he also made us sleep with our LCEs on, in the event the TOC got hit during the night, so we would just have to worry about instantly moving out to counter. Surprisingly, he did let us sleep with our helmets off.

I shared a hooch with Shaky and he said, "Fuck him, I ain't sleeping with that fuckin' thing on. I'm a grown man." I said fuck it and took mine off too. He couldn't fire both of us, right?

Anyway, we did the JRTC rotation in miserable, cold rain the whole time in the field. Actually, I think I would have rather been humping out in the bush; at least we would have been warmer.

We got back to Bragg, and I went upstairs to my A Team leader's room to find out how he'd done in Jumpmaster School. He had made it through the first time, which is not very common in Division. In Jumpmaster School, most people usually had to go back through the JMPI (jumpmaster personnel inspection portion) twice. It was called being "reentry qualified." If you failed the JMPI test, and in those days it was the final test, you had to wait for the next jumpmaster class and then you could start at the JMPI portion without having to go through the entire three-week course again. In order to become reentry qualified, though, you had to not fail any other portion of the school prior to it. That was the key.

Anyway, he had made it straight through, but had one little thing to talk to me and the platoon sergeant about. While we were gone, he had apparently gone to the battalion reenlistment NCO, who never had to go to the field anyway, unless a soldier was reenlisting out there. He had reenlisted to PCS to Italy, and it was coming up quick. As a matter of fact, he was going to begin clearing the unit in a couple of weeks. Unlike Ranger School, the unit could not hold a soldier on orders to PCS for graduating Jumpmaster School. Like I said earlier, they could only hold you a year after Ranger School graduation, and that had been about two years ago for him.

I warned him that Sergeant First Class P was going to lose his fucking mind. And he did. He took it as a betrayal of him and the company because companies usually don't get too many jumpmaster slots at one time. The battalion may only get between one and three at a time as a whole. They were pissed off at him—the platoon sergeant, first sergeant, and the CO. If I'm not mistaken, he ended up PCSing with an Army Achievement Medal, which is the lowest award you can get other than a certificate of achievement. I guess he was lucky he didn't leave with that. He had come in as a private three years prior, got his EIB first time go, graduated from Pre-Ranger Course and

Ranger School first time go, graduated the 82nd Airborne Division Advanced Airborne School first time go, and PCS'd with an AAM. The funny part was, he could give two shits about a PCS award. He was set for the remainder of his career in the airborne infantry and in the Army as a whole, and he knew it. That was the last time I ever saw or heard from him.

A couple of months went by, and it was EIB time again! This was going to be my third time and my last time because I was *not* going to fail again. Third time's the charm! I was the only squad leader in the platoon who still needed to get the damn thing and I had my good buddies Sergeant E and Shaky rooting for me. Oh yeah, Shaky had just graduated from Jumpmaster School and was getting ready to go to Pre-Ranger Course.

I remember talking to my squad prior to the training beginning. None of them had it either. There was no shame in my game. I told them we would all go through it together as a squad and earn it as a squad too. Sergeant First Class P called me into the command post the morning of the first day of training. He gave me his famous line. "Let me tell you somethin': if you don't get your EIB next week, I'm gonna fire your fuckin' ass. I'm gonna tell ya that right goddamn now."

"I'll get it, Sergeant." I did exactly that! In June of 1998, I earned the Expert Infantryman Badge. I passed that fucking hand grenade station with two grenades still left over.

They issued you five grenades. The first station on the lane, you had to throw it from the kneeling position into a large circle marked off with engineer tape. The grenade could roll as long as it detonated within the circle. The next station, you had to maneuver up by high-crawling and throw the grenade into a bunker, which was simple. Then was the dreaded twenty-meter throw into the fighting position. You got behind a stack of sand bags, took a peek, prepared your grenade, took one last peek, got up on one knee with the other leg kicked out, threw the grenade and got back down quickly behind the sandbags.

That son of a bitch went off and the EIB grader said, "You're a go." I jumped up and couldn't believe it. I still had two grenades left I could have kept trying with, had I failed the first throw. That was it! There was no way I could fail now, but I didn't get cocky, and I stayed focused. I still had to finish the day of other testing lanes. Too easy.

The next morning we conducted the twelve-mile foot march, which started behind Division HQ on Fire Break 6. They had a big-ass digital clock sitting on a desk set up in front of the gate opened in front of the firebreak. Next to it was a water buffalo (a giant potable water tank pulled on a trailer) and next to that was a field ambulance. We got our briefing from the grader, which was the EIB NCOIC. It was still dark out, so they issued chem lights for us to stick in our helmets. Out of my squad remaining, it was me and my B Team leader, who by then was my only team leader.

Fire Break 6 was a mile long of mostly sand. At the end of it, you hit a T-intersection and then paved road for the next ten miles. At the halfway point, you handed someone from the EIB committee a card they had issued at the start point. They marked the card in order to prove you went to the halfway point. Once they marked it, you turned around and went back. You had to jog at least half of the march, if not most of it, in order to make the three-hour time standard. Then that last mile was the sandy Fire Break 6 again.

I made it in like two hours and fifty minutes with quite a few paratroopers behind me. As I was coming in, I could see Shaky and Sergeant E cheering me on, and Command Sergeant Major X was hollering at all of us. The clock was moving, and I made it through the gate. I went over and turned in my halfway point card and was marked off as a go. If you happen to lose the card on the way back, you're an automatic no-go and have to do the march again the next morning, unless it was your third no-go: then, you were done.

I then went over to the fence line and sat down, leaned up against it and started slamming water. I can honestly say, I believe that was the most physically exhausted I have ever been. My whole body hurt. My team leader made it too and came over and sat next to me. We high-fived and didn't say shit to each other. Shaky and Sergeant E came over and filled up our canteens for us.

This is what I remember next. The time was burning up fast and troopers were still coming in and barely making it. At three hours on the dot, Command Sergeant Major X closed the gate. As he was closing it, there were soldiers struggling to finish on the other side, screaming, "NOOOO! No, Sergeant Major!"

Once the gate was closed, he stood there on our side and said to the candidates that didn't make the time, "Good job, Airborne! Way to finish hard! See ya tomorrow mornin' back here for the retest. Bye!" He then turned around and started walking away, and then stopped and went back. "Oh yeah, one more thing, Airborne: go home and drink plenty of water, rest yourselves up, and have yourselves an Airborne evenin,' Bye!"

I remember telling myself, *Wow* . . .

Shaky took our weapons back to the company for us and turned them in. We climbed into Sergeant E's car, and he drove us back. I got to the barracks and my room, took a shower, and collapsed in my bed. I didn't even go down to see Sergeant First Class P. I slept all day, and nobody bothered me, either.

The next morning I was sitting on Sergeant First Class P's couch. He came in from his meeting with the first sergeant, sat down, and stared at me with a grin on his face. He leaned back in his chair, put his hands behind his head and said, "You see? I told ya, Iiiii told ya . . . Around here, you gonna accomplish shit." He was telling me this as if he had gotten me the award and that I hadn't earned it myself. I didn't care, I was happy as shit. The next thing out of his mouth was, "Okay, you know what's next. Take your pick."

I said, "I'll go to PRC, Sergeant."

"Wait a minute," he said as he pondered. "We're short jumpmasters, especially after your former team leader fucked this company and the battalion."

I didn't argue with him, although I wanted to go to Pre-Ranger

Course and Ranger School first. I said, "Jumpmaster it is."

That afternoon at 1300 on Lindsey Field, I got to stand in Command Sergeant Major X's "receiving formation." The next week, I passed the jumpmaster pretest down at the school.

CHAPTER 6

STAFF SERGEANT PROMOTION

OUR PLATOON WAS going through some leadership changes. Actually, the company was, too. We had recently gotten a new first sergeant who had come right from our company. He was a platoon sergeant in the platoon that shared our command post, so he knew our drama with Sergeant First Class P pretty well. He had made the E-8 list and immediately got "frocked" and became our first sergeant. So really quick, let me explain what I just said. Senior NCOs (E-7, E-8, and E-9) got promoted off Department of the Army selection; no longer points like E-5 and E-6. You no longer physically sat in front of a board and got asked questions; instead, your records went in front of a board of E-9s, selected throughout the Army. They looked at your Enlisted Records Brief (ERB), one sheet of small print that had all your previous assignments, schools, awards, etc., that was your responsibility to manage and keep updated. So your ERB, last five NCOERs, and an official Department of the Army photo of yourself in your Class A uniform was what got reviewed and evaluated. The board determined whether you got selected for the next pay grade; if you did, you got a sequence number and became promotable. Back in the day, you'd find that out through the *Army Times* newspaper that came out once a month. It had the latest promotion board results, and that is how most NCOs had found out if they made it or not. Once your unit was notified that you had become promotable, if a next higher slot was available, with recommendations, you would normally be frocked (which means wearing the rank on your uniform) and put into that position. So even though this platoon sergeant was still getting paid as an E-7, he would wear first sergeant rank and begin his first sergeant-rated time, which was the real important step. Once his sequence number came up later on, he would then begin to start getting paid as an E-8.

So one squad leader in our platoon ended up PCSing to Fort Polk, Louisiana and Sergeant E left for Special Forces (SF) selection, which didn't go over too well with Sergeant First Class P.

There has always been some kind of stigma with guys that leave Division to go to SF. I think it's pretty much because the unit really doesn't have any control or say over whether or not you can go. By regulation, they cannot stop you from taking the PT test and going through selection, which is right there at Fort Bragg, actually on Camp McKall. Sergeant First Class P was disappointed but not pissed like he had been when my former team leader left. Sergeant E had served his time with this battalion and done everything he was asked to do. He simply wanted to pursue his dream of eventually becoming a Green Beret, which he eventually achieved.

Shaky ended up moving out of the barracks and into government housing on post because his wife finally moved back up to Bragg with his kids from South Carolina. Soon after, he went to Pre-Ranger Course.

Within a couple of weeks, the two squad leader positions were filled with two great guys, with whom I'm still friends with to this day. Staff Sergeant "S" came from another company within the battalion. I believe the battalion command sergeant major had a policy similar to when I got laterally transferred from company to company because of promotion. Staff Sergeant S was a team leader who had made the E-6 cut-off score and was promoted, then moved to our company to begin his squad leader time. Of course the same rule applied: if you were tabbed, you didn't have to move companies. By now, I realized that whole thing was a numbers game. Each company got to maintain their "victors" for their books. A victor is a skill identifier that is attached to your MOS.

So Staff Sergeant S came in and I believe he was dreading coming to our platoon because he already knew who Sergeant First Class P was and his hardcore reputation. As a matter of fact, I believe the whole fucking brigade knew who he was. I brought the new guy into my room and gave him a cup of coffee, and we smoked a cigarette and shot the shit. I remember him asking me how bad it was. I told him like Shaky and Sergeant E had told me eight months prior: "You'll get used to it." I also remember him telling me his goal was to get some squad leader time knocked out and he was going to put in for drill sergeant. I remember responding, "Good luck with that, with this guy."

Staff Sergeant S was Black and so was the platoon sergeant. So I wondered if there was going to be some kind of favoritism from him toward the new squad leader. Fuck no, there wasn't! Make no mistake about it, Sergeant First Class P only recognized two colors when it came to any soldier—black and gold when worn on the left shoulder—a Ranger tab.

About a week or two later, we happened to be in the field training on a defensive perimeter. It was nighttime, and here came the other new squad leader, Javier, I'll call him, primarily because that was his first name. He'll be the only soldier in this book with whom I worked that I'll actually refer to with his real name, just his first though. He showed up to the company and the first sergeant had happened to be back in the rear, probably taking back empty mermites from chow, so he'd snatched his ass up and brought him to the field to link up with Sergeant First Class P and the platoon. I don't even think Javier had a weapon or his field equipment put together. Anyway, he met up with Sergeant First Class P and they spoke a little and then he came my way. He was a real energetic, spirited person, with a funny sense of humor. We couldn't see one another because it was dark out. We began the normal introduction conversations. He was coming from Benning off the trail for three years, if I remember correctly, and he knew Sergeant First Class P from a previous assignment somewhere too. Either from when he was in Division before or down at Benning, either on the trail or Pathfinder School or something. Either way, he and Sergeant First Class P were familiar with one another, but of course, not best friends.

Our platoon was definitely diverse in its leadership. Me and Javier were Hispanic, Staff Sergeant S and Sergeant First Class P were Black, and Shaky was a blond-haired, blue-eyed Marylander. It sounds like the beginning of a racial joke that your drunk uncle would tell during family cookouts: so two Mexicans, two Black guys, and a White guy walk into an infantry platoon . . .

I thought Javier was tabbed and he thought the same about me. We were sitting there outside of a foxhole, shooting the shit, and he asked me where I had been. I told him that I had come from 3rd Battalion and had been here in 1 Panther almost a year. The next morning, when the sun came up, he said to me, "Augi, you're not tabbed?"

I said, "No, and you're not either?"

He said, "Hell no brother, I thought you were."

"Why would you think that?" I asked.

"Because you said you came from Third Battalion."

"Oh, shit!" He had thought I meant 3rd Ranger Battalion and I just assumed he was because he mentioned Pathfinder School and Benning. So we laughed it off. He had actually been one of our machine gunner's drill sergeants at Benning too. During breakfast chow, he pointed him out and started talking shit to him.

Shaky passed Pre-Ranger Course and was leaving for Benning in about a week, so he and I did some celebrating. I was getting ready to go to Jumpmaster School down the street around the same time. One morning before PT, we were sitting in our normal morning meeting with the platoon sergeant. He looked around and asked, "Which one of you motherfuckas smells like aaalcohol?"

I said, "I think it's Shaky, Sergeant."

Shaky looked at me and replied with a big old smile on his face, "Don't even try it, dude."

Sergeant First Class P looked at me and said, "Let me tell you somethin' motherfucka: you're gonna fuck around and become a goddamn specialist. I'm gonna tell ya that right goddamn now."

"Oh no, Sergeant First Class P, if you smell alcohol on me, that's not from drinking, it's the Rogaine I applied to my head this morning." I was going bald at the time and Sergeant First Class P's hair was thinning also.

"Does that shit work?" he asked.

"Oh, roger that, Sergeant, I already got little stubbles of hair coming in and shit."

Then he asked, "How much does that shit cost?"

"Ah, it ain't much, Sergeant, about ten bucks a bottle at the PX." I completely changed the subject on his ass, from smelling like booze to Rogaine for Men's hair regrowth formula. We got into PT formation and Shaky and the other two squad leaders couldn't stop laughing.

I made it all the way through Advanced Airborne School, with only one problem, I failed JMPI. Oh yeah, two problems: I wasn't reentry qualified either because earlier on in the course, I also failed the written exam the first time. So like I said before, you must pass all previous tests, first time go to be reentry qualified to come back and just test on JMPI or PWAC (practical work in the aircraft).

Jumpmaster School was a three-week course, with five major tests a paratrooper must pass to graduate: nomenclature, written exam, giving sustained airborne training or AKA prejump, PWAC, and the dreaded JMPI. PWAC was actually when you put jumpers out of an aircraft, usually a C130 for testing. As long as you covered all commands and didn't move your feet while holding onto your static line, you were good. You exited about two or three students and then you exit yourself. You didn't know if you were a go or a no-go until you got back to the schoolhouse later that evening and checked a sheet of paper taped to the wall with all students' roster numbers on it.

JMPI was the make-or-break test, and when I went through (both times) it was the last test. You had to inspect three jumpers, one *Hollywood*, and two combat equipped. Hollywood simply means with just helmet, main, and reserve parachutes. Each student got five minutes to inspect all three jumpers, and each were rigged with at least three deficiencies with their equipment. As you inspected, you had to remain in proper sequence, keeping your face approximately six inches from the items you're inspecting, calling out each deficiency on where it lay on the jumper, and do it all within five minutes or under. Each student got three attempts and two additional attempts if they were reentry qualified.

After I failed it, I got into my little truck and drove back to the company. I said this back then and I'll say it now: once you failed JMPI, the cadre should have made the student wait at least fifteen minutes before they allowed them to drive off because they were thinking about what they fucked-up on the rest of the day, not the road they were driving on. I walked into the company, and you know right where I had to go.

"Okay, when you going back for JMPI?" he asked me as if I were reentry qualified.

"I have to go back through the whole thing again, Sergeant."

"What the fuck for?"

"I failed the written exam the first time and had to retest on it."

"What the fuck! You mean to tell me you failed the fuckin' written fuckin' exam?"

"Roger, Sergeant."

"Get the fuck out of here. I swear I'm gonna make you a fuckin' SAW Gunner . . ."

Soon ORS (operational readiness survey) and DRF1 time came around again. ORS preparations were supposed to be a time to kind of relax, get your squad together, clean and do maintenance on all squad equipment, and fill out the proper maintenance. We were not in the field, we were in the barracks for the next couple of weeks. It was winter time outside and cold, and it was just nice to not have to be in the fucking woods for a change. We thought it was going to be nice and peaceful for the next couple of weeks before we got into the holidays. Nope. Did I happen to forget where I was at and what platoon I was in?

Shaky had unfortunately failed and been released from Ranger School. I think he had gotten injured on a fifteen-mile foot march. Anyway, now he and the rest of us squad leaders were all together every day in my room, cleaning our weapons. Staff Sergeant S lived off post and used to keep his ruck, LCE, and helmet in my room. Shaky lived in quarters and he started doing the same. Javier lived upstairs in Shaky's old room.

Javier was a geographical bachelor, meaning his wife and kids were still down at Benning off post, kind of like Shaky's had been. Actually, I don't blame Javier because he had a real nice house down there. His kids liked their schools, and his wife had a real good job. I believe his plan was to knock out a few years of line time and head on back to Benning.

Anyway, my room would start to look cluttered with their shit on my floor every day, and I used to joke and tell them, "This ain't no fuckin' storage area." They would joke back and tell me, "At ease." They were all E-6s and I was the only E-5 squad leader, so they used to fuck with me and tell me, "At ease, Sergeant" all the time. I would always reply back with, "Fuck you, Staff Sergeant."

Now both Javier and Shaky were both senior E-6s, and if I'm not mistaken, at the time they were both eligible for the next E-7 selection board. I'd have the coffee brewing and my room filled with cigarette smoke. Me, Shaky, and S all smoked. Javier was the only one who didn't, but it didn't bother him. This is how the first day of ORS prep went for us—smokin' and jokin' and letting our hair down a little bit. That party ended real quick.

"What the fuck y'all doin?" There he was standing in my doorway.

"Cleaning our weapons, Sergeant."

"No shit, I can see that. What the fuck are your squads doin'?"

"They're upstairs in the hallway, cleaning their shit too, Sergeant."

S said, "Yeah the team leaders are with them, making sure they're gettin' their shit done."

Javier told him that one of us squad leaders would periodically go upstairs and check on them and make sure they weren't in their rooms fucking off.

Sergeant First Class P yelled back with, "Oh, like you motherfuckas are doing right now? You motherfuckas need to be up their asses getting this shit done right. Y'all too busy worried about sitting down here in Aga-naga's room drinking fuckin' coffee and smokin' your fuckin' cigarettes." He looked at me and said, "Let me use your phone."

I said, "Go ahead, Sergeant." That was the only reason he had to come down to my room, to use my phone, which he did often. So he might as well give us a little ass-chewing while he was there. When he was done with my phone, he wanted all our 2404 folders that each of us maintained on all our squad's equipment.

"They're upstairs with the team leaders, Sergeant. We'll get 'em and bring them to you in your office."

He said, "That's right. I want to see all of them, to see how fucked-up y'all's shit is."

We all told him the same thing, "My shit's good, Sergeant. All up to date and everything."

"Yeah, we'll see."

We all ran upstairs, grabbed our shit, and made sure it was as good as we were boasting about to him. So after we checked it out, we handed them to Shaky and he took the whole pile of them down to Sergeant First Class P.

After lunch, we came back to my room and sat on my couch, feeling full and wanting to close our eyes. Our weapons were upstairs being guarded with the rest of the platoon's while everyone was at chow.

After about a half hour, we all woke up to, "Well, well, well. I didn't know it was motherfuckin' nap time in Sergeant Aga-naga's room. I didn't see that on the fuckin' training schedule. I must have missed that shit. Bring yo' fuckin' asses down to my office."

We all sat in front of his desk with our green books, waiting for the ass-chewing. "Why are all your 2404s lookin' all sloppy, like a fuckin' five-year-old wrote them?" he asked all of us. "Why ain't that shit typed?"

We thought this was going to be an easy answer. "We don't have a computer and a printer to use, Sergeant."

I asked him if he wanted us to use his.

"Let me tell ya somethin', fuckin' smart ass: fuck no you ain't usin' my shit." I got it again. "You know what? I'm about to make you a fuckin' SAW Gunner. Fuckin' bald-headed motherfucka."

Oh yeah, by this point I had stopped sugarcoating my hair and started shaving my head.

"You see what I'm sayin'? None of you motherfuckas are taken this ORS seriously. Let me tell y'all somethin', if this platoon fails ORS, there's gonna be four squad leaders goin' to the fuckin' S-4 Shop."

I remember thinking to myself and I'm sure the other three were too: *How is not having our 2404s typed up going to cause us to fail the inspection?*

The next morning's meeting before PT, he told us to grab a couple of our guys and bring them back to his office. When they got down there, he handed them his car keys and told them to go out and grab the computer and printer from his back seat. We all sat there looking at each other and didn't say anything. When the kids came back, they asked him where he wanted the pieces. He looked at me and asked, "Is your room open?"

"Roger, Sergeant." I looked confused, but not for long. We all figured out where this was going.

He sat back in his chair with his famous smile and said, "There y'all go. You got yourselves a computer and a printer to work with.

Now y'all have a means to have all your documents typed up, starting with your 2404s."

I had to ask, "So my room is now the platoon administrative office too?"

Sergeant First Class P said, "Why not? You don't do shit in there anyway, but drink yo' fuckin' coffee and smoke yo' fucking cigarettes! So I want all yo' shit typed up, startin' with those fuckin' 2404s before ORS Inspection. Got it?"

"Roger, Sergeant, " we all replied.

S asked him where he'd gotten the equipment.

P sat back in his chair and said to us, "You know what y'all's fuckin' problem is? Y'all don't know how to *network*. You motherfuckas need to know how to network if you wanna be successful around here."

Inspection time came and we couldn't wait to get it over and get Sergeant First Class P off our backs! We were in BDUs and upstairs in the platoon area waiting for the Division inspectors to come to the company. After formation and after each platoon got their briefing of what was going to be inspected, Sergeant First Class P called us into his office.

Surprisingly, he was really happy and excited. "Okay, y'all did it, you made it to this point. You just sit back and let the Division guys do their shit; your shit is done and complete. Now you motherfuckas can walk around and drink yo' coffee and smoke yo' fuckin' cigarettes."

I remember sitting there and telling myself *This wasn't hard, what was the big deal?* I guess we were all happy that he was in a good mood. Anyway, we passed ORS and assumed DRF1.

I woke up a little late one morning, threw on my PTs, slipped on my flip-flops, grabbed my green book, and ran down the hallway to the platoon sergeant's office. I ran in and sat on the chair next to the platoon leader's little file cabinet. The other squad leaders were sitting on the couch. "I'm here, I'm here, Sergeant, sorry, I woke up a little late," I said.

"What the fuck do you have on?"

"My PTs, Sergeant, with my shower shoes."

"Did you shave?"

"No, not yet, Sergeant, I just got out of bed."

"What the fuck does AR 670 dash one say about shaving and being in Army uniform?"

I was losing my patience and said, "I know what AR 670 dash one says, Sergeant."

He said, "Okay, motherfucka, tell me what the fuck it says."

"It says you must be clean-shaven and in the proper uniform."

He asked, "Unless?"

"Unless you're on shaving profile, Sergeant."

"Are you on fuckin' profile?"

I jumped up off the chair. "Fuck no I ain't on fuckin' profile! I ain't never been on fuckin' profile my entire life!"

He said, "Sit yo' fuckin' ass down, motherfucka!"

"No, fuck that, Sergeant! It's six o'clock in the fuckin' morning and you're bitchin' to me about 670 dash-fucking one! I'm sick of this shit!"

"You better sit yo' ass down before I—"

I cut him off and said, "What, fire my fuckin' ass? Fuck that, I quit!"

I got up and went down to my room, shaved real quick, put on my sweat top and bottoms, socks, shoes, and my PT Belt, and went outside to formation. As I stood outside in the cold, I thought to myself, *What the fuck did I just do? I just ended my career.* I felt terrible, but at the same time I was relieved that I had finally given it back to him. It didn't matter; I was going to lose in the end anyway for disrespecting a senior NCO. I wondered what platoon the first sergeant was going to put me in or if I was going to have to change companies.

Sergeant First Class P and Shaky never came out of the barracks to formation. Javier took over the platoon and dismissed us to go do PT. I felt sick to my stomach, turned it over to my A Team leader and went back to my room. I took a shower, got into BDUs, and waited for Sergeant First Class P to fire me. Around 0830 he knocked on my door and I said, "Yes, Sergeant."

He had a shit-eating grin on his face and asked, "Can I use your phone?"

"Roger, Sergeant."

I was confused. That was it? I never heard a word about it from him again. Later on, I found out that Shaky talked him out of doing anything and reminded him that I was pretty loyal to the platoon and not so bad of a leader.

Winter went by, the holidays came and went, and by May1999, we had a rotation at the NTC (National Training Center) at Fort Irwin, California. Unlike JRTC, this training environment is in the hot, arid, open desert and hills of the Mojave. Not really too much fun—of course neither was JRTC, ever. It was just one of those events in the Army that you suck up and drive on, and then you tell yourself in thirty days it's over and you go back to Bragg. Unlike JRTC, there were no old World War II barracks for us to use to prep for the field. Instead, they put us in large outdoor open hangers. We did all our preparations and precombat checks and inspections right out of these areas. There was definitely a lot of downtime there, and that was okay with us because the heat was dry and even dangerous at times.

So the NTC, back in those days, was designed generally for heavy units such as armor and mechanized infantry. I guess because it was open desert as far as the eye could see and it was a way for these vehicles to move more freely for training. This training facility was a gold mine for heavy units to train, especially after that ass-whooping we had laid on Saddam Hussein and the Iraqi army during Desert Storm a few years before. It wasn't the norm for the Army to send many light infantry units out there. They were mainly kept for training at JRTC, at the time.

Like at JRTC, our company had to go through a couple of live-fire maneuver ranges out there before we went into the desert for two weeks. I'm not quite sure what kind of range it was, but I remember they had us start early in the morning, before the heat really kicked. We still had the typical body armor, and we had to take our assault packs on our backs because everybody had to carry mortar rounds to drop off as we moved into our positions. Afterward, they got us into the shade to do our after-action reports and then move back to the hangers.

The whole two weeks in the desert, I'm not kidding, I believe we only conducted one force-on-force fight and that was the "grand finale" at the end, in which we were in a defensive perimeter on a hill. The heat index was too high for training across Fort Irwin, so units were told to keep their guys in the shade drinking water. I remember we were in a big-ass company perimeter for days. Everybody was to set up under their hootches and we made them stay in the shade pretty much while the sun was up. The four of us squad leaders took our ponchos, snapped them all together, and made ourselves one giant hooch. The commander, first sergeant, XO, platoon leaders, and platoon sergeants put up their hootches in between the two company Humvees. This was the first time in the Army that we had an area that looked like a "gypsy camp," and nobody said anything about it. It was awesome. If you're going to be in the field and sucking, this was the way to do it. Of course later on, after 9/11, we didn't get that luxury. It didn't matter if it was 120 degrees, you were out in the shit, but that's another book down the road.

Anyway, we stayed out of the sun, played a lot of cards, and just talked a lot to each other, mainly joking around and messing with each other. This is probably one of the reasons, other than having such a hard platoon sergeant, that we all got along great and remain friends to this day. We played a new game that sticks with me to this day, especially if you're sitting around a bonfire. I've introduced a lot of people to it over the years and it was created at my first rotation to NTC. It is called the "Name Game."

The rules are pretty simple: you name a famous person, real or fictional, such as a cartoon character. First and last name is given, the next person in clockwise order has to say another famous person, but his or her name has to begin with the letter of the last name that you gave him. For example, I say Willie Nelson to S. S has to respond with someone whose first name starts with N, like Nicholas Cage. It may sound stupid, but it sure as hell passes the time. Me, S, Shaky, and Javier played that game every day during our field rotation, and we played it so much we would run out of names and have to agree to start over.

It was getting crazy out there in the desert heat. It was nothing to see a soldier standing in an empty MRE box with a trash bag filled with water, taking a bath in the middle of the perimeter. I turned around one day and there was a "Joe" standing, butt-ass naked, washing his nasty ass in front of God and everyone. Nobody gave a shit either.

After our big two-hour battle on the last night, we rode back to main post in five-ton trucks, got assigned another overhead hanger, showered and got cleaned up, and put on clean BDUs. They had trailers set up for us with hot showers and toilets. So for the next few days before we went home, it was normal cleaning of equipment, and turning in our MILES Gear. Oh yeah, Sergeant First Class P didn't have us attach the harnesses to our LCEs like he had at JRTC. I guess not guarding the brigade HQs didn't have us in the limelight enough to get that detailed and OCD this time around. Plus, like I said, I only remember one major battle the whole field exercise anyway.

Something else I remember from that NTC trip that I won't forget—I finally made the E-6 cut-off score, after waiting for it since Korea. We were shooting the shit in the hanger one evening and Sergeant First Class P called me over. He was sitting with the first sergeant and the other two platoon sergeants.

"Congratulations, Staff Sergeant Aga-naga."

I said, "What?"

"Yeah, you made this month's cut-off." They were sitting there with an *Army Times* one of them had bought. I looked at it and saw my name on the promotion list. Back in those days, it also had my Basic Noncommissioned Officer Course date as well, which was right around the corner, too. The First Sergeant asked me if I wanted to get pinned on (promoted) in front of the company.

I said, "No, just want to sew it on when we get back to Bragg, if that's okay, First Sergeant."

He was cool with it and when we got back, I showed up with staff sergeant chevrons on my collar. When I was walking away to tell my buddies, Sergeant First Class P hollered out to me, "It's about fuckin' time!" I simply turned around and smiled at him, as he smiled back at me.

After the rotation, our battalion had fourteen days block leave coming up over the Fourth of July time period. I was going home to Michigan to visit family and friends, come back to Bragg, and pack up for the two months back at Fort Benning for my BNCOC class.

After block leave, I needed to go back to Michigan for an upcoming wedding the following weekend, so I put in for a four-day weekend pass. I would drive up Thursday night after duty and be back late Monday night before Tuesday morning formation. Too easy. I filled out the pass request and slipped it onto Sergeant First Class P's desk.

Later, I heard him holler. "Hey ahh, Staff Sergeant Aga-naga, get yo' ass down here!"

I walked in his office, "Yes, Sergeant."

"Why the fuck do you need to go on a four-day pass when yo' ass just got off block leave?"

So here came my explanation. "Ahh, Sergeant, I met this fine-ass girl that I'm kinda seein' now and there's a wedding she's going to this weekend, and I want to surprise her and take her to it."

"A wedding?"

"Yes, Sergeant, I'm gonna wear my class As, with my beret and jump boots, and I'm gonna be blingin'."

Here it comes, the most memorable line I ever heard from Sergeant First Class P. "Whoa, whoa, whoa, whoa! Class As? Why the fuck would you wear yo' Class As? You ain't got shit on 'em anyway, you non-Ranger, non-Jumpmaster, bald-headed motherfucka." Then I looked down and he was signing my pass request. Then he ordered me, "Here, go take this down to the orderly room for the CO to sign it."

I said, "Ahh thanks a lot, Sergeant, this is going to be the shit!"

Sergeant First Class P replied to me with, "Let me tell you somethin': you ain't back Tuesday morning in formation, I'm gonna fire yo' fuckin' ass."

I was so excited, I took my leave form and said back, "Oh shit, Sergeant, I'll be back by Monday night—too easy."

He just looked at me and said in a real low, sarcastic tone, "Class As . . ."

I had about five days before I was on my way back to Georgia in order to secure my new rank of staff sergeant by attending and graduating from the basic noncommissioned officer course. Back in those days, you had to graduate Primary Leadership Development Course to secure E-5, Basic Noncommissioned Officer Course to secure E-6, and Advanced Noncommissioned Officer Course to secure E-7. All three and any NCO academy require each candidate to first pass the Army height and weight and physical fitness test on day one in order to remain and start the course. Failing an NCO academy for any reason, especially height and weight or PT test, would be a career stopper for the soldier, but would also look terrible on the unit that had sent him or her. For that reason alone, the brigade command sergeant major had a policy that any NCO within the brigade who was going to attend any of the academies would have to pass a height and weight within five days of reporting to the school. Also, they would have to pass it by a senior NCO at Brigade HQ. The PT test was given at the unit level prior to them leaving, but the weigh-in had to be verified by Command Sergeant Major X first. Apparently, we'd had too many NCOs fail it in the past and he was doing everything he could to prevent it from happening again. He must have gotten his ass chewed by the division command sergeant major one too many times.

It just happened that one of my team leaders was scheduled for PLDC at the same time I was headed off to BNCOC. So he and I had to walk across the street to Brigade HQ and get our five-day-out weigh-in.

Now, Command Sergeant Major X's policy was that every soldier got their height and weight checked and received a tape test also. The tape test was given if a soldier was overweight by standard, meaning the number on the scale was too high for that soldier's age. If that happened, they would get a measuring tape test around the waist and neck to measure body fat percentage. For example, you may have a soldier that is overweight according to his height and age standard, but he may be built like a body builder. Therefore, he would get his body fat measured. If a soldier passed the tape test, they passed the weigh-in. Command Sergeant Major X's policy was that they had to pass both regardless. If they did not, obviously they would not be going to school until they did.

I passed both, but my team leader did not. It sounds weird, but he passed the height and weight test, but failed the tape test by a couple percentage points. The NCO giving the test told him he wouldn't be going to Primary Leadership Development Course for this upcoming class. I was pissed. Mainly because this whole concept was stupid. Nobody gets taped if they pass the height and weight standard in the first place. I argued with the NCO about it before he suggested I go see the command sergeant major. I agreed to in a heartbeat. I wasn't going to stand there and let one of my soldiers get screwed over because of stupidity like this.

"Get in here, Airborne! What do you got for me?" he bellowed when I showed up.

I attempted to explain my team leader's situation. Command Sergeant Major X replied, "That's fine, but he doesn't make the body fat."

I argued, "Yes, but Sergeant Major, he won't have to worry about the tape test because he makes the weight."

I got the same thing. "But he doesn't make the body fat."

I continued to argue, "But Sergeant Major, he won't have to worry about—" I got cut off real quick.

"Okay, I can see where the fuck this is goin'." Then he said, and

I'm not bullshitting, "Flip to the flap to the floop—Get the fuck out!" I didn't say shit. I assumed the position of attention, made a right face, and marched the fuck out of his office. I told my team leader he would not be attending this PLDC class. I told him to drop about ten or fifteen pounds and we'd get him in again later.

BNCOC was a pretty fun time. It was a three-hour drive away from my unit at Bragg and at first, I thought I was on a minivacation, which it was to a certain point. It was pretty much a party almost every night, especially in the barracks, which were right behind Airborne school, down the same sidewalk. The instructors were real laid-back and easygoing.

It was your typical NCO academy with test after test in the classrooms, and a day and night land navigation course. We also had to go through a small field exercise where we were evaluated on infantry battle drills and patrolling according to FM 7-8, which was actually easier than what Sergeant First Class P used to put us through. I passed everything with no problem. It also was my first opportunity to interact with other 11 series soldiers from all over the different units in the Army. Since this was my first time with other infantry MOSs, I noticed there was another reality I hadn't really been aware of at the time. There was a prejudice that existed in that school environment as well. No, not a racial prejudice, an MOS prejudice. The light infantry and mechanized infantry guys seemed to have a problem with each other. Hell, that's the way it was across the Army when it came to the light and heavy units. It was crazy and foolish, but it doesn't mean it didn't exist. Especially with how young we all still were at the time. Most of us were staff sergeants, still in our twenties, and had a lot of testosterone to throw around, like we had something to prove. Even the cadre had their problems with classes mixing students that were light or heavy.

The 75th Ranger Regiment guys pretty much stuck to themselves, except for one student who had longer hair, all combed back. They seemed to cling to him, wanting to hang out with him all the time. He wore a maroon beret with the Special Operations Command patch and had a Ranger tab above that. It was the first time I had come into contact with a real Delta Force operator. This dude was a stud. Hell, even the instructors were having him give us classes on building- and room-clearing techniques when we were in the field. I used to wonder what the hell he was going to gain from this school, but like it was for the rest of us, it was mostly a check in the box for him. He had his Ranger Battalion buddies be his demonstrators. It was pretty cool. Anyway, it was a pretty fun and educational time.

"Oh you upset because the party's over?" This of course was the first meeting back with my platoon and the first question Sergeant First Class P asked me.

I quickly responded, "Oh it wasn't a party, Sergeant."

He quickly rebutted, "Oh, bullshit! You can't bullshit me motherfucka. I know BNCOC is a party. Wait till you go back there for ANCOC."

I didn't mention the kegs of beer that we had in the latrines in the barracks down there. One per floor on the weekends. Hell, our senior instructor had come from 2 Panther and he kept a refrigerator full of beer in his office downstairs on the first floor. I asked him one time how he ended up at Infantry BNCOC. Come to find out, that poor bastard had broken his back on a nighttime jump. He had landed on the hood of a Humvee that had been dropped in prior to the personnel parachuting.

"Now that that shit's over, you know where you have to go back to now right?" Sergeant First Class P reminded me.

"Roger, Sergeant." It was time for me to get back to Jumpmaster School once and for all. It had been a few months since my last class, so I would have to take the pretest again to get in, but I wasn't worried about that. I was ready and couldn't wait to go back.

Before I left for the next class at the Advanced Airborne School, the word was that our famous platoon sergeant had made the E-8 promotion list, which meant it was time for him to move companies soon. It was still in question where or what exact company the brigade leadership was going to put him in. It is common that battalion command sergeant majors assign platoon sergeants and brigade command sergeant majors assign company first sergeants. It's actually properly pronounced "command sergeants major" for plural, but it just never sounded right to me. Everything in the Army as far as leadership assignment and evaluation is always two commands up. I didn't have time to think about it much because I had to get myself ready for school. I passed the pretest on a Friday and over the weekend I was getting prepared. I had my face in that study guide. I stripped the camouflage cover off my ballistic helmet and put new parts onto it, such as a headband and chinstrap. You have to get your helmet ready for day one, and before you leave on day one, your roster number gets taped on the front and back of it. I stripped off my E-Tool and two-quart canteen from my ALICE pack and was ready to go.

The first two weeks of Jumpmaster School came and went, and I passed everything, first time go. This obviously put me in the safe zone to be reentry qualified, if need be, but I wasn't worrying about it then. Monday morning was day one of JMPI. If I remember correctly, the last two days of the week were the infamous test days. That weekend, I went out to loosen up and have a good time. Shaky and I went out to a couple of bar and grills in Fayetteville and simply had a relaxing weekend.

I did some *shadow-boxing* in my room on that Sunday. Shadow-boxing is going through the JMPI sequence without having an actual jumper in front of you. You simply go through the sequence, using your hands and eyes, and just run through it the way the Black Hats taught us.

During the first two weeks that I was in Jumpmaster School, Sergeant First Class P did get frocked to first sergeant and was moved over to another company within our battalion. Shaky was our acting platoon sergeant. I think there was a little animosity between him and Javier because Javier had more time in grade as an E-6 than Shaky, but the fact of the matter was that Sergeant First Class P wanted Shaky to be the platoon sergeant because he had been our weapons squad leader the whole time he had been in the platoon. Shit, I didn't have time to worry about their little spat. My "fifty-meter target" was getting through JMPI and graduating Jumpmaster School.

Since I'd failed my first two tests, the pressure was on. I had failed for time, not for sequence violation or missing deficiencies, which was a good thing. I had it all right, I just needed to pick it up a little bit. This last test, I finished the third jumper and the Black Hat showed me my time. It was like 4:54. He didn't say anything at first, just, "Here's your time, Jumpmaster."

I asked, "Did I get all my deficiencies, Sergeant?" I know I wasn't a sequence violation because they stop you right on the spot if you are.

"Yes, you did, Jumpmaster. You're a go." He signed my grade sheet and told me to take it to the grading table around the corner. I ran my ass over there and if I could, I would have been backflipping all the way there. I handed in my go slip and the instructor said, "Congrats, Jumpmaster, and don't ever JMPI three jumpers that fast ever again. You take your time for every jumper." They tell you that during the course because three jumpers in under five minutes is for test purposes. If they see you do it on the street, they may disqualify you for being unsafe. Yes, jumpmaster instructors come to the units on Ardennes Street during their Mass-Tac exercises periodically, to evaluate the unit jumpmaster teams, or at least they used to.

He then told me that our graduation ceremony was 1300 the next day. I got into my truck and drove back to the company. I got into the barracks, reached into my refrigerator, and popped open a beer. I sat down on the couch and just savored the moment. I remember the company was empty. Maybe they were at a weapons qualification range or something. Hell, I didn't care. I was still "hands off" from the company until after graduation.

I did feel sort of empty that I couldn't walk down the hallway to my old platoon sergeant's office and talk a little shit. I could have imagined him telling me, "I told ya, Iiiii told ya." I almost walked down to his new company, but I didn't. I could only imagine what that unit was going through with that new hurricane coming. I wondered if they even knew what they were getting. I'm sure they did. Everybody knew who he was. As I took a sip of beer, I remember thinking that I had thought my name had changed to *Motherfucka* for the last year and a half.

Like I previously mentioned, Shaky was the new acting platoon sergeant. He had one of his gunners running the weapons squad. He was a pretty squared-away kid. Actually, the two machine gunners in a rifle platoon are usually two of the most squared-away soldiers, or they wouldn't be in the positions.

They pretty much have it down to a science. They know how to set up the machine gun with its tripod and put it into operation within seconds. They go through drills on it constantly. With Shaky in the command post, our platoon also got a new platoon leader as well. I'm not sure where our old one went at the time, he may have been branch detailed, which means he was of another branch such as signal or perhaps military intelligence. Branch-detailed lieutenants usually knocked out two years as an infantry platoon leader and then they went back to their original branch they were commissioned in, which meant moving units.

One thing I will say: I mostly found that branch-detailed platoon leaders were more squared away than the actual Infantry branch ones. That's just my opinion and experience during my time in a line unit.

I remember running into our old platoon leader at Fort Riley, Kansas about ten years later at a computer-simulated center for training. He was a major and was in Special Forces, getting ready to deploy again to the Middle East. We hung out that whole day and reminisced about the "Sergeant First Class P Regime" days, where he'd only had a little file cabinet for a desk in the command post.

Our battalion had another alert coming up that everybody already was aware of. We knew we would be going through the eighteen-hour sequence, which meant spending time over at the PHA again. I'm telling you, if you spent any time in the 82nd Airborne Division, these training exercises became more and more routine the more the years went by. This was a good opportunity for Shaky to get his debut as platoon sergeant and some good rated evaluation time for preparing and getting a platoon through an alert process, followed by an airborne assault, with a two-day follow-on mission.

Prior to the actual callout, we did our own preparations to get ready the day before. We had all the soldiers out on the rocks with their ALICE packs (I couldn't call them rucksacks anymore because I was now a current, qualified jumpmaster, and damn it felt great. ALICE pack is the only name for that piece of equipment to jumpmasters). We inspected their packing list by having them empty everything out and as we called each item out, the soldiers held it up and then put it back in their ALICE packs. The last items we inspected to ensure that everyone had were their air items, which enabled them to lower their equipment during a jump. Those are pretty much the most important items in a paratrooper's packing list. As we checked them, they put them away on top of the rest of the packing list. Everybody had all equipment during this inspection.

The reason I am emphasizing this is because of one of my soldiers in my squad. Remember the kid nicknamed Jack I mentioned? Well, Jack got his name because he was all "jacked the fuck up" all the time. "Mr. Former Navy SEAL Trainee" was a nonperformer. Not because of laziness or anything like that, but he just couldn't connect to get it done. He was "jacked up." He wasn't even a real shitbag either. He did great on PT, was always on time and in the correct uniform, and was always respectful. His match just didn't light the fire most of the time.

So the next morning at zero dark thirty, we got on the cattle trucks and headed down to the PHA. After we were complete with some rehearsals, we received our combat orders from the new platoon leader and had our guys start rigging their equipment to jump. Well, guess who was missing a major air item? Jack! He came up to me with his team leader. I looked up at him and just knew something was wrong.

"What's up?" I asked.

The team leader told Jack, "Go ahead, tell him."

"What? Tell me what?"

Jack said to me very humbly, "I forgot my 'rig,' Sergeant—"

"Your rig? What the fuck is a rig, Jack!" I knew what he was talking about, but I couldn't believe it. "Do you mean your harness single-point release, Jack?" I don't know what I was more pissed about, him making up his own nomenclature for air items, or the fact that he had forgotten the largest air item there is. "How the fuck do you forget the largest air item there is, Jack!" I can see forgetting or misplacing a small item such as a quick-release snap, which was pretty common at times, and we even carried extras because of it, but a fucking harness single-point release?

Just to give a quick explanation of what this item is used for, to those not familiar, it is the harness system that you wrap your ALICE pack in in order to lower it to the ground before the jumper impacts.

"Oh, and by the way, Jack, we don't normally carry extras of those, you fucking dumbass! We're not allowed to go back to the unit area to get you another one either. So your ass is pretty much mission incapable because you won't have your equipment!"

Then I really got pissed when he asked me this, "Does this mean I can't jump tonight, Sergeant?"

"Oh, fuck no, motherfucker! Your fucking ass is jumping, don't you worry about that, Jack!" I asked, "Is that why you took it out of your ALICE pack, because you thought that was going to get you out of this jump tonight?"

"Negative, Sergeant, I think I took it out to get something out of my ruck last night and forgot to put it back in, Sergeant."

Even after we told the whole platoon to not open their ALICE packs after the previous day's inspection.

"Get this motherfucker out of my face, Sergeant," I said to his team leader. I went and told Shaky about Jack's little problem. I asked him if he wanted him to leave his ALICE pack with the supply sergeant and just have him jump with his weapon. The next day or so, we could figure out how to get it back out to him.

Shaky said, "No, I'll take care of it. We're gonna get hot chow; I'll have the supply sergeant bring him out one when he comes back with dinner."

I told my buddy, "Roger that. Thanks, brother."

Jack's team leader had him in the front leaning rest and on his back with his feet elevated the rest of the afternoon.

Tonight's airborne operation was going to be my first official jumpmaster duty. Shaky was going to be the primary jumpmaster and I was going to be one of his safeties. We were jumping out of a C-130, with the same old timeline of 0100 or 0200 TOT. This time it was over the biggest and easiest drop zone on Bragg—Sicily. The reason I say easiest is that it has the easiest reference points to identify in the air, day or night, for the two JMs on each door of the aircraft. I believe Holland was my second favorite.

Anyway, all chalks were now going to be C-130s for the next few months because the Air Force had recently gotten rid of the classic C-141s. They were done with them and weren't making any more. The new larger jet aircraft that would be used in the near future and is still used today is the C-17 Globemaster. This aircraft could hold and deliver one hundred paratroopers. I called it the "Cadillac" because each jumper had more room, with their own individual seat that they got to put down and put back up themselves. You just had more room all around, and once I performed jumpmaster duties out of one, I never wanted to go back to a C-130 again.

So let me briefly explain what is required to receive your Senior Parachute Wings in the Army. One has to be a current, qualified jumpmaster, have a minimum of thirty jumps, and perform an assistant jumpmaster duty during a nighttime combat equipment jump. Now before a new jumpmaster can perform an assistant jumpmaster duty, according to the Division policy, they must complete at least two safety duties first. At least this used to be the standard fifteen to twenty years ago, so it may have changed since then.

Now, a jumpmaster team of an aircraft consisted of a primary jumpmaster, who was overall in charge and responsible for all jumpers, an assistant jumpmaster, and two safeties—one per door. The safety's primary duties are to annotate names and social security numbers of each jumper on the manifest and seat all paratroopers onboard the aircraft prior to station time. The entire airborne timeline is based off backward planning from the station time of the operation. That is when all paratroopers for all chalks are seated and ready for takeoff. The jumpmaster ultimately fails their duties if they do not make station time.

Finally, the safeties are responsible for controlling each paratrooper's static line as they exit the aircraft. Once all jumpers are airborne, the safeties do a final check outside the aircraft to ensure there are no towed parachutists. They both come back inside, give each other a thumbs-up, and then pull the static lines back inside the aircraft. Usually, the Air Force loadmasters helped out with that. The safeties do not parachute; instead, they land back at Pope Air Force Base and have to turn in the parachute deployment bags, which the static lines are attached to, from their respected chalk. In between rigging and loading the aircraft, safeties obviously help JMPI the jumpers as well. So that night was my first safety duty as a new jumpmaster.

After we JMPI'd all the jumpers on our chalk, we were standing around waiting for the Air Force to come get us to load up. All of a sudden, we heard, "Well, well, motherfuckin' well!"

"Oh shit, I know that voice," I said. I turned around and there he was, First Sergeant P. He had come over to say hi. "Staff Sergeant Aga-naga, what the fuck you got that red arm band on for? Don't tell me you a fuckin' jumpmaster now."

I said, "Hell yeah, First Sergeant, I finally got that shit."

"You doin' your first safety?"

"Roger First Sergeant."

"Who's yo' primary jumpmaster?"

I said, "Old Shaky, First Sergeant."

Shaky came over and shook his hand. "How you doin' as platoon sergeant, Shaky?"

"It's goin' smooth so far, First Sergeant," Shaky responded. He looked back at me and said, "You know what you have to do now, don't you?"

I said to myself, *Here we go.*

"I know, First Sergeant, PRC and Ranger School."

"That's right, don't lose focus on that shit."

The Air Force guy came to get us to move out to our bird.

First Sergeant P said to me, "Next time I see yo' ass, you better be on your way to Ranger School."

"I will, First Sergeant."

He replied sarcastically, "Yeah, we'll see." He always had to get the last word in. But I actually felt bad that for a change, he hadn't referred to us as "motherfuckas." Maybe making first sergeant had made him more politically correct? I don't think so.

Once all of us safeties got back to the base and turned in our D-bags, we linked up with a battalion S-4 soldier who loaded us up on a cattle truck and took us to Sicily DZ to link up with our units. They dropped us off. I locked and loaded my M4 with blank rounds, threw my ALICE pack on my back, put my night vision over my eyes, turned on my radio, and headed in the general direction I knew my platoon would be in off the drop zone.

Our follow-on mission was to secure an intersection about four or five hundred meters off the drop zone to allow follow-on forces to maneuver through. When I approached the opposite corner of the drop zone, I took a knee and tried to call Shaky on the "horn." He answered and told me their location, which was close by in the wood line, just off the drop zone. When I got to them, they were in a triangle security perimeter just waiting for the CO to order us to move out.

After about two hours and some snoring from the troops, the CO called the platoon leader and told him to move us out to secure our objective. We all got up and moved out. Like I said, we only had a few hundred meters to move. As a matter of fact, we squad leaders had pretty much figured what intersection it was. It was generally two main firebreaks off the northeast corner of the drop zone. The OPFOR was made up of three or four broke soldiers from the battalion headquarters that couldn't jump. They were at a checkpoint on the intersection, basically behind two or three pieces of plywood with a few sandbags around it. We attacked just as it was getting daylight and quickly secured the site.

The new platoon leader called the CO and gave the report, then he came back and started getting crazy on us with FM 7-8 shit. He told Staff Sergeant S he wanted him to set out a listening/observation post (LP/OP) about two hundred meters into the wood line.

Staff Sergeant S started sharpshooting him by asking, "An LP/OP, sir?"

We understood the concept of early warning from incoming enemy or enemy in the area, but in reality, we knew it was going to be a matter of minutes before we were going to be ordered to move again. We had seen this "movie" a time or two out here.

"With what radio, sir?" S asked him.

The only radios we had in those days, again, were for the squad leaders, platoon leader, and the platoon sergeant. Shaky came over and took the new platoon leader back over to the center of the perimeter with the RTO (radiotelephone operator) and medic. Later on, we asked Shaky what he had told him.

He said, "Hey, this ain't Ranger School. You're not gonna get a no-go out here. Just wait for 'Six' to give us the order to move out, which will be very soon."

About ten minutes later, the CO called end of mission and ordered the other two platoons to move in our direction, toward the main firebreak. About a half hour later, here came about four five-ton vehicles down the firebreak to pick us up and take us back to the company. We got back to the battalion and grounded all our gear on the rocks, put out one guard per platoon and the first sergeant told us to go to the chow hall and eat breakfast—that's the way you finish off an airborne operation: when you get back in the next morning, you're still in time for breakfast.

A couple of months went by, and we had some changes within the platoon again. We finally got a new platoon sergeant who had come in from the Brigade S-3 shop. Javier made the E-7 list and Brigade moved him over to 2 Panther to start his platoon sergeant time. Staff Sergeant S finally got his wish and when Sergeant First Class P got promoted and moved to another company, he put in his paperwork to request drill sergeant school (DSS) and got it! So he was about to leave for DSS down at Fort Jackson, South Carolina and then come back to Bragg, clear the unit, and PCS to Fort Sill, Oklahoma to be a basic training drill sergeant.

Last but not least, Shaky came down on orders to go back to Korea again for another year! No way. That would suck. *There goes my good buddy,* I told myself. At the time, I had been focused on getting into Pre-Ranger Course, so I had been doing Ranger PT every morning with the battalion scout platoon for the past month or so. It was ass-kicking PT. I'm talking eight-mile runs and shit. They'd have us in the pool for two hours—damn, they were trying to drown our asses— but I was in shape and ready to get to the next class.

Somebody else had recently just left, but not from our platoon or company. The legendary Command Sergeant Major X had left Brigade and moved on to the Fort Bragg NCO Academy as their new commandant. Normally, when that happens to a brigade command sergeant major on Ardennes Street, they usually end up being the division command sergeant major within the next year or two.

Oh yeah, and one more change I almost forgot to mention: I had recently gotten married and was living in a pretty nice condo in Fayetteville. I married the girl from my hometown in Michigan that I had to convince Sergeant First Class P to let me take to her friend's wedding.

We were sitting in the platoon sergeant's office as he went over the changes he was going to make with leadership positions in our platoon. A replacement had come in for Javier. He was an E-6 coming in also from the brigade S-3 shop. S's squad was turned over to his A Team leader for the time being until another E-6 came in. He moved me to weapons squad leader and had my A Team leader take over my squad. I didn't say anything, I just sat there and nodded my head. Actually, I was pondering on my Pre-Ranger Course packing list while the new platoon sergeant was telling us his agenda for the platoon. I remember staring at his desk. It was the usual old metal desk you commonly saw throughout offices in the Army. It was all cluttered with loose papers and whatnot. He had one of the old metal bookshelves with a few regulation manuals just stacked on top of one another. The command post was definitely a different scene. Oh yeah, the platoon leader had his own desk as well. Wasn't used to seeing that.

The new platoon sergeant was a good guy. He had been "born and raised" in Division from a private to a sergeant first class. He wasn't tabbed, had his combat infantryman badge from Division during Desert Storm, and had master wings with over a hundred jumps. He had a real strong Southern accent and a sense of humor. He used to compare everything we would do to the way it used to be fifteen years ago. It was kind of weird at first, because he seemed to be too nice to us, and that's something we were not used to. It was definitely a change but looked to be a positive one. He sort of reminded me of how the platoon sergeants used to be in 3 Panther back when I was new to Division. They were more laid-back, not such Ranger "fanatics."

I said goodbye to my two good friends, Shaky and Staff Sergeant S. I wished them luck and told them I'd be right there in 1 Panther still when they got back from their next duty stations, especially Shaky because his tour in Korea would only be twelve months. His family was still staying in post housing while he was gone. His plan was to come back to Bragg anyway. As far as S went, I would get to see him when he graduated DSS and came back to clear the unit and the post before he moved out to Oklahoma. As far as Javier, he would stop by periodically to say hi. He was enjoying his time in 2 Panther as a platoon sergeant. Just like that, I felt alone for the first time in this company. But I had to remain focused on my next career move: the 82nd Pre-Ranger Course, followed by US Army Ranger School.

I have a confession to make. Even though I was married and lived off post, I still maintained my room in the company across from the CQ desk. I never did turn in the key, and nobody said shit about it either. So I still had the computer and the couch, and I generally used it as our squad area. Now if a new single NCO had gotten assigned to the company and the first sergeant had needed to give him the room, of course I would have turned in the key. But for the time being, nobody said anything.

One morning, I had weapons squad in there and we were cleaning the two guns and going over our 2404s. While in our rooms during duty hours, we always kept our doors open while we were working out of them. The first sergeant came to my door and had a serious look on his face. "Staff Sergeant Augi, come on down. I have to talk to you, bud." I thought to myself that something had happened to a family member back home or my wife or something. I went to his office, and he told me to come in and just sit down.

"Okay, Augi, here it is buddy. You report to Fort Jackson Drill Sergeant School in about ninety days. Afterward, you'll be stationed at Fort Jackson for two years as a Basic Training drill sergeant. Your report date for drill sergeant duty is in about six months. Just like your buddy S that just left, once you graduate DSS, you'll come back here and clear, go on leave for a while, then report to Fort Jackson."

I actually thought I was going to start crying. Instead I got pissed. "Fuck that, First Sergeant. I ain't going. You have to step in with the battalion and brigade command sergeant major and help me get out of this shit. I know out of the three of you, someone has a connection to Infantry Branch at Department of the Army that can get me out of this bullshit." I threw the Ranger thing at him and said, "First

Sergeant, you know I've been doing PT with the scout platoon for the past two months at least. I just took and smoked the Ranger PT test and the swim test with them last week. I was planning on taking the Pre-Ranger Course PT Test down at Towle Stadium the next class, which I think is less than two weeks away."

He cut me off and told me, "I want you to shut up for a minute and listen to what I have to tell you, young man. I know you're all pumped up and ready to go to Ranger School, but it just ain't your time, and I'm not your old platoon sergeant either. I know what you guys had to hear every day under the 'P Regime.' He was the old platoon sergeant that was on the other side of our command post and yes, I'm sure he used to hear it all."

The first sergeant was also a former drill sergeant at Benning before he came here and started his platoon sergeant time. He asked me, "When do you think I went to Ranger School young man?"

I replied, "I don't know—when you were an E-4 or E-5, First Sergeant?"

"No, Augi, when I got done off the Trail as a new E-7. I left drill sergeant duty and went to Ranger School before coming back here and starting my platoon sergeant time. Listen to me, go knock out your drill sergeant time and you will secure your E-7 selection, I guarantee it. Ranger School isn't going anywhere, trust me. Now, don't go down to DSS and fuck it up either. That is still considered an NCO Academy and if you fail it or go down with an attitude like you have now, once you come back, your career will be ended. I can assure you the brigade command sergeant major will have no mercy on you for failing DSS."

"Okay, First Sergeant," I said, still in disbelief. But he had put it all into perspective for me. In those days and probably now, nobody was getting out of drill sergeant or recruiter duty once you were selected by the Department of the Army. After I thought about it, I was going to be the next class down there after Staff Sergeant S.

My next goal before I left for DSS was to get my other safety and my assistant jumpmaster duty knocked out because I'd be damned if I were going to leave Bragg again without my senior wings. The only problem was our battalion didn't have any jumps scheduled until later on around Intensive Training Cycle time again.

So what was a man to do? How could I accomplish this task? Man, this was Fort Fucking Bragg, there was a jump every day of the week. I just had to go out and find a unit up and down the street that would let me tag along. Too easy.

First and obviously, I went to 2 Panther and 3 Panther's S-3 shops to see if they had any upcoming jumps, and they didn't. So I went down toward All-American Highway to the corps support units and started going into their headquarters asking if they had any upcoming jumps. I found one unit that had a jump coming up, a detachment from the 18th Airborne Corps Engineers. They agreed to allow me to be one of their safeties. A daylight Hollywood jump at that. Way too easy.

I went back to my company and got permission from the platoon sergeant and first sergeant. Hell, they didn't care. Our unit wasn't doing shit that day anyway. Plus they knew I was on a time crunch.

I showed up in the morning at the unit conducting the jump, a daytime Hollywood jump over Sicily DZ out of a C-130. It was a beautiful, sunny fall morning, and one couldn't ask for a better day to jump. As a matter of fact, I couldn't remember the last time I had even seen a jump during daylight hours, let alone a Hollywood jump, other than Jumpmaster School. I was excited for this and glad to get a break from a line company for a day. I showed up with my ballistic helmet and my red armband on my right sleeve. I met and shook hands with the primary jumpmaster, assistant jumpmaster, and the other safety. They already had the manifest done and typed up. I was like *Shit, this is going to be an easy, stress-free day.* After they did prejump and parachute landing falls, I got into my truck and headed down to Green Ramp.

When I got there and parked, my mind really got blown away. They had a grill out and some of the spouses were cooking hotdogs and hamburgers for the unit before they started doing mock door training and parachute issue. *Shit! I'm gonna have me a hotdog and a hamburger*, I said to myself. I couldn't believe it. This detachment had turned this airborne operation into a party day. Nobody was stressed, nobody was cursing or threatening each other. Hell, they didn't even have to put paint on their faces. It was a great jump and a great time. It was good to see how the other side of Fort Bragg lived. As I drove home, I remember thinking that I used to live that lifestyle in the Army. Had I made a mistake going to the infantry life over six years ago? Fuck no! I loved it.

My last Intensive Training Cycle in Division before I left to become a new drill sergeant was here. I was all pumped up too. "Let's do this shit!" I told my squad before we headed out to the field. They were all great kids. They all knew me well and knew I was close with their previous squad leader—Shaky—who was well into his first month in Korea again.

We got out to the field and the company started with fire team blank- and live-fire certifications, and then two days later, we'd move to squad blank and live. One thing I quickly realized was that weapons squads didn't have to go through these lanes, that they were mainly for line squads to go through. So we stayed back, rehearsed our drills, and helped out with ammo and water for the lanes.

It wasn't until the next week when we were doing platoon certifications that I had my most memorable live-fire training exercise in my military career. We were tasked with assaulting a trench complex. My squad was responsible for the platoon support by fire. In addition to the M240Bs initially "lighting up" the objective, we had to take out two enemy positions on its far side. This would be achieved using AT-4s. Like we had at any other live-fire maneuver range, we had it down to a science. As we got into our position, we had to wait for the engineers to blow the wire outside the trench. When it was blown, that was our signal to initiate fire on the objective. After about thirty seconds of fire, I pointed at the first AT-4 gunner to fire. *BOOM!*

I then pointed at the second gunner. *BOOM!* Back in those days, most of us squad leaders did not wear ear plugs because we had to be able to communicate through our radios, especially during live-fires because everything had to be so precise to remain safe. After the two AT-4s went off five feet from me on both sides, my hearing gave out. Everything went silent and all I could hear was a constant ringing. My head was a little rocked also. I remember feeling like Tom Hanks in the beginning of *Saving Private Ryan* when he went down on the beach and lost his hearing for a minute. Thank God for visual signals to shift and lift fire because everything was still silent, and I wouldn't have been able to hear through my radio if I had wanted to.

The first VS-17 panel went flying through the air from the assault squad below. I banged on my two gunners' helmets to shift to the left. They had already traversed their guns because they knew what the signals were anyway. Great kids, and they were on their A game. I pulled out my VS-17 and threw it up and out to the objective so the assault squad leader knew we had confirmed the shift. I would wrap and tie off my VS-17 panels around rocks, so the damn things would get some distance. That was crucial. At nighttime, we used chem lights for our visual signals.

The assault maneuver obviously was coming from our right into the trench and moving toward the left. Once they came in contact with the first bunker, they blew it and moved forward. The front man for the lead squad would carry a long stick with a VS-17 panel tied to the top like a flag. This was referred to as the "maneuver front line trace." Once they cleared the first bunker, that was our key to lift fire. I still couldn't hear, but I yelled into my mic, "Lift fire, lift fire confirmed, over." Then I threw another panel out for the visual.

My guns stopped and the remainder of the line squads went to work and cleared the trench. By the time we did our AAR with the battalion commander, my hearing was back, but a little low. Anyway, my first live-fire as weapons squad leader was successful. Other than my hearing, it had gone off without a hitch. Oh yeah, my two AT-4 gunners got props from the battalion commander because they hit and destroyed both positions. One thing I learned during all these live-fires throughout the years, the field grade officers that evaluate and certify their subordinate units want to see two main things: safety procedures being used (so nobody gets shot) and shit blowing up and being destroyed. It was a great life.

The last big event for the field exercise was a "hot load" jump on Sicily DZ. *Hot load* meant the aircraft would land on the airstrip of the drop zone. The paratroopers would load on it, and the pilot would take off, go for a little distance, turn around, and drop the troopers onto the drop zone as normal. It's awesome because it cuts the hour-long flight time we normally have to do in order for the pilots to get their time credit. I believe we had two C-130s that were going to do a total of six drops, three apiece, or something close to that. The reason I remember this drop in such detail was because it was my first assistant jumpmaster duty, which was going to be my last jump in Division prior to PCSing and mostly due to it being my last certification to be able to get my senior wings.

We stayed the night at the platoon live-fire range. The next morning after mermite chow, we marched a few miles to Sicily DZ. Once there, we put everybody in the shade and relaxed for a few hours. We had to make sure everyone was drinking plenty of water. I was stoked! The first sergeant was making up the manifests for our company. After noon, we linked up with the battalion air officer and got our airborne briefing. I was a jumpmaster on chalk 1, which was the first lift, and I remember being nervous because I had to have it be dark out to get credit for a nighttime assistant jumpmaster, which again, was the standard to qualify as a senior parachutist.

We started doing the airborne timeline around 1800 with final manifest, then I gave the chalk prejump, parachute landing falls, then mock door training. We then did parachute issue, rigging, and JMPI. By the time we wrapped all that up, it was dusk. We had the chalk sitting in order, waiting for the birds to show up, land, and have us load up. I was good. It was going to be dark when we would be loading then jumping.

My assistant jumpmaster duty went off without a hitch. When I landed, I policed up my parachute and reserve, walked off Sicily to the bleachers, and waited for our company to get 100 percent accountability. The cattle trucks were already waiting for us. We got back to the barracks, wiped down our weapons, and turned in our sensitive items. The next week was dedicated to detailed cleaning and maintenance of all equipment, we called it "refit."

That next Monday morning after PT, I put together my paperwork with a copy of my jump log and went to turn it in to Division Headquarters myself. I didn't even bother with the battalion S-1, which was normal protocol. Less than a week later, I had my orders for the senior parachutist badge. About two weeks after that, I reported to drill sergeant school at Fort Jackson, South Carolina.

CHAPTER 7

US ARMY DRILL SERGEANT SCHOOL
GOING BACK TO BASIC TRAINING AS A STAFF SERGEANT

BASIC COMBAT TRAINING is the initial nine weeks that every soldier endures in the Army. Jobs in the Army are also known as MOSs (military occupational skill), and most combat arms MOSs in the Army have their own basic combat trainings. These training cycles are extended for twelve to thirteen weeks, which includes an additional month of specific job training. These MOSs usually consist of Infantry, Artillery, and Engineers and, at the time I was going through, were all male only. Any other basic combat training programs were designed to be coed, with separate barracks for male and female recruits. Each platoon consisted of approximately three drill sergeants—two male and one female—and one of them was usually a combat arms MOS. The average was three drill sergeants to approximately sixty to seventy recruits.

Fort Jackson, South Carolina, was the premier Army basic combat training installation in those days and probably still is today. The coed environment was still a relatively new concept that was introduced around the mid-1990s throughout the Army. Some leaders during this time period still had issues with this concept, for more reasons than one. It wasn't about physical stamina, training standards, or even the different appearances of the recruits. It was the reality of having both male and female eighteen-year-olds spending twenty-four hours a day with each other for a nine-week cycle. This added more stress to an already stressful environment. The term *fraternization* became as common in the basic combat training environment as the term *training* itself.

I may repeat this periodically throughout the next couple of chapters. The success of a good drill sergeant is not how much you can scream and holler at someone. The success of a good drill sergeant is being able to teach—period. For two years on the Trail (what we called drill sergeant duty), I witnessed drill sergeants fail with their jobs because they could not connect with the recruits. All they could do was scream all the time at them, day in and day out. As time went on—and not too much time, either—the recruits simply would lose all respect for that particular drill sergeant that just screamed at them all the time. A recruit, or any other subordinate soldier back in a regular unit, will respect a leader that can teach them something instead of yelling at them consistently. I am not at all suggesting being soft on them—and I was not—but there definitely is a time when effective teaching can be done without raising your voice.

After one basic combat training cycle went by, I realized that the recruits were giving themselves a sense of pride in learning something, especially when it came to learning soldier skills. A successful drill sergeant must also realize that these young eighteen- and nineteen-year-olds volunteered to be part of this environment and that they were not drafted, as some of our fathers were. They actually wanted and craved to be there in order to be a part of a premier military force. I also was not afraid to tell them, "Good job" when they completed a task that they learned to do to standard. By doing this, I and many other drill sergeants earned their respect, which goes a long way in that environment. I still remember what my boss, the senior drill instructor of our platoon, told me when I first got on the Trail. He said to me, "Your success for the next two years isn't what you accomplish anymore but what your soldiers accomplish."

I had never wanted to nor expected to ever become a drill sergeant. As a matter of fact, I'm quite sure that 80 percent of drill sergeants or former "drills" never expected or wanted to, either. Just like most Army recruiters do not wish to be or have not asked to become recruiters. Drill sergeant and recruiting duty in the Army are additional duties that about 50 percent of sergeants, staff sergeants, and a few sergeants first class get levied for throughout their military careers. *Levied* is a nice military term for being drafted to a duty station or an additional duty.

Like I've said, I wasn't a big fan of being here, especially coming from a combat arms MOS and going to a coed basic training environment. Many of us NCOs throughout the Army had already heard of the horror stories of male drill sergeants getting into trouble with the female recruits. There were many rumors, supported by factual incidences throughout the Army during this time, that some drill sergeants were being charged, and even went to prison for abusing and having sexual affairs with new soldiers they were in charge of during basic training. It even got to the point that many NCOs would say that if they were ever to be levied for drill duty, they would demand and fight to get stationed at Fort Benning or another basic training installation where it was strictly combat arms, so they would be surrounded by all male soldiers instead.

I remember thinking that all I needed to do was be disciplined and do the right thing, and I would have nothing to worry about. However, the Army was starting to go through a time of political correctness, and adding a coed basic training to it could add fuel to the fire. What if I found myself in a situation where I did the right things, but a female recruit claimed differently? Would I find myself in a guilty-until-proven-innocent situation? One fact about being a drill sergeant in the Army—and after talking to some other drills from the other branches of service, it seems to be true for them as well—it either makes or breaks a career. I have known some individuals that experienced the latter. These were some of the thoughts that ran through my mind as I mentally prepared for this upcoming change of life and duty assignment.

Like everything else in the Army, I treated it as a "one step at a time" scenario. Before I had to worry about being a drill sergeant, I first needed to worry about getting through Drill Sergeant School itself. Everybody knew that this was not an easy task by itself, either. One has to modulate almost all drill and ceremony steps and procedures in order to graduate. *Modulating* is reciting word for word each sentence and page of a marching movement, straight out of the Army Field Manual or Regulation. I remember when I was at the Basic Noncommissioned Officer Course at Fort Benning, a couple of years prior, there were guys walking around behind the barracks we stayed at, and they were talking to themselves. The US Army Drill Sergeant School at Fort Benning was behind our company. Come to find out, they were DSS candidates that were practicing their modulating on drill and ceremony movements. They would be out there all hours of the night, too. I would walk down to the latrine at midnight to take a piss and would hear a guy talking to himself. I'd look outside the window, and see someone smoking a cigarette, pacing back and forth, modulating to himself. You have to modulate to graduate. During this timeline, the Army had three drill sergeant schools: one at Fort Leonard Wood, Missouri; one at Fort Benning, Georgia; and another at Fort Jackson, South Carolina. Today, there is only one at Fort Jackson, the United States Army Drill Sergeant Academy.

I remember there were two of us within my battalion at Fort Bragg that were heading off to DSS, but to two different locations. The other NCO was heading off to Fort Benning, and I was heading to Jackson. The battalion school's NCO advised us to prelearn the first three modules and the Drill Sergeant Creed prior to reporting to school. We were confused and had to ask if we were going to get tested on the modules during the first week. He told us no, but it would make our lives easier for that first week's transition if we already had them memorized, the logic being that, during the transition of going back into the basic training mentality ourselves, with drill sergeants over us, knowing these modules would be one less thing to worry about and study for. So I learned the first three, which were the position of attention, rest positions at the halt, the hand salute, and the Drill Sergeant's Creed, which was a couple of paragraphs by itself.

The battalion command sergeant major also came out to give us some last-minute words of advice. He reminded us that we were heading to an NCO academy and to not take it lightly. NCO academies have an academic evaluation form attached to them, which gets filed in your official Army records upon your graduation. The academic evaluation is the DA Form 1059, and it was pretty much thrown in our faces for the entire nine weeks that we needed it to be successful. Receive a substandard 1059 from any military leadership academy and it could be the difference of not being selected for the next promotion. Even though I was not excited about becoming a drill sergeant initially, when I received my levy notice, I still had every intention of giving 110 percent at the school and afterwards giving the same effort as a drill itself for the next two years.

Fort Jackson was only about a two-and-a-half-hour drive from Fort Bragg, so the trip down there was easy. The most difficult part was finding the school itself once I arrived on post. These were the days before smartphones and the GPS systems that everyone uses today, so I had to use signs to get there. DSS on Fort Jackson is on the backside of the installation, away from the main post, so it took some searching before I finally found it.

As I entered the building, there was a DSS (drill sergeant instructor) sitting at a desk as soon as I walked in. As I stood in front of him, I noticed he and I were the same rank: staff sergeant. He asked me if I was reporting to DSS. I replied with, "Yes, I am." He looked at me with a strange look in his eye. Before he even said anything back to me, I knew what was going to come out of his mouth next.

"Yes, I am—Drill Sergeant," he said to me with a confident tone in his voice.

I repeated, "Yes, I am, Drill Sergeant," as I half-ass slid into the position of parade rest. He handed me a form to fill out and asked if I had driven my own privately owned vehicle.

"Yes, I did, Drill Sergeant."

He then instructed me to go get all my gear from my vehicle and lock it up because it would be the last time that I would have access to the parking lot for the next three weeks. He then called for another drill sergeant candidate, who walked out of an office down the hallway. He instructed him to take me upstairs and get me squared away.

"Sergeant, he'll take you upstairs and show you your room, bunk, and wall locker. Take all your gear up to your room. Do not unpack. Do not make your bunk. Get into PT uniform and be standing out front here for an 1800 formation, where we will conduct an introduction to the school, followed by a weigh-in."

"Yes, Drill Sergeant," I replied. I assumed not unpacking our gear was protocol in the event that someone showed up overweight. That way, they weren't wasting time setting up their area in the barracks. They could simply pick up their negative DA 1059 and drive their butts back to their duty station. It made sense to me.

Formation was not what I expected. I was guessing that it was going to consist of a lot of yelling and in-your-face shit from the drill sergeant instructors (DSIs). It wasn't any of that. Instead, it was very professional, with all the DSIs lined up at parade rest with the company senior drill sergeant out front. All of us candidates were already assigned to platoons and squads and, prior to the formation, were instructed to move into our correct spots. Actually, for the first initial formation of about 120 candidates, I was impressed on how well organized this group of cadre were executing it. I could tell this was not your usual NCO academy where the cadre seem to come out lackadaisical at first until the groups get themselves organized. These were professionals that knew their jobs inside and out, and after completing two years on the Trail, one could understand how simple it was for them to be subject matter experts at this environment. These were the cream of the crop drill sergeants that had already completed two years of successful time as basic combat training drill sergeants. Most of them were volunteers for a third year to be conducted at the School House on Fort Jackson. Like I said, though, they had to complete their two years down where the rubber meets the road, in the hostile chaos of the basic training environment, and do it without a blemish on their record, in order to get into the School House.

The senior drill sergeant started the formation by citing the Drill Sergeant Creed to us all. After he was finished, he began giving the introduction to us. "Welcome to the United States Army Drill Sergeant School. Congratulations, you all have been selected as the top ten percent of the noncommissioned officer corps, and we are in charge!" This was basically the speech that he gave the company before turning our platoons over to our DSIs. They got us back into the barracks and began the weigh-ins. I believe one drill sergeant candidate did not meet Army height and weight standard, and he or she was immediately removed from the school and sent home. There's always one.

After the weigh-in, we were sent upstairs to unpack and get our bunks and wall lockers squared away. It was back to the basic training wall locker and bunk display that every soldier, airman, sailor, and marine hated. During this time, they even had us bundle up our civilian clothes that we had worn there and turn them in downstairs. Just like brand-new recruits, each drill sergeant candidate was allowed to bring one personal gym bag to store all of our civilian clothes and even our vehicle keys in. They were not kidding. You were not going to get access to that parking lot for the entire Red Phase of training, which was the first three weeks. With each passing moment that first night, reality was setting in that we were going back to basic training. The only difference this time was that they called you "Sergeant" instead of "Private." Back when I had gone to basic training, ten years prior, they called you some more colorful names such as "shithead," "shit for brains," or "dumbass."

Day one of DSS began at around 0530 with a room, wall locker, and bunk inspection by the DSIs. I had my shit squared away because I'd stayed up pretty much most of the night getting it done. As I had loaded my wall locker, the memories were all coming back, especially when I had to start canoe rolling my socks. Each hanger had three fingers space in between them with our unit insignia or patch on our BDUs facing toward us. Some others in my room chose to blow off getting their area set up and perhaps get to it some other time.

When the DSIs came into our room of six candidates, not one of us had our displays to their standard, which we had pretty much predicted. The one or two NCOs in our room that chose to do nothing all night really drew in the attention of the drills for simply not complying with their instructions to have it all completed by first call. We even had to have our last names and last four of our social security number stenciled on a piece of masking tape on the foot of our bunks and on the upper right-hand corner of our wall locker. "Hey, Sarnt, why did you choose to not comply with our instructions to have your displays finished by first call this morning?" We quickly learned that "Sergeant" turned into the one-syllable word "Sarnt" by the DSIs.

"I fell asleep," my roommate responded.

I thought to myself, *Damn, he didn't even call him "Sergeant" or "Drill Sergeant," for Christ's sake.*

"You fell asleep, what?"

"I fell asleep, Drill Sergeant." The DSI did something at that point that made me and everyone else in the room realize what their strategy to earn our obedience and compliance with their instructions was going to be from here on out: they were going to take our time from us, and time in DSS is precious.

"Okay, Sarnt, after the APFT and chow this morning, you will be setting up your wall locker and bunk displays to standard. At 0900, we will begin our first demonstrated class on the first three modules that you will be tested on next week. Instead of receiving our much-needed demonstration, you will be in here setting up your area." That was it. The DSIs walked out of the room and went into the next, and we went down to formation in our PT uniforms, bringing one canteen of water. There was no screaming or making anybody do push-ups or any of that; simply taking time away on a critical event such as our first module demonstration. That's how they knew they had us. Fail any written or verbal exam in this leadership academy and you will fail the school and your military career will probably end. It was that simple.

The 0600 formation started off with the senior drill sergeant calling out one candidate to come out front and begin the Drill Sergeant Creed in front of the company. As he or she said each line of the creed, the rest of the company had to repeat it loudly and thunderously. This would occur every morning for the next nine weeks. Everybody was going to get an opportunity to be out front, so it behooved everyone to learn the damn thing.

The Army Physical Fitness Test, or the APFT, or as we referred to it most of the time, the PT Test, was the first evaluation event of day one. They marched us down the hill to a large outdoor arena area with a track. We began stretching and counting off the seconds of each stretch to their standards. Each event was graded to Army standard. If the candidate failed any event of the PT Test, they were given one opportunity to conduct a retest. If they failed it twice, they were removed from the course as a PT failure. Try going back to your unit and explain that one to your first sergeant or command sergeant major. The standard of first passing an APFT before continuing on in a course was not limited to drill sergeant school but was the normal procedure for all other NCO academies throughout the Army. Nevertheless, we lost another two or three candidates for being PT failures that first day.

We were moving fast that first day, and there was no slowing down. Like the DSI had said in our room earlier, at 0900, we received our first demonstrations on the position of attention, rest positions at the halt, and the hand salute. All three modules would be tested on week two. Being tested on all three modules that were presented at the beginning of the school week only happened once throughout the school. These three modules in particular every drill sergeant candidate had to say, verbatim, in order to pass. After that, the number of modules increased depending on the drill and ceremony subject. For example, the subjects consisted of facing movements at the halt, steps and marching, basic manual of arms, advanced manual of arms, and squad and platoon drill. Each subject had between three to eight drills we had to learn within them.

DSIs would demonstrate all the modules of that particular subject for that week to learn and study, but we would only have to say or pitch one or maybe two of them. We just didn't know which one it would be, so we couldn't blow any of them off. We had to learn all of them verbatim. When it came test time, it would be one-on-one with us and a DSI that would grade us. We normally would be allowed to have one demonstrator, which was another candidate. If we were doing a marching module, we could have several individuals demonstrate for us while we pitched the module to the DSI. The DSI picked which movements we would modulate by having the candidate to be tested roll a die. Whatever number our die landed on was the module we got tested on. If we had to do two modules within that subject, we would simply roll the die again.

It definitely was a fair concept, but I'll be damned if I always rolled the hardest module for that particular week. I mean *every* time. It was a good thing that I had already memorized all three for that first week, because it did make that initial change of environment easier. The DSIs warned us not to get ahead and try to learn more than what we were presented for each week. The logic was that we did not want to overload ourselves. Module testing was not the only testing we had for any given week, either. There would be written exams, and any other events that all candidates had to pass in order to graduate, such as weapons qualification, and every other basic training graduation requirement that a new recruit had to do.

We were in Red Phase, which meant total lockdown. No phones, no vehicles, only written letters, and no leaving the school area. We had the red guide-on (flag) in front of each platoon. Our structure was the exact same as that of a basic training company. Each platoon had a platoon guide out front. Next to him or her was the guide-on bearer. Each platoon was broken down into four squads with assigned squad leaders for each. Some of us candidates were still in shock that we were having to transition back into a basic training mentality. Some of us couldn't get over it, either.

During that first week of school, there was one sergeant first class (E-7) candidate that simply could not accept the fact that he was there and that he was on his way to being a drill sergeant for the next two years. This guy had a piss-poor attitude from the start and bitched about everything. Yeah, it sucked, and we all preferred to be somewhere else, doing something different, but we weren't and had to suck it up and drive on. This guy refused to accept being there and would tell me he had no intention of staying. I used to ask him how he planned on getting out of the school, and he would tell me that he was going to talk to the commandant and get the hell out of there.

The commandant of any NCO academy is a command sergeant major, which is the highest enlisted rank in any branch of service, and you usually are not going to bullshit them, either. The guy trying to get out was assigned to Fort Bragg prior to school and was Infantry as well. According to him, he had just begun his rifle platoon sergeant time and needed to get back to continue it. I just remember thinking, *Well, good luck thinking you're going to get out of here on a positive note. The cadre here, in this place, isn't going to give two shits about your platoon sergeant time at Fort Bragg.* My logic happened to be spot on. He went to our senior platoon DSI and complained, which ended up with the company senior DSI, and finally with the commandant of the academy.

The next day, I asked him how it had gone with the commandant. He told me that they all were trying to convince him to stay and that it would be beneficial for his career progression, which was absolutely true. He felt differently because he was already an E-7. I told him that it would probably guarantee him his E-8 promotion. How convenient would that be? Start off as a senior drill sergeant for a little while, make the E-8 promotion list, and move right into being a basic training first sergeant. This seemed pretty simple to me. Nope! This guy was "Ranger Rick" and wanted to get back to "Ranger Land" at Fort Bragg—no matter what it took to get there. He was pretty much an asshole with an attitude like he was beyond becoming a drill. At least that was my perception of him. I ran into a couple of those guys during my time on the Trail. He had admitted to me what his plan for getting out of there was going to be. He intended to purposely fail the first written exam twice, so that he would be an academic failure for the course. I asked him, "You sure you want to do that, Sergeant? You know you're going to get a bad 1059 on your record, right?"

He replied, "I don't give a shit about all that. I'm gonna get the fuck out of this place and get back to a line unit where I belong. Besides, I already got instructor time. I was an RI for two years in the mountains." I just shook my head in disbelief. I didn't want to be there, either, but I wasn't going to end my career over it. Instead, I had every intention of doing my best both in the school and on the Trail.

So he failed the written exam both times, and his release procedures began immediately. When he came out of the commandant's office, he was pissed. Apparently, the commandant had called his battalion command sergeant major back at Fort Bragg, and he was notified that for his actions of purposely failing DSS, he would also lose his opportunity to be a platoon sergeant back there as well. When he told me this news, I wasn't surprised at all. Coming from Fort Bragg myself, I knew the politics of it, and he should have also. He said he had a connection in Ranger Branch and that he was going to go back to Ranger Training Brigade at Fort Benning, where he would finish out his career as an E-7. I told him good luck and maybe I'd be seeing him around someday. Unfortunately, that's exactly what happened. About three years down the road, he would end up being one of my Ranger Instructors, and I would regret that I had ever even met him. I will talk more about him later on.

Marching into the chow hall was not an easy task anymore, either. We would march in as a platoon and file in by squads. I'd hear the order, "File from the left, column half left!" As the First Squad leader, I would look over my right shoulder and give the command, "Column half left!" The first morning, when the DSI gave the command, "March," I stepped off with the wrong foot. He immediately caught me and got into my face. "You stepped off with the wrong foot, Sarnt. RBI that and have it on my desk prior to morning formation tomorrow." He wanted me to write a response based indorsement, known as an RBI. Yes, I am aware that the word *indorsement* is misspelled. Or is it? *Indorsement* is still in the dictionary and has the same meaning as *endorsement*. Anyway, in Drill Sergeant School, having to RBI a drill and ceremony movement was considered punishment. The DSIs would argue that it was a learning tool to correct our mistakes. Both are correct. Again, either way, that shit took time away from us, time that could be used for studying a module or for an upcoming written exam. When you were told to RBI a movement you may have screwed up on during the training day, that meant writing out by hand the correct way to perform it, right out of the Drill and Ceremony Field Manual. And that took away from our personal time. Anyway, I RBI'd the correct foot to step off with on a column half left movement and had it on the drill sergeant's desk that evening.

Marching to cadence while singing was the only way of life those days during Drill Sergeant School. "One, two, three, four! DSS, DSS! One, two, three, four! DSS, DSS!" We were getting on buses and being taken over to main post, straight in the heart of basic combat training land. We were about to do Fort Jackson's Victory Tower for the next few hours. Victory Tower was a forty-foot rappel tower with other rope-bridge obstacles around it as well. Each candidate is given a class in the rope corral pit on how to properly put on a rappel seat prior to walking up the steps to the top of the tower. Once on top, the drill sergeant would link the candidate into the main rope and send them over down the tower. The most difficult part was getting each student into a proper L-shape before sending them down. Later on, we found it to be the same challenge with the recruits once on the Trail.

The entire morning at Victory Tower, I was waiting for the range cadre or the DSIs to show us how to run the range itself as drill sergeants. That never happened. We would simply run through these ranges as if we were basic trainees ourselves, and that was it! I soon figured out that learning how to run these training facilities was going to be taught by our drill sergeant buddies once we got to basic combat training. Most of the Range NCOs, the facilitators for each particular range where training took place, in this environment were ex-drills or NCOs that were broke. Most of them pretty much acted as if their job was more important than ours. I also learned this really quick when I got on the Trail. The funny part is that any basic combat training drill sergeant could do their own job plus the other NCO's job, any day of the week.

Our instructors would get us together as platoons every so often and talk to us about the realities of the Trail. "Hey, sarnts, I know this sucks for ya. It did for us, too. Who the hell wants to leave the regular Army and come into this environment? We sure as hell didn't want to either. But let me tell you something, sarnts, being here in Drill Sergeant School is nothing compared to the world you all are about to enter in a few weeks. DSS is a frickin' cake walk, sarnts. The basic combat training world is insane. You'll be dealing with sixty-five eighteen-year-olds day in and day out. Getting them through the chow hall is a task by itself. They ought to allow us to give you a class on that by itself, but they won't put it in the curriculum. It's going to stink. I mean literally your barracks, being in a closed setting with all those kids, is going to smell. Some of them are not going to shower or the air conditioning is going to give out in your bays, and it's going to stink. So prepare yourselves, sarnts. Later on, in Blue Phase, you'll have an opportunity to go spend a day in basic combat training, as kind of a hands-on training day, so that you can see it up front for yourselves."

After the bayonet assault course, the Fort Jackson Obstacle Course, and the gas chamber, on top of more module testing and written exams in between, we were ready to change the guide-ons to mark the White Phase. We were put into a company formation with the traditional Basic Training Phase Change Ceremony, where the DIs would change each guide-on from red to white. This meant more to us than just knowing we were moving on to the next phase of the school, but that we were going to get a little more freedom given back to us. Like I said, this was designed to take us through almost identically what the privates go through in basic combat training. That weekend was going to be the first time in three weeks we could leave the academy area on our own. We were even given the opportunity to go on a pass for the whole weekend. The DSIs opened up the storage closet in the barracks and let us get our personal bags with our civilian clothes. I ended up driving back to Fort Bragg to stay with my pregnant wife for the weekend. Honestly, instead of relaxing all weekend, I ended up having her help me study for the next group of modules I had to learn for the upcoming week.

White Phase, just like basic combat training, was primarily focused on marksmanship training and qualification. Every soldier must qualify with an M16A2 rifle to graduate from basic training. Same rules applied to DSS candidates. The M16 was the assault rifle for that time but was still considered old for most infantry personnel because we had mostly already switched over to using the M-4 carbine. The M-4 is a smaller, lighter version of the M16 but has the same mechanical functions.

"One, two, three, four! DSS, DSS! One, two, three, four! DSS,

DSS!" We marched with our rifles at the position of port arms and filed onto the buses, heading to our first rifle range. Once there, we filed into the bleachers, and the DSIs began to give us our range safety briefing. This was the zero range. *Zeroing* is putting the bullets or rounds on your point of aim through your sites on the weapon. This is done by adjusting windage and elevation on the sites (up and down, left and right). The standard is placing five consecutive rounds, out of nine, inside a four-centimeter circle on a target while in a foxhole-supported position. The target is twenty-five meters from your position.

The briefing also consisted of the DSIs telling us that if we were combat arms MOSs to not do our own thing while setting up our foxholes for firing. It was almost insulting to have someone tell us how to properly set up a supported firing position, but it was part of the standard training, and we would have to comply—just like every other aspect of the school. I remember getting into the foxhole, by command of the range tower, and placing our nonfiring arms out on the dirt in front of us. We were then instructed to draw a line along our arm and then cross it where our wrist lay. That's the spot we would set up our sandbags to lay our nonfiring arms. I remember thinking how ridiculous this was.

The weapons qualification portion of DSS was painful, due to having to comply with these little rules that were given to us, but at the end of the day, most of us qualified and passed another mandatory test in order to graduate. Notice I said, "most of us." Yes, there were some NCOs in the school that had problems qualifying, but if memory serves me correctly, they eventually did. The problem was we were moving along with the other required classes and testing at the school, and not qualifying meant a DSI had to take them back out to the range. The rest of us were moving on while others were getting behind, still having to worry about qualification.

The school moved on, and eventually, we entered the final three weeks and Blue Phase. The testing was getting more difficult, especially the modules. By this final phase, we were being tested on squad and platoon drills. Of course, as I explained earlier, I rolled the die on the more difficult modules such as count off, stack arms, and take arms during squad drill. During platoon drill, I rolled counter column, and I believe everyone had to do opening ranks and closing ranks, according to academy standards. When a candidate was finished with their module, the DSI would sound off with, "Close it out, Sarnt." The candidate would reply with, "At normal cadence, at ease." The term "close it out" was a way of the Trail. From DSS until my two years ended at Fort Jackson, saying "Close it out" was a more respectful way of saying "Shut up." Forgive me if I continue to say, "I believe" or "if I remember correctly." After all, this was more than twenty years ago for me. Just typing that sentence alone makes me feel old.

We did have our visiting basic combat training for a day during Blue Phase. We got dropped off at a basic combat training battalion just prior to their PT formation. We were broken down into platoons and sent to the respected platoon offices or command posts. I know for a fact that the drill sergeants did not want us there and didn't need or want our help, either. I remember going through the ranks in the morning looking at the recruits and yelling at some of them for moving during the position of attention or whatever. Their actual drill sergeants just looked at me with disgust in their eyes. I immediately got their vibe and backed off. I went to the back of the formation and simply sat back for the rest of the day and observed. How do I know they did not want us there? Simple: when I was on the Trail, I too did not want those damn "schoolhouse candidates" yelling at or telling my soldiers what to do, either. I'll get into this a little later, but a certain bond develops between a drill sergeant and their recruits. Almost like a mother figure protecting her own from outside elements. That's how it was with a drill and his or her soldiers.

They took us over to the uniform issue facility, not to be mistaken for the clothing issue facility, but where the recruits got their phase two clothing issues. This consisted of their dress uniforms issue, fitting, and altering. Phase one was done while they were in the Replacement Center, and that issue consisted of their basic issue of uniforms such as their battle dress uniforms, PTs, socks and underwear, etc. Tactical gear, in those days, was issued at platoon level by their drill sergeants in basic combat training.

This was actually our first site where we were taught, and given a walk through, on their clothing issue procedures. After that was complete, we were taken over to the post clothing issue facility, where we were issued our first drill sergeant campaign hats. We were issued these during the end of the course because it was part of the graduation ceremony. When we got back to the academy, the DSIs took us to our platoon classrooms and gave us a block of instruction on how to put them together with the leather strap, how to properly fit it to our heads, and finally, how to wear the damn things.

We took the final PT Test, which prevented me from getting Distinguished Honor Graduate by a couple of points. The honor grad got a perfect three hundred on the test, and I got like a two hundred ninety–something. However, I did make the Commandant's List, and that was okay with me, since I had never done that good at any other leadership academy prior to. Hell, now that I look back on it, the Basic Noncommissioned Officer Academy had just been a two-month party for most of us, which I was simply lucky I graduated from.

With that in mind, prior to the end of the course, we were allowed to leave post overnight if we wanted to. It was like an overnight pass like the recruits get in basic training prior to their graduation. I decided to stay in the barracks and not test Murphy's Law. In other words, I didn't want to risk anything that was going to cause me to be late or get me into trouble, period. Every class always has one. One candidate ended up getting a drunk driving charge and was immediately dropped from the course. Damn! Only a couple days left, and he was out getting into trouble. His career was shot as well.

Nine weeks after arriving at DSS, it was finally graduation day. It was a pretty prestigious ceremony. All of us were dressed up in our

Class A uniforms. Prior to walking across the stage, as they said our names, we were handed our campaign hats. It was a well-rehearsed procedure from the day prior. As we placed our new campaign hats on our heads, we would take both hands, fingers and thumbs extended and joined, and would trace them over the circular brim of the hat. After we quickly traced over the brim, our hands went down to our sides with a sharp, snapping motion. Once at the position of attention, we would march across the stage and were handed our graduation certificates.

Most of us were skeptical about our upcoming futures on the Trail. We were nervous and knew we were about to enter a changing world of working seven days a week at times and spending more time at our basic training companies than we would at home with our families.

I had a little bit more on my plate during this time that I needed to accomplish. I had to get back to Fort Bragg, clear my unit and the installation, sign out on leave, and get up to Michigan (where me and the wife were from), so that she could give birth to our firstborn. At the time, she was already pushing nine months of pregnancy. After this was complete, we were to drive back to Fort Jackson, sign in to the installation, find a place to live, and then I could begin my two years on the Trail. In October of 2000, I graduated from the United States Army Drill Sergeant School and was officially a basic combat training drill sergeant for the next two years.

CHAPTER 8

MY TWO YEARS AS A BASIC TRAINING DRILL SERGEANT

SECOND BATTALION, 60TH Infantry Regiment was my new battalion of assignment for the next two years. My starship was my place of work and my home. "Starship" is what we called the battalion area because it was shaped in a hexagon with six companies at each apex and the battalion headquarters out front. Not to mention the Army referred to them as the "Basic Training Starship Barracks." They were built in the 1970s. There were eight basic training battalions at Fort Jackson in 2000.

I was assigned to Alpha Company, 4th Platoon. I would be living with the logos for the Alpha Gators and the 4th Platoon Mad Dawgs from there on out. I reported to the first sergeant, who introduced me to the company commander and then took me upstairs to our platoon bay and introduced me to the platoon sergeant. His official title was platoon sergeant, anyway; most would refer to him as the platoon senior drill sergeant, or the boss, or their friend and mentor. I preferred the friend and mentor method, and so did he; it made the environment much easier to be in. All three drill sergeants in the platoon knew who was in charge, and we also knew we had to come together as a team in order to accomplish each day's tasks. For privacy purposes, I will only use first names of personnel that I was close with on a daily basis. Some I may not remember, so I will refer to them by a nickname, or simply Drill Sergeant So-and-so.

The first sergeant left us and went back downstairs to his office. "You got any paperwork for me, like your last NCOER (noncommissioned officer evaluation report) or anything?" my new platoon sergeant asked.

"Yes, Sergeant," I replied. "Or do I call you Drill Sergeant?" I stood in front of his desk at parade rest.

He told me to sit down at the empty desk in the office, which was mine to have. He immediately went into our introduction—the way he wanted it done, not the formal military style of parade rest and handshakes. He then went into his concept of working together in this environment. "Okay, my name is Tim. I would prefer that you call me by my first name. In front of the privates, you will refer to me as Drill Sergeant So-and-so (his last name). I would like to refer to you as your first name, and in front of the privates, same rule applies, unless you have a problem with that. If you do, I will call you Drill Sergeant—I can't pronounce your last name."

I said to him, "It's pronounced Aga-naga, and I'm good with the first name thing, Tim. I actually prefer 'Augi' when I'm referred to by my rank or Drill Sergeant. Aga-naga has way too many syllables, and most people just end up screwing it up anyway. So I always go by 'Sergeant Augi.'"

Tim nodded and said, "Okay, sounds good."

Tim was a staff sergeant promotable at the time and was just waiting on his sequence number to come up for promotion to E-7. As a matter of fact, during this time period, all drill sergeants were staff sergeants (E-6) and sergeants first class (E-7). There were no sergeants (E-5). The only E-4 or E-5s assigned to a basic combat training company were the supply room and administrative representatives. Other than the first sergeant, executive officer, and company commander, everybody else was a drill sergeant. There were twelve total drills per company, three per platoon, with four platoons. Of course, very seldom were there three per platoon at any given time.

Back to Tim. He had come from the Special Operations community within the Army prior to getting levied for the Trail. He was Aviation Branch and previously was assigned to the 160th Special Operations Aviation Regiment (Airborne) at Fort Campbell, Kentucky. So he had more of the laid-back, Special Ops mentality, and coming from the insane, fast-paced Bragg, hooah, hooah mentality, I was okay with a little calm. Make no mistake about it, though, Tim was a no-shit guy that would tell you like it was. If you were fucked-up, he'd tell you in a heartbeat, especially when it came to getting the mission accomplished. Tim said, "Look, I try to find a way to make our lives (the three of us assigned to the platoon) easier among each other in order to get our jobs done to standard. If me calling you 'Nate' or you calling me 'Tim' makes our communication with each other easier, then so be it. Because the second we walk outside that door"—he pointed out to the bay—"the insanity begins."

At the time, the Company was gone to the uniform issue facility getting their class A dress uniforms issued to them. They were just finishing up White Cycle and had qualified with their assigned rifles. It seemed a little early for dress uniform issue, but it was the month of December, and they were getting ready to leave Fort Jackson for Christmas exodus for two weeks. Tim had stayed back because he knew I would be coming in, and our other drill sergeant was with the platoon. Clothing issue was one of those basic combat training events that required minimal drill sergeant supervision for the day. The other drill was Christi, and I would meet her the next day. She had been there about two basic combat training cycles before me. She and Tim both had their previous plaques and pictures on the wall behind their desks, and Tim suggested to me that I put mine up because it showed the privates that I had accomplishments in the Army outside of the basic training environment. He said not to worry about it for the time being, because I had plenty of time to get all that done during Christmas exodus. Instead, he told me to go get my official drill sergeant photo taken, which meant going to a little studio down the street from our battalion. I had to have my picture on the company wall downstairs. He asked me if I was married, and I said yes with a newborn at home. He then told me after I got my photo done to go ahead and go home and do whatever I needed to get done, such as unpacking or whatever. I said, "Oh no, Tim, I can come back. I'm ready to jump right in and get my feet wet a little bit."

"Don't worry about that, bubba. You'll have plenty of time to get your feet wet after exodus. Trust me. Right now, you got here at a downtime that really only happens once a year. Take advantage of it, because when we get back off exodus, it's gonna be nonstop." Tim had a habit of calling his friends 'bubba.' He was born and raised in Kentucky and was a good ole country boy.

I said, "Okay, sounds good. I appreciate you letting me take off, and I will see you in the morning."

He replied with, "Yep, be here at 0530, and I'll start showing you how it starts here every morning." As I started walking out of the office, Tim said, "Oh, yeah, and Nate, remember this: your success from here on out is no longer measured on how well you do but how successful they become during their nine weeks with us."

"Roger that," I said and walked out into the bay and through the doors out of the platoon area. I remember telling myself that I thought I was going to like my new boss Tim.

The next morning I walked in, and there was a line of soldiers outside of the platoon command post. I walked into the office, and Tim was sitting at his desk filling out sick call slips. "Drill Sergeant Augi, can you break this line off and take some of these sick calls for me?" So I did and started signing their slips. Most of the sick calls were colds and congestion problems. Almost all year long in these bays, a lot of privates were sick all the time. You could not deny them sick call, only recommend that they not go and either suck it up or go back some other time after a big training event. After the last one had left, Tim told me exactly that. Right now, right before exodus, there was nothing going on for training, so it wasn't a big deal having that many sick calls in the morning. Christi came in, and we were introduced to each other. Tim gave me a blue vest to put over my PT jacket, and we went downstairs. All drills on Fort Jackson wore a blue vest so they could easily be identified as cadre.

It seemed pretty routine. The first sergeant came out, received the accountability report from all four platoons, and then released the platoons to the drills to conduct PT. Tim marched the Mad Dawg Platoon outside of the starship onto the open field to our platoon PT platform area and immediately got them into an extended rectangular formation. That first morning, he stretched them out and took us on a little run around the block a couple times, and that was pretty much it. I was waiting for him to introduce me to the platoon, but that came later that evening. I guess that first morning I was eager to jump in and get ready to be a drill sergeant for the first time. Like he told me the day prior, there would be plenty of time for that in the next two years.

All the other drills in the company were curious about me, and most of them came up and introduced themselves. It was pretty cool getting to know them all. There were the drills from 3rd Platoon that was right across the bay from us. The 3rd Platoon "Bushmasters" were led by Chuck. It was Drill Sergeant Chuck and Drill Sergeant Mac. Drill Sergeant Mac was funny and mouthy. She did not put up with anyone's shit, especially from privates. Chuck's other drill sergeant was an Infantryman who wasn't bad but was a little too serious about life at times. Downstairs was 1st Platoon, and I cannot remember their motto. Their platoon sergeant was Drill Sergeant D, who was an E-7 from Fort Bragg as well. As a matter of fact, he and I went to DSS together but were in separate platoons, so we really didn't know much about each other. His experienced drill sergeant was named Long. Drill Sergeant Long looked identical to Tiger Woods—I mean they could have passed for identical twins. He was funny and happy-go-lucky all of the time. He made time on the Trail go by easier, and he and I eventually became good friends. I think I'll refer to him throughout the rest of this as Tiger. As far as 2nd Platoon, their platoon sergeant was a former Special Forces NCO that didn't want to be there or have anything to do with any aspect of the program. Everyone could tell that it was a struggle for him to even be there every day. Actually, I sometimes wondered how he had even graduated from DSS at times. He had a drill sergeant that was a bundle of nerves all the time. He just seemed on edge twenty-four seven. I don't know if the Trail was taking its toll on him or if he was having marital problems or both. Anyway, these were the drills that I would be spending most of my two years with at Alpha Company, 2/60th at Fort Jackson.

All the drills called each other "battle." This was short for "battle buddy," which was the cornerstone for all privates in the Initial Entry Training (IET) environment. A private was not allowed to go anywhere by themselves. They had to have a battle buddy with them at all times, especially when talking to any drill sergeant one-on-one. If that soldier did not have his or her battle buddy with them, we had to turn them away until they had one. Usually, they had the same one that they would pick from the beginning of basic training, but during training, there were times they simply had to grab whoever was around them when they needed to talk to a drill about something pressing at the time. I was quickly confronted with this, too. One thing I learned really quickly was a new drill sergeant better get their ass on board as fast as possible, because the basic combat training world doesn't wait for you to catch up. The privates damn sure don't care that you are new to the basic combat training environment. All they see is the round brown hat, and you had better be able to answer their questions and fix their problems. Oh yeah, that's something else that was different from the School House. Nobody here ever called the soldiers "recruits." They were referred to by the drill sergeants as "the privates" or simply "soldiers."

Exodus was just a couple days away, and there literally wasn't anything to do but get the soldiers packed and make sure their class

As were worn properly. Tim had asked me if I'd be okay with being late man for my first time. "Yeah, no problem. It's my turn anyway," I told him. Actually, I felt relieved that he had trusted me enough this early in my time there to stay until lights out by myself. What I didn't know was that I was about to be thrown in react mode as soon as kitchen patrol (KP) was over for the night.

There I was, by myself for the first time with the Mad Dawgs. Most of them were downstairs in the formation area sitting on the bleachers, shining their boots, and writing letters. Others were on the payphones. Lights out was 2100, if my memory serves me, and first call was at 0500. I was sitting at my desk in the office when I got a knock on the door. It was a female soldier that had just returned from KP duty, standing there with her battle buddy. "Drill Sergeant Augi, I have to talk to you about something."

I said, "Okay, c'mon in. What's going on?" She went on to tell me her story of what had happened to her on KP. She claimed that the KP drill sergeant had pushed her in the back in the mess hall. I immediately thought to myself, *Oh shit. My first night actually being alone with these soldiers and I get thrown into a cadre abuse charge.* There was no wasting time for me. This was the shit they had told us about in DSS, and I got it immediately my first week on the Trail. "Did anybody see him push you?" I asked her.

"No, Drill Sergeant, but it did happen. It was Drill Sergeant So-and-so from Bravo Company, and he had gotten mad at me because I wasn't moving fast enough for him. He yelled at me, and then he pushed me."

So, before I caught myself starting to become an investigator or a barracks lawyer, I knew the first thing I needed to do was to find the blank sworn statement forms. We had a filing cabinet in the office, so I opened up the drawer that was labeled "blank forms," and found the sworn statements right in front. I had her sit down at Tim's desk and her battle buddy sit down at Christie's. I had her fill out the sworn statement, and we both signed it.

Afterward, I told her, "Okay, I'm going to take this up with Drill Sergeant Tim in the morning, and he will be getting back to you tomorrow." I hated throwing the ball in his court, but honestly, I really didn't know how this was going to work. This was a time when I actually could say that I was the new guy who didn't know enough yet. Tim knew the drill sergeant in question, and he had been there for over a year already and had known this private for some time as well.

The next morning before PT, I told him about it and showed him the sworn statement on his desk. "Okay, I'll take care of it," he said to me. That was it. The subject was never spoken about again. It wasn't mentioned by Tim, the other drill—who obviously never got into trouble because he was still there—or the soldier. It was a situation of a fire that was put out, and I never did find out how, nor did I ever ask. I'm not suggesting anything got swept under the rug, but I can say that whatever the outcome was, neither party involved had a problem with each other again. It made me feel somewhat relieved, too, because that was the point when I realized that Tim had our backs and wasn't going to play the game of somebody getting into trouble because of accusations without proper investigation. My opinion of the whole thing after it all ended was that she was angry at that particular drill sergeant, accused him of abusing her, and perhaps took advantage of the situation of a brand-new drill (me) being there that night. Perhaps she could have gotten more satisfaction from a new drill sergeant than she would have gotten from someone who already knew her and what her personality was like. Throughout my time on the Trail, I continuously witnessed some privates wanting to test the waters with the system.

A couple of weeks went by and the privates came back from Christmas exodus. It was somewhat chaotic in the formation area. All the drill sergeants were present, hollering at the soldiers coming back in. The impression in the company was that they went home for the holidays and got all lacksey-daisy and lost all their discipline from the previous six weeks of basic combat training. It really wasn't, at least for the majority of them, but it was the drill sergeants' thing to get all spun up about. It was funny for me to see some of my battles in action with their privates.

"Oh, look! They just come back on in here, bebopping like they're back on the block!" Another drill would say something like, "Oh, yeah, just take your sweet ole time getting into formation!"

Then you'd hear something like, "Oh, hell no! What the hell is that on your neck? Is that a damn hickey? Oh shit, drill sergeants, we got ourselves a loving man over here!"

I think the funniest one of all of us talking shit was Drill Sergeant Mac. Some of the shit that came out of her mouth, you would literally have to turn around and laugh so that you weren't seen doing it in front of the privates. It was priceless. Some of the female soldiers would come back with too much make-up on while they were in their uniforms. "You'd best take your ass upstairs and wash some of that shit off your face!" It was comical to the point that you realized that these soldiers were damned if they did and damned if they didn't. They were going to get it either way. It was the drill sergeant's way of saying, "Welcome back to basic training, privates."

The next day, we had our Blue Cycle ceremony. Like the rest of basic combat training, Blue Cycle was pretty crammed with events and graduation requirements such as EOC testing (end of cycle), D&C competition (drill and ceremony), a couple of tactical ranges, the Victory Forge field exercise, and the most important event of all: the final APFT. The reason I refer to this as the most important event is because if they failed, they did not graduate, and it flat-out looked terrible on the cadre for failure to get a trainee in enough physical condition to pass the Army PT test.

One thing I was beginning to notice that used to bother me, probably the most when I first got on the Trail, was that there was almost a hatred of cadre among other companies. It was like the competition didn't end with the privates competing but with the drill sergeants as well. I guess at first I wasn't used to that, coming from infantry battalions in the regular Army. It wasn't like that there at all. Here in basic combat training, it was a continuous sharp-shooting competition between cadre. It always happened when we were mixed together for an event, especially at the chow hall. The chow hall was a basic combat training experience all on its own. Talk about a chaotic environment. Go inside of a basic combat training chow hall sometime and you'll see the definition of a hostile environment, especially when a new drill sergeant enters, like myself.

The dining facility, or mess hall, or chow hall, was split up between two dining areas. Alpha and Bravo Companies were on one side and Charlie and Delta were on the other. There was one empty company area in the battalion, and that was for Foxtrot Company during the summer months, known as the "summer surge." It was a company of reserve drill sergeants that would come into Fort Jackson for two basic combat training cycles during the summer surge in order to augment the battalion for the abundant number of trainees that would come in during that time period. Each company in the battalion would usually task out one drill sergeant per company to assist the reservists. Ours was Fox Company—don't ask me why it wasn't Echo Company to fill in the correct sequence.

Getting back to the hostile crowds in the chow hall, the row of tables that were for cadre only was verbally insulting at times. "Hey, Drill Sergeant, I just seen one of your privates grab a fucking soda out of the machine! It must be Candy Land over there in Alpha Company, as usual!" This is the kind of shit I was talking about that literally threw me off when I first got there. Hell, I was thinking to myself that perhaps they were allowed to have sodas during Blue Cycle, I didn't know. Come to find out, the answer was no. During my time on the Trail, we never authorized the privates to have anything other than water, milk, or juice from the chow hall. The reality was that this particular drill sergeant from Bravo Company was fucking with me because I was new to the game, and he was feeling me out. I remember his face, too, but not his name. He was a Bravo Company platoon sergeant who had been there probably as long as Tim and Chuck. After a couple of cycles, I was cool with him, but not so much that first couple of weeks. There were a couple of other asshole drills from the other side, too, that would wander over to our area and run their mouths. That was okay. In the back of my head, I knew they didn't know where I came from, and being an asshole definitely can go both ways.

It happened again about a week later. "Hey, Drill Sergeant, one of your privates just snuck a cup of coffee from the dispenser!" I looked around toward the last of the Bravo Company trainees and saw one private with his boot laces out of his boots. "Hey, soldier, stand the hell up. Who is your drill sergeant?" I asked. He pointed over at the big mouth and said his name. I said, "Hey, Drill Sergeant, this private can't even wear his uniform correctly in Blue Cycle! His damn boot laces are all over the damn floor and shit! Hell, I thought I was gonna start rappelling off those sons-of-bitches! Is this your product of leadership? Fucking weak!" I then sat down two tables away from him and started eating my breakfast. He just looked at me with a smile on his face. I never heard anymore shit-talking from him again, at least not toward me anyway. As a matter of fact, he was cool with me from that point on. Years later, I ran into him at Fort Lewis, Washington, at one of the shops, and we shot the shit for a few minutes. It was a small Army. I still had to shut the other drills up from the other side, and eventually down the road I would.

One morning Tim and I were sitting around getting the soldiers' graduation packets started, checking through them to ensure they had the correct items in each. He was going through them and telling me what had to be in each by the time they graduated, and we sealed and sent them off to AIT (advanced individual training—for their military occupational service "job") with the soldier. Christie was with the soldiers out in the bay, going over barracks maintenance with them.

"Hey, bubba," Tim said. "I'm going to need you to pitch inspection arms to them this afternoon, if you're up to it."

I said, "Yeah, no problem." Tim was going to have them draw their weapons so that we could start going over drill and ceremony competition sequence with them. He told me he wanted me to take that task over, marching them in the competition. I was pumped up to do it, because I happened to like doing D&C and wanted the challenge. He was going to march them this cycle and have me watch. The next cycle was going to be all mine. I asked him, "Hey, Tim, where do you want me to form them up to give the module?"

"Module? No, sir, we don't do that here. Just go through the task and teach them so that they'll understand it. Trust me, they'll get it faster, and it will make more sense to them." I was so relieved. There would be no modules during my time on the trail. Those days were over for me. Tim told me, in the most respectful way, "You're gonna find out that we do things a little different in reality here in basic combat training than perhaps you were taught over at the School House."

"Roger that, understood," I replied. I was still relieved. We still taught them every single D&C movement to the set standard; we simply didn't make every single step an individual lesson. My God, how the hell would you have time in this place? I did hear that there were units on Fort Jackson that would make it mandatory for every movement. That seemed to be adding to the timeline that was already packed full.

"Nope, just line them up here in the bay and go over it with them step-by-step until you feel comfortable that they have it down. I already taught them all other advanced manual of arms, except for inspection arms. Next week is the competition before Victory Forge, and I want them to be squared away," Tim instructed.

After lunch, Tim had them in formation downstairs outside of the arms room cage. He was teaching me the formalities on how they drew their weapons. He sounded off with, "In weapon number sequence..."

The privates would sound back off with, "In weapon number sequence..."

Then Tim finalized it with, "Count off!"

The privates would all sound off with all the numbers of weapons assigned to the platoon. At the same time, they would fall out of the formation and line up at parade rest in a single file line outside of the arms room cage. Once they received their weapon, they would look down at the chamber, pull the charging handle back, release it, and place their weapon on safe. They would then fall back in at position of attention in the formation area.

Tim got in front of the formation and sounded off with, "Drill Sergeant Augi!" I ran in front of the formation, stopped, did a left face, and saluted him. Tim then told me, "They're all yours, Drill Sergeant. Take them upstairs and conduct advanced manual of arms training with them."

"Yes, Drill Sergeant," I replied. I dropped my salute, took one thirty-inch step forward, conducted an about-face, and told the platoon, "On the command of 'Fall out,' get upstairs and toe the line with your weapons and stand by for my instructions. Fall out!"

I had them lined up with their rifles in the platoon bay, toeing the line in front of the bunks. There was a square line painted on each bay floor of all the barracks in our company, and that was where we would have them lined up inside. "Okay, listen up. I'm going to talk you all through inspection arms with your assigned M16A2 rifles." Without thinking about it, I started modulating unconsciously. "Inspection arms from order arms is a seven-count movement. The command is 'Inspection arms.' On the command of 'Execution, arms,' execute port arms in two counts. On the third count, move the left hand from the hand-guard of the weapon and grasp the pistol grip, thumb over the lower portion to the bolt catch." I actually caught myself and remembered what Tim had told me that morning. He was right; only about half of them understood what the hell I was saying to them. So I grabbed one of the rifles and talked them through it as I did it with them. After about half an hour, they were getting it, and it was running smoother and smoother. Tim was in the office, probably evaluating whether or not I could teach them something or if I was a screamer and that's it.

Nope, I was teaching, and they were learning. I was actually enjoying it—until the bay door opened up.

Another drill sergeant from Bravo Company came in and started yelling at one of the soldiers over something. He stood in the bay as if he were evaluating me giving my class. I remember saying something about it being a seven-count movement again, and that's when it happened. He started sharp-shooting me. "No, Drill Sergeant, it's an eight-count movement."

Now I was on the spot. "No, Drill Sergeant, it's a seven-count." Then he wanted to argue with me. That was mistake number one—I was new at this, but I knew these simple rules. He countered my instruction. Mistake number two, he did it in front of the soldiers. Not to mention, he was flat-out wrong about it being an eight-count movement.

He said, "Listen up here, soldier, this is how it's done!" One thing I remember about him was that he never said their names; it would always come out as "dummy" in a very sarcastic manner.

The next thing I heard coming from the office was Tim. "Hey, Drill Sergeant So-and-so, I need you in here." He went in, and the door shut. That was my first impression of him in the training environment. I knew it was going to be a long road with him, and I hoped I only had to see him in the chow hall. I went back to teaching by myself after Drill Sergeant Tim pulled this other drill off the scene.

The next day, we had a surprise health and welfare inspection in each of the bays. First and second platoon would conduct their inspections downstairs in their bays, and us and third platoon would do our inspections in our bays. I guess this was routine, especially since they had just recently gotten back from exodus. Again, I sort of sat back and observed how this was going to play out. It was exactly what I expected, too. Wall lockers were getting pillaged, drill sergeants were climbing up on bunks in order to look inside of the ceiling tiles with flashlights and they were looking through the latrines. I don't know what it was, but the privates always thought they could hide stuff in their long dress coats. That first inspection, we found like three cans of chewing tobacco, a Walkman radio, and—no shit—Drill Sergeant Mac found a cellular phone. Remember, this was in 2000. Cell phones were definitely not a thing yet. "Oh hell, NO! What the hell is this? A mobile phone? What is this for, so you can get booty calls in the middle of the night?" It happened to be a female soldier that had it hidden in the ceiling tile above her bunk. It was nice, too, with a leather case and everything. There it sat on the desk in the front of the bay. Punishments for contraband at this point were loss of phone privileges for the rest of basic training. It may not seem like a lot to the average person, but phone privileges meant everything to a basic trainee.

It was also Army values training time for the final values class for these soldiers' journey through basic combat training. Army Basic Training used to be eight weeks. That's what it was when I had gone through ten years prior. The Army had added an additional week for values training. The seven Army values were the acronym LDRSHIP, which stood for loyalty, duty, respect, selfless service, honor, integrity, and personal courage. The last class that Tim was about to present was personal courage. He had the platoon sit around the desk in front of the platoon bay. We had a butcher-block table set up with all the Army values, and he quickly reviewed each of the previous six, then he went into the final one. It was interesting watching him teach it, because he turned it into the light at the end of the tunnel for them in order to gain their interest. He had a way of engaging them in noninteresting subjects. For each values class, we gave them the Army definition and then would have them give us examples and then would compare the value toward upcoming training events that they were about to execute during that week. Tim used personal courage as an example of our upcoming ranges for the next week, such as hand grenades, US weapons, the night infiltration course, and the Victory Forge field exercise.

The next week was busy, busy, busy, and we were on the go. All the ranges I just mentioned, the D&C competition, and the end of cycle testing. EOC was an entire day event for first aid, communications, nuclear biological chemical, map reading, etc. Pretty much we were going over all soldier skills testing. The soldiers were definitely under the stress of passing all these events. Other company drill sergeants would test our soldiers on these events, and we would do the same for theirs as well. For us, it was mainly Bravo Company that tested our soldiers. If your platoon won any of these events that were graded or judged at battalion level, you would be awarded a streamer to place on your platoon's guide-on. It was a competition, and it meant a lot to us as drill sergeants as well. It was a rite of passage to talk shit to others within the company and the battalion. We would say shit like, "Our platoon's guide-on has so many streamers, we're gonna need two privates to carry it." The soldiers loved it, and I'm not going to lie, the drill sergeants had pride in it, too. It was a mark to show how much your training paid off and the quality of your platoon.

Out of all the ranges for basic combat training, the hand grenade range always had us a little nervous. After all, these were new trainees throwing two live grenades, which was also mandatory for graduation of basic combat training. The range cadre at hand grenades truly earned their pay. I believe during my two years on the Trail there were two separate incidents where the range cadre had to grab a private and throw them and themselves over the berm from a live high explosive grenade being dropped by accident. Of course, the soldiers spent half the morning at the practice portion of the range, and they had to certify with practice grenades before they could go over to throw live. It definitely was a little bit more of a tense range than the others.

It was my first Victory Forge field exercise and another great learning experience. Tim broke it down to me right off the bat. He made sure I understood that this was basic training, not the 82nd Airborne Division, and not to get too spun up if this wasn't field training like we were used to in the active Army. I understood and had no problem with it being more laid-back. Victory Forge was a three-night field exercise, and on the fourth evening, right before dark, we took off for a ten-to-twelve-mile foot march back to the battalion.

The soldiers would dig foxholes to standard so that we had a company defensive perimeter. They would man these positions with their battle buddies. We taught them to always improve their positions with camouflage and constantly fortify them to make them stronger. Some were actually impressive. If these privates got anything out of Victory Forge, it was how to build a two-man fighting position according to Army standard.

Once the perimeter was generally set with minor fortifications, we took the soldiers out and taught them some basic patrolling, such as conducting a reconnaissance, an ambush, and a platoon attack. It was good old-fashioned Army training. We also got them introduced to some great Army terms, such as, "If it ain't raining, we ain't training!" Also, "It doesn't rain in the Army, soldiers, it rains *on* the Army!" They seemed to get a kick out of it. As far as having enemy personnel to play the opposing force (OPFOR), we would get our own cadre or our supply guys or administrative NCO with a couple of drill sergeants to run around and pop off a few blank rounds at the soldiers. We coordinated all operations over our radios whenever we wanted them to hit the trainees. We made it as real and as exciting as we could with the equipment we had. I used to get them spun up by going from hole to hole and telling them stuff like, "Whoa, what is that out there, soldier? You guys better get ready. I think they're gonna hit us any time now." They would get all into it and have their weapons at the ready.

We would finish off the field exercise with a grand finale firefight in the defensive perimeter. We'd throw smoke grenades and maybe even a CS gas grenade (riot control gas) or two since they had their protective masks on them at all times. After it was all over, we would have them conduct an extensive police call of the entire training area. They would fill in their fighting positions and picked up all the brass from their blank rounds. In between events for that finale day out in the field, we would show them how to clean their weapons in the field by breaking down the upper receivers and wiping the bolt carriers down, getting all the dirt and sand off them. "Do not, for the love of God, break down your bolts!" We preached that to them in the event they would lose a small piece of their weapon, such as one of the pins in the bolt assembly group, while we were in the field.

The final foot march out of Victory Forge was a pretty big deal in basic combat training. It was a mandatory event for graduation, and it ended with the Victory Forge ceremony back at the battalion. The march was a long, straightaway movement conducted in the hours of darkness. Like I said, it was between a ten- to twelve-mile road march with all their equipment, which included a thirty-five-pound rucksack, with their helmets on and weapons at the ready. We stopped them along the range road approximately two, possibly three, times, depending on the heat index, for water breaks along the way. The pace was relatively slow due to us preventing heat casualties among these new trainees. Their bodies were not used to conducting a fast-paced forced foot march in the South Carolina heat, especially when it was during the summer surge. Although some of them physically could if we had pushed them to.

Once we got to the end of the road march, outside of the battalion area, we would halt everybody, get them some more water, and have them get their composures back. The first sergeant would get on his radio with the Battalion S-3 (Operations) NCO. Once they were ready for us, we would form our companies up and march them over to the Battalion Headquarters, where they would have a large bonfire lit up and burning. We would form all companies in the front of Headquarters 2/60th and receive a speech from the battalion commander. He would congratulate the soldiers for completing all major events of basic combat training and tell them that they were well on their way toward graduation in a little over a week. He would then command each company to issue each soldier their values tag.

We would open ranks within the company, and all drill sergeants would go through and issue their soldiers their tags. These values tags were to be placed on their identification tags or dog tag chains. It was a pretty important event of basic combat training prior to finishing up a cycle.

The only two major events left on the calendar were the battalion final inspection and the final APFT. For the final inspection preparation, all equipment, including each soldier's tactical gear, weapon, wall locker, and barracks as a whole, would be inspected by the battalion commander and command sergeant major. The drill sergeants would take our own money and purchase mass amounts of shaving cream and the spray canned air for weapons cleaning. Tim would even bring in a couple of power drills to rod through the barrels of the M16s with metal brushes. We would spend about three full days preparing for the inspection. Tim taught me to break it down in phases. Day one, get all the equipment cleaned, and while it was drying, start on the weapons. The bay cleaning should be held for last. We had the latrines so clean you could have literally eaten off the floors.

The final Army Physical Fitness test was graded by Bravo Company drill sergeants, and we graded their soldiers in return. It turned into drama at times, like everything else in this environment. You'd see drill sergeants bringing them out coffee; some would even have breakfast muffins or Krispy Kreme doughnuts for the other drill sergeants. It got to the point where I would see straight-up ass kissing from one company to another over a PT test. I guess in the reality of it, every soldier had to pass to graduate, and some thought that those soldiers that were on the edge of failure were in the hands of these other drills. I didn't kiss any of their asses. As a matter of fact, I wouldn't even talk to them. I had a mentality of "do your job." I didn't need to kiss their asses for them to do their jobs to standard. I'd be damned if I ever offered those Bravo Company assholes any cups of coffee. I'm telling you, they rubbed me the wrong way from the beginning. The reality of it was if any of my trainees failed the APFT, they're going to get retested by somebody else. So I wasn't kissing anybody's ass.

I missed my first sequence of graduation events, which were the rehearsal, family day, and graduation itself. I got tasked that final week of the cycle to become the company primary hand-to-hand combat or unarmed combat instructor. There was a week-long class at Fort Jackson that we had to take and pass. A team from Fort Benning came up and taught us classes on the new Brazilian Jiu Jitsu style hand-to-hand fighting techniques that the Army was changing over to. It was pretty intense. I actually broke a finger during the training. Who knew? My first broken bone in the Army and it was done being a drill sergeant at Fort Jackson, SC.

My first full basic training cycle was pretty chaotic, as all are. One drill sergeant per platoon usually went over to the Replacement Battalion to pick up the new soldiers. The unwritten rule was that we did not interfere with or yell at the new trainees while they were still under the control of the Replacement Drill Sergeants. This was going to be my first full basic training cycle, and Tim wanted me there for the whole thing, including Replacement pick up, in order to get the full experience. This I can still remember as if it were yesterday. It was Drill Sergeant Mac, Tiger Woods, me, and the platoon sergeant from 2nd Platoon.

You would have thought that this group of privates were best friends with their current drill sergeants they had from Replacement. I mean, they weren't even referring to them as "drill sergeant." On this subject, I am going out on a limb and am going to go ahead and say this now: A drill sergeant during my time on the trail used to receive an additional $275 per month for special duty pay by the Army. I'm sure it was supposed to be in accordance with working seven days a week, along with the daily hours that went with it, especially the first three to five weeks. Replacement and AIT drill sergeants received the same extra pay as well. These particular drills should not receive $275 or whatever the pay is today for special duty pay. This isn't just my opinion but that of almost any other basic combat training drill sergeant out there. Replacement and AIT drills are not with the soldiers twenty-four seven. Especially AIT drills that usually do PT with the trainees and then march them off to their MOS training NCOs that have the soldiers all day. There are separate cadre that teach them Monday through Fridays on their specific MOS training. It is not the responsibility of the drill sergeants, as it is in the basic combat training environment.

A Replacement drill sergeant's number one job is to get the new soldiers in-processed into the installation and to ensure they can run a mile without passing out before they can send them to us. In actuality, most Replacement drills used to be basic combat training drills anyway and would probably agree with not receiving the additional pay. Most of them volunteer for a third year on Fort Jackson for whatever reason, such as having children in school, other family reasons, or they simply do not wish to go back to the regular Army to do their jobs right away.

I remember telling Mac, "These soldiers seem to be a little close to these drills over here."

She replied with, "Oh yeah, Augi, we see this every time we come over here at the beginning of a cycle. When you hear the term 'Candy Land,' this is where it really is, battle. Don't worry about it. I know it's hard to watch this shit and keep your mouth shut, but that shit's about to end real quick," she said with sarcasm. She leaned into me and told me to keep quiet on the bus ride back to the battalion, too. She said to wait until we tell them to get off the buses and then all hell would break loose on them.

I honestly couldn't wait, because the way they were acting and were allowed to act with these drills was pissing me off more by the minute. It took me back to when I had gone through basic training ten years earlier. I remembered as well that the Replacement drills were more laid-back than the basic combat training drills, because when we got off the cattle trucks from Replacement to our basic combat training battalion, it was pure chaos. That feeling always sticks with any soldier, even us drill sergeants who were about to instill the same shock factor here in the next hour or so. We just stood off to the side until they began loading on the buses. On the way to the battalion, we had them place their heads down on their duffle bags that were on their laps. We gave them specific instructions not to talk to one another and not to look outside the windows, just to keep their heads down on the duffle bags. They were still acting all lacksey-daisy for the bus ride over. Once the buses stopped in front of the battalion, I asked them politely to look up at me. They did. I then asked them to do me a favor. I then said to them, "Get your fucking asses off this fucking bus now, goddamn it! Move your sorry asses, privates! Get the fuck off the bus!"

All the other company drills were outside the starship hollering at them to hurry up and move. It was utter chaos at the time, soldiers dropping their bags, mass confusion, and some crying as well. We put as much stress onto them as anybody could think of. We did everything but place our hands on them, of course.

Once in the company formation area, we had them drop their bags and move to the bleachers. It was quick and fast, not too formal of a class, but fast and furious. We had them line up in a single file line and file into the bleachers from top to bottom, yelling at them the entire time. "Who the fuck told you to sit down, soldiers? Stand your sorry asses up until you're told to sit down!" Once all the soldiers were in the bleachers, one of us gave them the command, "Take seats!" The company commander and the first sergeant then came out and gave them their introduction into basic training and introduced each drill sergeant to the entire two-hundred-fifty-soldier company.

Once the introductions were complete and the first sergeant turned the company back over to the drills, we had to form them up by platoon and get them into dinner chow before we got them upstairs to the bays. Forming up, marching to, and getting into line in the mess hall was a task by itself in the basic combat training environment. One drill sergeant per platoon would have to move up and be present at the podium in the entrance of the mess hall in order to take head count.

There were three separate pages that needed to be recorded. Active Duty, Reserve, and National Guard had three separate sheets. Each soldier was to sound off with, "Drill Sergeant, Active Duty, 7249, Drill Sergeant!" The number was the last four digits of their social security number, which was what the drill sergeant had to write down on the correct component sheet. As soon as the soldier was through sounding off with their last four, the next soldier would sound off with his or hers.

It got pretty intense inside that walkway, especially when you had drill sergeants screaming the whole time they were in there. The head count drill couldn't even hear the trainee and had to tell them to sound off again. Once the cycle got going a few days and the soldiers were used to this pattern, the Charge of Quarters (CQ) drill sergeant would do the head count for his entire company. Male drills were responsible for CQ duties throughout the entire battalion, and females did the battalion staff duty. There was a reason for this. No male drill sergeant could enter a female bay after lights out; they needed to be escorted by a female drill for headcount purposes twice throughout each night.

Once the entire platoon was in the dining portion of the mess hall, the last soldier for that platoon would sound off with, for example, "Drill Sergeant, last Mad Dawg seated, Drill Sergeant!" From that point, they had seven minutes to eat and start heading out to formation. No talking, no looking around, head and eyes on their trays of food, and that was it. When their seven minutes were up, we'd say, "That's it, you're done with chow. Get up and get out in formation—move your asses!" Actually, it was only the last soldier that was timed for the seven-minute period. The platoon did not have to wait on him or her to sit. Once they sat down, no matter what order they were, they could begin eating. Only the last trainee was timed after they sat down to get out of the dining facility.

Once back in the company area, we had them fall back on their bags, grab them, and head upstairs to the platoon bays. The first thing we showed them was toeing the line painted on the floor. "Every time we tell you to get upstairs and toe the line, this is exactly what you will do, Mad Dawgs! Understood?"

All answered, "Yes, Drill Sergeant!"

We then had them dump their duffle bags on the floor. Immediately, we conducted basic clothing issue inspection. This is pretty routine for all basic training in all branches of service. The drill sergeant calls out each item of clothing, and the private holds it up above his or her head. The other drill sergeants walk down the line, and once we saw the item of clothing, we would tell them to pack it back up in their duffle bag. "Don't be getting your shit mixed up with your buddy next to you, because if you screw this up, soldiers, you're going to dump them and start all over. It doesn't matter to us what time you get to bed tonight. Either way, first call tomorrow morning is still at 0500. It doesn't matter to us how much sleep you get!"

This went on for the next eight weeks, and then again, and again, and again. I went through eleven basic training cycles in two years, after which I was pretty on edge the rest of my military career. I still am today, but not as bad as when I first got out thirteen years ago. I still get awakened by my wife all the time for cursing and screaming at soldiers in my sleep. I don't think it'll ever go away.

One thing that was forever engrained in my mind during my time on the Trail was my individual experience of what happened to our country on September 11, 2001. Everybody has their personal time or experience of what they were doing or where they were that horrific morning, right? Mine was being a drill sergeant on Fort Jackson, South Carolina. September 11, 2001, was actually the day before one of our graduations for that particular cycle. The soldiers were to graduate the next morning and move on to their advanced individual training elsewhere.

We were conducting graduation rehearsal for the next morning of this particular cycle. We were right in the middle of our rehearsal when all of a sudden, we were ordered to report to the front of the parade field. "All cadre immediately stop all procedures and report to the bleachers for a mandatory briefing by the battalion commander."

We really didn't think anything of it, other than it was sort of unusual to stop us from conducting a rehearsal for graduation that was happening the next morning, but whatever. It must have been something important.

Man, it was definitely important.

What I heard from the battalion commander's mouth would change our lives forever. Not only to us as servicemembers, but to the country as a whole. "Company commanders and drill sergeants, there has been a terrorist attack in New York City. Two civilian airline aircraft have flown into the two towers of the World Trade Center in Manhattan. Our orders are to cease all training and immediately return to our battalion and inform these soldiers. All soldiers that are from New York or have parents or any family members that live and work in Manhattan are to call home immediately. Understand?"

We all replied, "Yes, sir."

When I climbed into Tim's truck with him to head back after the soldiers got on the buses, he had the radio on. It was live radio when we heard that a third plane had crashed into the Pentagon in our nation's capital. Tim immediately put his truck into park. He looked at me, and in the most serious voice I ever heard him speak, he said, "Hey, Nate, our country is under attack . . ." I never forgot that tone or that statement he made to me. As I write this now, I have goosebumps on my arms.

When we got back to the battalion, we had the soldiers call home, and drill sergeants that were from New York called home as well. There was only a small number of soldiers that needed to make a call. Actually, I told all the soldiers to call home, because this was something that was so emotionally devastating to all people—not just to the military, but to all human beings across the globe.

None of us could go home that afternoon, as we would have been able to regularly. Actually, the day before graduation day in this environment was usually the earliest days we got home to our families, but September 11, 2001, was not. I remember thinking to myself that on that day, our way of life had just changed forever—at least for the rest of my life on this earth. I remember thinking that at this point, I wished I was back on Fort Bragg, in the 82nd Airborne Division, because I knew they were going straight to Afghanistan to kick Al Qaeda's ass, and they did just that. I wanted to be part of it, not be stuck at Fort Jackson, South Carolina, as a Basic Training drill sergeant. Don't worry, I would have my chances to fight this Global War on Terrorism in the future.

After my two years were finished, it was time to leave this environment. I was on orders to head back to Fort Bragg for the third time in my career, and I was excited, too, because by this time, I was an E-6 promotable and was sure that I would be a rifle platoon sergeant. Not only was I leaving basic training forever, but I was going to be able to fight in this new war as well. In the near future I would learn the meaning of the phrase *be careful what you wish for*.

DRILL SERGEANT AUGI 2000-2001

CHAPTER 9

THIRD TIME AT BRAGG WITH A VERY DISAPPOINTING START

MY WIFE (AT the time) and I had just bought our first house in Raeford, which was about fifteen miles from Fort Bragg. With drill sergeant time behind me, I couldn't wait to get back into the 82nd Airborne Division. I was still on PCS leave for the first couple of weeks back, and I used that time to get our house moved in and everything set up.

Our neighbors were cool and brand-new to this neighborhood as well. Actually, since they were still putting houses up around us, I guess everybody else was pretty new too. Our next-door neighbors moved in almost the same week we did, and the husband, Staff Sergeant D, was also going back to Division for his third time. The only difference was he was coming back from recruiting duty. He had been around the 325 Airborne Infantry Regiment most of his past time in Division. I remember at that time wanting to go to the 325 this time, primarily because I found out that Shaky and S were both there, but I think in different battalions. All I knew was that they were both E-7s and platoon sergeants by now. Shaky had already been there over a year and S, just recently coming off the Trail himself, had been there only about two months. Honestly, at the time, I just wanted to get to a unit that was about to deploy to Afghanistan so that I could get into the fight as part of the Global War on Terrorism.

By this time, Fort Bragg had just finished construction of a second main PX and another commissary. That place had gotten bigger with some changes in the past two years since I was gone. We had heard that Green Ramp over at Pope AFB had reconstructed a new and much larger airborne preparation facility. So we drove out there to check that out. It was nice, with new mock door overhead hangars, and the indoor facility was big enough to hold an entire brigade taskforce. On the airfield behind the facility were C-17s lined up, which made me remember that the old C-141s were no longer in use. Me and Staff Sergeant D started reminiscing about how uncomfortable those bastards were. They were basically like a larger C-130 that you could pack twice as many paratroopers in.

So that week we did all our in-processing, took a PT test and weigh-in, and got our welcome briefing from the division commander and command sergeant major. Oh by the way, that turned out to be no one other than the infamous Command Sergeant Major X. He had finally made it to the top in Division, as predicted.

After they were complete with their briefing, the division command sergeant major took all the NCOs in a back conference room and gave us our internal briefing—and it was in classic Command Sergeant Major X format. "All right, newly assigned NCOs, for how many of y'all is this your first time in my Division?"

Out of about twenty of us, the majority of the hands went up.

"All right, I'm gonna find out which of you that failed the PT test or height and weight, Airborne."

I thought to myself, *Here's that height and weight thing with him again.*

"Now if you come here and can't pass the goddamn Army Physical Fitness Test, this ain't the place for you, Airborne! Now you supposed to be goddamn NCOs. So every time you pull out that ATM card outcha wallets and stick it in that machine to get yo' dollars out, remember what the fuck you get paid for in the first place, Airborne!

You better come here ready to lead from the front! I don't want to hear all the bullshit either, like all the excuses why you can't meet the physical standards. I don't wanna hear, 'Well, I came from Korea,' or 'I came from recruitin''. You's a goddamn NCO, Airborne, so you better live up to it in this place, or don't even botha unpackin' yo' shit! I'll send yo' asses right down the street or across Bragg Boulevard to a corps unit, where you can fail all the PT tests you want, Airborne! Now, I'm gonna get those names of y'all that failed the PT Test and weigh-in."

Me and Staff Sergeant D were good, so we got to leave and go back out to get our brigade assignments. As soon as we walked out of that room, we laughed our asses off and probably for the rest of the day after that. Like I said, that was classic Command Sergeant Major X. His briefings were nothing more than a threatening ass-chewing. Like he said, it was "his Division," and well deserved.

By this time, the 504th had gone and fought in Afghanistan first, then they were followed by the 505th, who had just gotten back within the last month or two. The 325 were slotted next and that's what everybody on Ardennes Street was talking about at the time. This was January of 2003, so we had not gotten involved in Iraq yet. Bush 43 was still in the negotiating phase of trying to get Saddam Hussein and his two sons to stand down from power. So me and Staff Sergeant D were hoping to get into the Falcon Brigade this time in Division.

We happened to both be told that we were going to the 505th and received orders for the Panther Brigade. I was good with it because after all, it was where I had grown up in this place almost nine years earlier at this point. My neighbor wasn't too happy at first; he just wanted to go back to where he grew up in Division too, but like I said earlier, every battalion on the street was the same, each just has different PT T-shirts and flashes on their berets. Everybody was going to run up and down Ardennes Street every morning and parachute out of jet and rotary wing aircraft. Down the road, they'd throw in back-to-back combat deployments—coming soon to a theater near you.

We in-processed in brigade headquarters. I figured already being assigned to 1 and 3 Panther in the past, it was my time to go to 2 Panther. No, it was back to 3rd Battalion! I was excited because I was getting an opportunity to go back to where I had started off. Actually, there were about twenty of us that got assigned over there. They had obviously had a big troop turnover after they got back from combat a month or two earlier.

That is common, to have troops come back and get sent by the Army to other assignments, especially E-5 and E-6 turnovers. Many of them get levied to go to recruiter or drill sergeant duty. E-7s finish their two-year platoon sergeant time and move on, usually to staff and wait out their time for the E-8 list to come out, and in this place, they usually make it if they had a successful two years.

I was excited to get my first platoon. It was time and I was ready. I couldn't wait to get my own desk in a command post and meet my four squad leaders. There happened to be another E-6 promotable who was going over to 3 Panther with us. I want to say that this was his first time in Division, that he was previously in 75th Regiment. He had a combat scroll from back in Somalia.

We got to the battalion headquarters, and because there were a few of us signing in, they put us in a small room across from the staff duty desk. The S-1 staff came over and took the packets we got from Brigade and we were told to stand by for the battalion commander and command sergeant major. I remember being excited about what company they were going to put me in. Would it be one of the two that I had been assigned in the past? It didn't matter to me because I was about to begin my new journey as a senior NCO and a platoon sergeant.

They both came into the room and the battalion commander started first. He introduced himself and welcomed all of us to 3 Panther. He called for a show of hands of who was coming back and if anyone was coming back to this specific battalion. Of course I proudly raised my hand and I believe I was the only guy who did.

"Oh, when were you here before, Sergeant?" he asked me.

"I was here in '94 through '97, sir." He replied, "Oh good, that's awesome, where you coming from now?"

"Drill sergeant duty, sir."

"Hooah," he answered back. He then told everybody to go get in-processed, that he had a busy couple of hours in front of him, and that he would give us an initial briefing in a couple of days. He then turned it over to the command sergeant major and then left the battalion HQ. The command sergeant major came in and looked around at all of us standing there and said, "All right, welcome to 3 Panther."

"If you don't know, this battalion just returned from an eight-month combat deployment in Operation Enduring Freedom. So the paratroopers that you'll be with are sharp and they know what they're doing. So listen to them and take their advice when they offer it to you. Now that's for junior enlisted and NCOs as well."

He seemed like a good guy and was down-to-earth, as I was about to find out in the next twenty minutes or so. He was a younger command sergeant major, a good-looking guy with solid eyes. I had seen plenty of them in the past with this look in their eyes, which meant they weren't to be fucked with. Very serious—they would joke around, but then go back to no-shit serious. He told us all to stand fast and wait for the S-1 Shop to tell us what companies we'd all be going to. Then he looked around and said, "Now where's Staff Sergeant So-and-so."

It was the other promotable E-6 who raised his hand and said, "Here, Sergeant Major."

"Okay, you're promotable, correct?"

"Yes, Sergeant Major."

"Okay, come on back with me to my office so I can do a one-on-one with you. I have a platoon for you." So they both walked out of the room and headed down to the command sergeant major's office. I stood there confused and thought he just wasn't aware that I was promotable too. My neighbor looked at me and told me to follow them down to his office. I thought I would wait a few minutes, so that I wouldn't interrupt the two. Eventually, after about five minutes, I said the hell with it and went down. He was still in there talking to the other NCO. I knocked on his door lightly. The command sergeant major said to me, "Hey, what can I do for you?"

I said very humbly, "I apologize, Sergeant Major, for interrupting you two, but I don't think you are aware that I too am promotable." He replied very calmly, "Oh yeah, come on in here and let's talk about that, and I'll explain it all to you."

"Thanks, Sergeant Major." I sat down on his couch. The other staff sergeant was sitting in a chair in front of his desk.

The command sergeant major looked at me and gave it to me straight. First, he asked how to pronounce my name. I told him and he asked, "Can I just call you Sergeant A for now?"

"Oh, roger, Sergeant Major."

"Okay, thanks, Sergeant A." I remember feeling kind of weird, as if this guy was being overly nice or maybe sarcasm was about to come from him. "Sergeant A, this is how it works in this battalion. All platoon sergeants and platoon leaders will be Ranger qualified before myself or the battalion commander will allow them take charge of a rifle platoon. This is my and his policy for this battalion, and we have no intention of changing that policy. Do I make myself clear?"

"Roger, Sergeant Major." I had just seen my entire career come to a screeching halt before my eyes.

He then continued, "Now if you choose not to go to Ranger School, then I'll just keep you in my S-3 shop until you leave here someday."

I replied to him, "No, Sergeant Major. I have every intention of going to Ranger School right after ANCOC, for which I have an upcoming class date in a few months."

He said, "Okay then, sounds like a plan, Sergeant A. You want to just go to the S-3 shop until your class date?"

I said, "Roger, Sergeant Major, that'll work."

Then he looked closer at my BDUs and said, "Oh you're jumpmaster qualified? No, I'm going to put you in Charlie Company as a squad leader." Just when I thought this couldn't get any worse.

"Sergeant Major, could I just go to the S-3 shop for a little while before ANCOC? I mean, I already have four years rated squad leader time as of two years ago."

He said uncaringly, "No, you're going to Charlie Company as a squad leader and I want you to go report there as soon as you leave here, roger?"

"Roger, Sergeant Major."

"Okay, Sergeant A, if you don't have anything else for me, go ahead and take off."

"Roger, Sergeant Major." For the remainder of this book, I will refer to this guy as Command Sergeant Major Z.

I walked out of his office white as a ghost. I went back toward the entrance of the building and there was Staff Sergeant D waiting for me. "So what happened, did you get a platoon?"

"No, I can't until I graduate Ranger School first."

"Whaaat? Are you serious, dude?"

"Yeah, man, this ain't no joke." He had happened to get assigned to the same company and he and I walked down there together. I said, still not believing what had just happened, "This is definitely not the same battalion I was in a few years ago, and definitely not the way this shit's supposed to go."

Staff Sergeant D replied, "And he's making you be a squad leader again? Augi, you need to say fuck that, and go see the brigade command sergeant major and get moved to another battalion."

I asked, "Are you fucking kidding me? And if the brigade command sergeant major tells me too bad—because he's tabbed too—I'm truly fucked because it'll get back to our new command sergeant major that I went above his head. I know how this shit works around here, trust me. I've just never seen the Ranger School thing this bad."

I remember thinking back to a few years earlier about a specific platoon sergeant I'd had across Gela Street, and how he'd given me so much shit for not being tabbed, but he never kept my career progression back for it. I definitely had some serious challenges ahead of me during this time back in Division.

Staff Sergeant D and myself walked into our new company, the old company in which I had been a team leader and gone to Panama. Nobody was still there from those days, but it gave me some quick memories as we walked inside. We went straight to the orderly room and then the first sergeant's office. It was a pretty simple process. He gave us his welcomes and sent us both to our platoons that he was assigning us to. I went down to my command post and there was the platoon sergeant and a couple of E-6s sitting in there, which I assumed were his squad leaders.

Staff Sergeant D was in the same command post with the other platoon. Sergeant First Class W was sitting in there with a big old dip of Copenhagen in his mouth. He was a tall, slender guy, balding but not keeping his whole head shaved, so he looked older than he probably was. Either way, he did look like he could use a break.

"Hey, Sergeant, I'm your new squad leader." I didn't even wait for him to offer, I just found an empty seat and sat my ass down, still having a bit of an attitude from my initial encounter with the battalion command sergeant major.

He looked at me and said, "Ahh man! It's about time we got another jumpmaster in this fucking place." The other platoon sergeant on the other side said, "Hey this one is too," referring to my next-door neighbor. I just sat there and didn't say anything. I leaned over to him, shook his hand, introduced myself, got up and shook the other two squad leaders' hands and sat back down.

Without hesitation, Sergeant First Class W said, "Yeah, we're pretty busy around here with just coming back from Afghanistan and we've have a couple mass-tac jumps, which I had to be primary jumpmaster for on both. We need to get you two over to the jumpmaster refresher course over at the school ASAP, unless you've been already?"

"No, Sergeant. We just signed in from Replacement."

He then threw in the fact that in about two weeks, we were headed into Intensive Training Cycle and everything that came with it. Sounded like a standard couple of months in Division. It also sounded like this was his first time in the 82nd and perhaps that this place was getting to him. He then went on to tell me that he had well over two years already as a platoon sergeant and that he was just waiting for his replacement to come in. My stomach just churned a little more because that could have been my position and then this could have been a win for both of us. This guy looked worn out and ready to take a break.

Since he hadn't asked anything about me yet, I figured I'd just come out and tell him my status, so that maybe he wouldn't get too many high hopes about my longevity. "I'm leaving for ANCOC in a few months and plan on walking onto Ranger School from there, Sergeant, so I won't be here too long." He quickly sat up in his chair and got real serious on my ass. "You said you're going to ANCOC? What are you, promotable?"

I replied, "Roger, Sergeant. I thought I was coming in this battalion as a platoon sergeant, not a fucking squad leader again." I looked at the other two sitting in there and said, "No offense, but I already finished that job over two years ago, fellas." They both nodded their heads in agreement, "Oh yeah, we hear you." Neither were tabbed or jumpmaster qualified either.

Sergeant First Class W jumped up and said to me, "Wait here and don't go anywhere. I'll be back in a few." He went down to the first sergeant's office and shut the door. Apparently nobody in that company was aware they were getting an E-6 promotable but me. All I knew at the time was that it had changed Sergeant First Class W's attitude real quick.

Without knowing exactly what they were saying to one another in the first sergeant's office with the door closed, I pretty much had an idea of what was going on. I even got a little hopeful that the first sergeant was on the phone with Command Sergeant Major Z and that he was going to give in and allow me to start serving as a platoon sergeant right away.

Sergeant First Class W came back into the command post and asked me, "Hey, Sergeant A, you do plan on going to Ranger School from ANCOC right?"

"Roger, Sergeant, I have every intention to." I really did. I then was convinced that they had the command sergeant major on the phone and that they were trying to finalize this transaction. It almost felt like a business deal going down. Either way, I felt pretty positive for the first time since I had walked out of Battalion HQ. They were in there about an hour, I'm not kidding. The other two squad leaders left the command post and went down the hallway to the platoon.

He came back in, and he didn't sound too positive. "Well, I'm sorry, Sergeant A, but the sergeant major is not going to budge on this situation." You can tell Sergeant First Class W wasn't having it either and probably felt as bad as I did. He said, "All right, this is what me and the first sergeant came up with. Since you're scheduled to leave for Benning in May, you'll be a line squad leader here and go through ITC with us in a couple of weeks. After that, we'll be pretty much hands off you so that you can get ready for ANCOC and Ranger School. When you come back from Benning someday, if and when you graduate Ranger, the command sergeant major will move you to another company that needs a platoon sergeant. Roger?"

I replied, "Roger, Sergeant, too easy."

He then said, "Okay, in the meantime, before ITC kicks in, get to jumpmaster refresher and get that knocked out because we have a couple of big jumps coming up and we can use all the help we can get these days. This battalion in particular is running low on JMs."

"No problem, Sergeant."

He told me to go home, and I couldn't wait to leave. I snatched up my neighbor, who had been waiting forever on me, and I drove us home.

The next day around 1300, we had our official battalion commander welcome briefing in the battalion conference room. He came in and made it clear right from the start that this was his and the command sergeant major's battalion, period. There was an arrogance about him, particularly about the battalion's recent success in Afghanistan and how that reputation throughout the division must be maintained. He gave us almost every statistic on how 3 Panther had crushed the Taliban in their assigned sectors and that they had made a name for themselves over there. Then he went into the whole Ranger-qualified battalion policy.

"In this battalion, two schools are encouraged at all times, Ranger and jumpmaster. We take pride in 3 Panther because of our reputation on the street of having the most Ranger- and jumpmaster- qualified paratroopers anywhere else in Division. We expect those numbers to increase also. Staff Sergeant So-and-so from Bravo company just graduated from Ranger School a few days ago and was also the distinguished honor graduate from his class! That is fucking awesome!"

He then went into positioning leadership roles for those who were Ranger qualified and those who were not, of which I had already been made aware the day prior. "The sergeant major and I have a policy in this battalion: no paratrooper will serve in platoon leadership without being a Ranger graduate. I manage the platoon leaders and the sergeant major manages the platoon sergeants."

After we all left the "welcome briefing," I realized that this wasn't just Z's policy, but a consolidated team effort and mentality among the two in charge of this battalion. It also was made clear that it was a numbers competition within the nine infantry battalions on Ardennes Street. It always was, and I believe it still is today. I guarantee that's a very strong evaluation bullet for a battalion commander and command sergeant major to have: "His leadership has influenced subordinates to constantly learn and improve themselves, resulting in having the most Ranger- and jumpmaster-qualified paratroopers throughout the entire division."

Yeah, I've written an evaluation or two during my twenty years in the Army.

For two or three days, Staff Sergeant D and I were back at the 82nd Airborne Division's advance airborne school going through their jumpmaster refresher course. If I remember correctly, I believe the first day is based on indoor classes on the 82nd Airborne standard operating procedures. The focus was on all airborne procedures, drop zones, and timelines. Nomenclature class was given again with a test to go along with it, but for the refresher I don't believe it was for pass or fail. Actually, there was no fail course, just a crash course on current standard procedures. We went outdoors and each conducted a mock door procedure of both safety and primary jumpmaster or assistant jumpmaster duties. By the afternoon, it was in the sawdust pits going over JMPI (jumpmaster personnel inspection) for the rest of the day and the entire next. By the end of day two or three, we had it back, all down to a science. One would be surprised how fast all that comes back to you.

When we were done with the course, we took our certification slips to the Battalion S-3 air officer. Within the next two weeks, we both had a safety and our assistant jumpmaster duty knocked out. Again, we were both current, qualified jumpmasters coming back into Division. As a matter of fact, that assistant jumpmaster duty was a nighttime jump into Intensive Training Cycle for the next two weeks in the field.

This was an Intensive Training Cycle on steroids. What I mean by that is I remember every blank and live certification was increased. For instance, a line squad would certify on the typical squad live-fire maneuver range, and then as we moved to the platoon certifications on a trench complex, the squads would have to certify there individually before the battalion leadership would change it over to the platoon as a whole. Another intensity increase of this training cycle was that there was hardly any vehicle transportation from each of these certification ranges. The battalion commander had each element move as a platoon from range to range by foot, tactically through the woods, using compass direction and pace count. I will give that man this, he pushed that battalion to the limits and required excellent performance from all soldiers, rifleman through platoon leader. Being combat-ready was definitely his priority and he did a great job enforcing it too.

The equipment changes that the line units had in Division from two years prior were mainly on the weapon and night vision systems. Everything from the M4 carbines to the M249 SAWs, to the M240B machine guns all had the new rail system on them. The rail systems were designed to attach optics, infrared laser components, flashlights, and additional hand grips. We also had a new night-vision device called the PVS-14, which went over one eye only, instead of both like the old PVS-7B. Having only one eye covered with night vision helped the soldier's depth perception, assisting him to maneuver more easily. The body armor had recently changed as well to the Interceptor body armor system (IBA), which is equipped with a Kevlar plate in the front and back.

We got to the platoon live-fire range, which, again, was a trench complex. As I said, each squad had to go through it individually and certify blank and live before battalion would change it over to platoon. Each would be executing this as the initial assault element, entering and clearing the first row of the trench. The toughest part was getting from the cover and concealed positions in the wood line to the trench itself. It was about a two-hundred-meter movement in the open, which meant three-to five-second rushes by teams and individuals to get up to the entrance position of the trench. They even had a squad from another company demonstrate the assault for the whole platoon before the first squad's turn. It must have been their favorite squad leader in the whole battalion—because he was tabbed, was loud, and apparently didn't even have to wear a helmet. Instead he had a do-rag tied around his head, looking like he thought he was John Rambo or some shit. I watched the demonstration and just shook my head. This dude would have been annihilated in any other unit on the street for being out here looking like that.

So my squad went through the range without a hitch. We certified both blank- and live-fire. Then afterward, we had an after action review conducted by the battalion commander. Like I said, this was the first battalion commander I had ever seen get down to the squad level to evaluate training, but he was all over it.

After the review was complete, we started walking off and he called out, "Hey, squad leader, stay back here with us for a minute." I walked back over to him and the crew that was also standing around, such as the CO, first sergeant, Sergeant First Class W, and Command Sergeant Major Z.

"Yes, sir?" I said.

He told me, "Hey Sergeant A, you've got to get into shape, my man. You looked like you were struggling coming across that open area before you got into that trench. I mean your fat gut was hanging out of your IBA, for Christ's sake. But don't worry yourself, I'm not going to fire you or anything. You were a great leader in the trench. I mean you gave clear, concise combat instructions the whole time, and I was impressed with that."

Sarcastically—and I shouldn't have said it, but at this point, I didn't give a fuck—I said, "That's because I did this shit as a squad leader for four years straight before I did two fuckin' years as a drill sergeant." I don't think I even said *sir*. My fat gut? I didn't have a gut and I had just gotten a 290 on my recent PT test at Replacement before I had gotten to this fucking place.

The command sergeant major was staring at me and didn't say a word, but if looks could kill, I would have fallen back into that trench, deader than a doornail.

"We're done here, Sergeant," the commander said to me.

I then moved back to the squad and got them ready for the next event. That group stayed back there, and I could tell they were talking about me. I thought to myself, *Fire me, motherfucker. I leave for Fort*

Benning in a few weeks. For at least five or six months, I could give a fuck.

After we were done with that range, we tactically moved as a company a few miles away to the last objective. On our way, the first sergeant came up to me and walked beside me. "Hey, how you doing, Sergeant A?"

"I'm good, First Sergeant, what's up?"

"Oh, nothin'. I'm just making my way through the company, shooting the shit as we move along."

I remember it being cold and raining and it was midday, so he asked me about my new boots: "Hey, are those new boots?"

"Roger, First Sergeant."

"You like 'em?"

I asked him, "Okay, what's up, First Sergeant, why you askin' about the jungle boots I got on?"

He said very encouragingly, "Hey, man, don't let those guys get to you. They obviously got it out for you, Sergeant A."

I replied, "Well, what the fuck did I ever do to them, or what have I fucked-up?"

He said, "It's that whole platoon sergeant thing when you first got here. They look at you like you're an outsider questioning the system they've had in place as long as they've been here, and they resent you for that." He continued, "I've seen it since you showed up that first night and so did Sergeant First Class W."

"So what do I do about it, First Sergeant?" I asked.

"Nothing. Just do your time here before you go to Benning, and don't highlight yourself in the meantime. Once you leave, put this place behind you and concentrate on what you have to get done down there."

"Roger that. That's what I intend to do, First Sergeant."

After the long movement, each platoon broke off and conducted their portions of the assault, which was a small force-on-force with blanks. Live-fires were over, and it was time to get the fuck out of this field exercise.

As the weeks went on, tensions between President Bush and

Saddam Hussein were building, and the world was standing by to see if the United States was putting on a major bluff. I knew we weren't because after 9/11, I remember what the president's warning was to the rest the world. He had said, "You're either with us or against us." When I had seen Saddam Hussein, live on CNN, pick up that silver-plated pistol and fire it into the air in celebratory response to the attacks on us during 9/11, I knew his time was coming. It was very tense on Ardennes Street during the month of March 2003. Some elements of Division HQ, along with the entire Falcon Brigade, were already gone and in Kuwait. I was thinking about my two buddies over there, Shaky and S. On the morning of the invasion of Iraq, me, Sergeant First Class W, and the other squad leaders were having breakfast in the 3 Panther chow hall watching Baghdad get lit up like a Christmas tree on the news. They also were showing clips of the 173rd Airborne Brigade Combat Team out of Vicenza, Italy, parachuting into Northern Iraq. We were sitting there talking shit, being jealous, watching these guys get a combat jump on CNN while we were eating chow in the mess hall at Fort Bragg. Operation Iraqi Freedom had begun.

The next few weeks, there were some changes in the platoon and the battalion. Sergeant First Class W finally got to leave the company and go to Battalion Operations, and well deserved. He had had an excellent platoon sergeant run and it was his time to move on and let someone new begin their time. He could simply sit back and wait to make the E-8 list. The platoon ended up getting the staff sergeant promotable that was the recent honor graduate from Ranger School, who was also scheduled to go to the upcoming ANCOC class with me. Actually there were four of us from the battalion that were going to this class: the E-6 promotable I gad signed into the battalion with, the new platoon sergeant, and a guy in the S-3 shop that wasn't tabbed either. So there were two of us that would be moving onto Ranger School and staying at Fort Benning after the three month ANCOC class. The battalion commander left also. His time in command was up.

We all took the PT test and weigh-in prior to leaving for Benning. We had our travel pay coordinated with our S-4 officer, which issued our travel credit cards. I was even able to knock out my first primary jumpmaster duty prior to leaving as well. Too easy.

One thing I didn't do was go see my old platoon sergeant from 1 Panther, who was now a first sergeant for HQ Company, Division. I was still bitter and didn't want to hear his bullshit anyway. For all I knew, he was in Iraq too. We knew the division commander and command sergeant major were there. As I drove my truck south on I-95 out of Fayetteville, I told myself I wouldn't be back for some time, until almost winter. I put all the bullshit of the last few months out of my head and focused strictly on school. I looked at it as a two-part task: first, graduate ANCOC to secure the rank of sergeant first class, and then, graduate Ranger School to secure a platoon sergeant position. I graduated ANCOC with no problem. While I was there for the three months, I busted my ass doing PT intensely for preparation of Ranger School. I was ready for one of the biggest challenges of my military career—at age thirty-one. It had been a long time coming.

CHAPTER 10

RANGER SCHOOL
RAP WEEK

I DROVE MYSELF to Camp Rogers around 3 a.m., with a report time of four o'clock. There were about four or five other ANCOC graduates reporting there along with me, so we huddled together in the parking lot until we were called over to enter one of the buildings. Camp Rogers was as old as Ranger School itself. Most of the buildings were the old-style steel-arched Quonset huts. Once inside, we were told to take a seat and fill out the green cards they handed out to us. There were no tables. We sat on the floor and filled out our green cards as fast as we could because the RIs (Ranger instructors) were yelling at us to hurry up and get outside to form up for the Ranger physical fitness test. The cards we were filling out are mandatory for every student who walks through the door on zero day of Ranger School. It asks name, rank, social security number, unit of assignment, and how many attempts this is for each student going through this course. Supposedly, it is kept on file for eternity at RTB (Ranger Training Brigade) in order to maintain a record for every servicemember that starts the school, which is open for all branches of the military, not just the Army.

We were told to go get our two duffle bags and stack them to the side of the building we had just left and to stand by. We were then marched to the hand-to-hand combat pit across the street from the buildings of Camp Rogers, where we would be conducting the fitness test. The standard to pass the test was fifty-two push-ups in two minutes, sixty-two sit-ups in two minutes, run two miles under fourteen minutes and fifty seconds, and six dead-hang pull-ups immediately after the run. I'll admit that I was anxious and nervous about taking the Ranger PT test due to the hype leading up to this point—hype that had been built up over years of horror stories from guys that were Ranger qualified back at Bragg. Listening to them, you would have thought that this PT test was virtually impossible to pass. In fact, it was just the opposite for me, as I focused on it one event at a time.

I knocked out my fifty-two push-ups without having to repeat, and the same went for the sit-ups. I knocked out the run in great time and got in one of the dozens of lines for the pull-ups. You couldn't use your legs to kick or move any part of your lower body for momentum to assist pulling your chin over the bar. The RI grading you would say, "Mount the bar, Ranger." Once you were free-hanging, with your elbows locked, he would give the command, "Begin, Ranger." Once your chin was over the bar, you came down until your elbows were locked again, and then he would count the repetition, "One." You did that six times and the PT test was over. He then told me to move to the formation on the left side. The other formation on the right was for failures. Every student was afforded two chances to pass each event. For example, if one failed the push-ups twice, they were out of the course. As I stood in the "passing formation," I glanced over to the "nonpassing formation," and there appeared to be about twenty students that had failed the test. I remember saying to myself at that point, "There's nothing that's going to stop me now." I wasn't worried about the upcoming swim test, which was the other mandatory event you had to pass to get through zero day of Ranger School.

After the last of the students were complete with the pull-ups, we were instructed to go to our duffle bags and change into BDUs (battle dress uniform), boots, and a patrol cap. Every student was to have a two-quart canteen of water strapped around our necks as well. There was no changing area provided; it was right there, bare ass out in the open in front of God and everybody. We were instructed to pack another set of BDUs, an additional pair of boots, and another T-shirt. We were to pack them in a wet-weather bag and get on one of the two or three buses that were parked outside of the camp. We headed for Main Post to one of the swimming pools as the sun was just coming up. The swimming pool was right across from Airborne School, and on the other side of the two-hundred-foot towers, which were a pretty famous and common sight on Fort Benning.

As the bus pulled out of Camp Rogers, I noticed the PT failures sitting on their duffle bags, awaiting dismissal from the course. One of them was a fellow student from my ANCOC class. I remember looking out the window at him thinking that perhaps he should have worked out a little more while at the academy, rather than partying so much, but I was not judging. At this point of zero-day testing, I only needed to worry about my own ass.

The ride to Main Post was an irritating one. The students from the 75th Ranger Regiment were young and obnoxious. They were singing the whole way to Main Post, which was about a twenty to twenty-five-minute ride. The songs they were singing were old military chants. When I think back, it was sort of funny because these were young Infantry soldiers that treated Ranger School like it was a retreat away from their difficult units. Most of them, if not all, had already served at least one combat tour in Afghanistan by this time. Ranger battalion boys, or as the rest of the Army simply referred to them, "Bat Boys," were the equivalent of the young Marine mentality of "nobody can compare to us" within the Army itself. So, the majority of us just tried to maintain our sanity on the bus ride to the CWST (combat water survival test) while these young gung-ho warriors sang their songs in cheer and celebration.

When we arrived at the outdoor pool, the RIs had us file into the locker room and set our wet-weather bags on the benches and then move outside to the pool. The water test consisted of three events. The high drop, where the student is blindfolded and walks to the end of a diving board wearing BDUs, boots, and LCE (load-carrying equipment), while carrying a rubber duck, which is a slang term soldiers call a fake or simulated M16 assault rifle. Once at the end of the diving board, the student must step forward, about five meters above the water, while holding the weapon straight out in front of them. The student then steps off the board on command of the RI, falling into the water without letting go of the weapon. If they drop the weapon when submerged in the water, they must repeat the event again. If they fail it twice, they're dropped from the course. Same standard as the PT Test; if they fail any of the three CWST events twice, they're dropped.

The next event, and not in this particular order, is the backward drop. The student leaps into the water backward from the side of the pool, again into the deep end. While underwater, they must remove their equipment (LCE and weapon) and swim away from it. When they reemerge to the surface, they must have their equipment separated from their bodies.

The final event, and the one that causes the most failures of the CWST, is the fifteen-meter swim with LCE and weapon. Each student must swim the distance with their heads and the barrel of the weapon above water. Weak swimmers usually will fail this event as they may begin to panic and move to the side of the pool or drop their weapon and reach for the side. If they touch the side of the pool at all, they are an automatic failure for that event. We lost another twenty to twenty-five students on the CWST. Altogether, by around 11 a.m. when we finished the CWST and got back on the buses, out of approximately two hundred students that started that morning, about fifty were already failures and out of Ranger School. Out of the four or five other fellow ANCOC graduates that I had showed up with, I was the only one left before noon on zero day, which was not over by far.

The bus ride back to Camp Rogers was even more obnoxious than it had been earlier. The Bat Boys were singing their songs and playing grab-ass games again. I swear if I didn't know any better, I'd have thought they were on a fucking vacation. They were like little kids just arriving at summer camp, away from their parents for the first time. But it's funny when I look back at it today.

I sat next to this guy who just looked at me and shook his head at all the noise the Bat Boys were making. I asked him where he was from in the Army. He was coming from Germany, assigned to a reconnaissance unit). He looked and acted a little older, so I asked him what his rank was. In Ranger School, the students must strip their uniforms of rank, unit insignia and all special skill badges in order to have zero identity other than last name and US Army, or whatever branch of the military they belonged to. All heads must also be shaven bald prior to showing up on zero day.

He happened to be a staff sergeant (E-6), and this too was his first time attending Ranger School. So, he and I shot the shit on the bus ride back to camp and got along right off the bat. I told him if we ended up in the same platoon, we could be "Ranger buddies." Every student must have a Ranger buddy throughout the duration of the sixty-two-day course. He said, "Hell yeah, that's cool." I had met my first friend in Army Ranger School on zero day.

When we got back to Camp Rogers, the chaos began. "Rangers, get your asses off the buses, put your wet-weather bags over by your duffle bags, and get the fuck back here in formation! Swim test no-gos, sit on your duffle bags and stand by for further instructions! I'm not telling you what to do with your wet gear, Rangers, but if it were me, I'd pull that shit out and lay it on your duffle bags so it can dry out! Now hurry the fuck up and get into formation; we got training to start!"

After laying out our wet BDUs and boots, we formed up and were marched across the road back to the hand-to-hand pit. I remember looking up at the entrance of the pit area, which was pretty intimidating because there were two large, towering utility-pole logs with a huge Ranger tab hanging in the center of them. We got pretty used to seeing this pit and got very familiar with it over the next five days and nights.

We were in a column formation, and one of the RIs got out in front and commanded, "File from the left, follow me, Rangers!" We filed into the pit at a double time and jogged around for about fifteen to twenty minutes in a single-file line. Our two-quart canteens were slung across our bodies, and we were told to drink water whenever we wanted to, without having to be told when to do so—just don't stop running while you drink.

One of the RIs hollered out, "Quick time, Rangers! Walk it off!" We walked around the pit for about two laps and were told to stop and face the center. Two RIs jumped on the demonstration platform in the center of the pit and began our first block of instruction, which was our first hand-to-hand takedown drill. They weren't bullshitting; we were going right into training. I guess any in-processing we were going to do was totally complete when we had filled out that green card at 0400 that morning.

The instructors would demonstrate each drill and then turn it over to us to practice and then go full force on one another. All of us were paired off—not chosen by the RIs, but random or whoever was closest to us. After doing each hand-to-hand move a few times on one another, we would be instructed to run around the pit. We would switch off from having to bear crawl and then conduct buddy carries when told to do so. This went on for the next few hours.

"Let's go, Rangers, move your asses! This shit is just beginning! None of you should be tired yet! If you are feeling tired, you might be in the wrong fucking school, Rangers—move it!"

I remember thinking that I would sure like to eat something, since my last meal had been dinner the evening prior, and it was already about 1600. Lo and behold, we were finally instructed to exit the pit and form up. On the way to forming up we were told to stop off at the water buffalo and top off our canteens.

"We're going to eat chow, Rangers!"

The formation cheered like we were at the Super Bowl. We marched back onto the camp and straight to the mess hall. Outside, we were taught the Ranger School standard of entering any mess hall during any of the three phases. Six students would volunteer to step in front of the formation, and each would sound off with a portion of the Ranger Creed, and the rest of us would echo that portion until the entire Ranger Creed was complete. Afterward, each student would move to a row of pull-up bars and knock out six pull-ups before entering the chow line inside the dining facility. Again, this would be the standard during the entire sixty-two-day course.

Now, I've heard all the urban legends and horror stories of previous students saying that their initial chow hall meals in Ranger School were simply chaotic, and that the students were not even allowed to sit down and eat their meals but were to eat as much as they could while walking their trays to the trash cans before going outside. Another rumor I had heard from past students was that the RIs would force you to eat your whole tray of food, and then take you outside and "smoke" everyone until they all threw up.

I will say that I did not experience this. During my initial meal at Camp Rogers, we were afforded the opportunity to sit down and eat our dinner chow. I'm not calling those that have told these stories liars but am just saying that I did not experience that. However, we could not sit there and just shoot the shit, but rather had to eat our meal in its entirety, then hurry up and get out to formation, like any other military school. I believe that first Ranger School meal was chili mac, and it was the best chili mac I'd ever eaten in my entire life.

After chow, it was back to the hand-to-hand pit for more training, more bear crawls, more buddy carries, push-ups, flutter kicks, etc. Simply put, a continuous series of "ass-smokings" well into the night and literally into the next morning. It was well after midnight when we finished in the pit for zero day. We formed up and marched back across the street, and were told to secure our duffle bags, which had been in the same spot since 0400 the morning prior. We thought they were going to take us to our barracks and bed us down for the night. Unfortunately, we were gravely mistaken.

There were about 140 of us remaining from the little over 200 that had started that morning. One of the RIs marched us over to the headquarters building and told us to relax, drink water, and to check out the rosters on the bulletin board outside the main entrance. They covered what our roster numbers were, and our company and platoon of assignment. They broke us down into two companies— Alpha and Bravo. Within each company, they broke us down into two platoons. The RI came back out and told us to get a leader for each company and one each for the platoons.

"Don't worry about platoon sergeants and squad leaders at this time, Rangers. That'll come later, as I'm sure y'all are aware. Right now, for Assessment Phase Week, we only want to contact a company commander or a platoon leader. So, figure out who they're gonna be by the time I get back out to you in about ten minutes, Rangers. Also, you all need to get a Ranger buddy that's assigned to the same platoon. So, your task, Rangers, is to have two companies, four platoons with a company commander, a platoon leader for each, and everybody has a Ranger buddy. See you in ten minutes, Rangers."

That was easy. Me and my buddy from Germany ended up in the same platoon, so we were officially Ranger buddies. I believe commissioned officers stepped up for the initial leadership roles required for the upcoming assessment phase.

When the RI came back out, we were still all standing around in a gaggle. He didn't take a great liking to that, so he told us to get on our backs for about another ten minutes of flutter kicks.

"Let's go, Rangers! Get up and get your asses in the four platoons according to these rosters and give me a fucking leader standing in front of each. Move! We're on your time now, Rangers! You can get three hours of sleep or an hour. It don't make any difference to me. I'll be here all night anyway, Rangers." We got into four platoon formations, but it was sloppy, and some students had already forgotten which one they were to get into. The sleepiness and disorientation were starting to set in for some of the students.

"Stop, Rangers, just stop! Get on your backs and start fluttering again. We'll stay out here until the next formation, which will be in about three and a half hours, Rangers! It don't mean two shits to me!" After about another ten minutes he yelled out, "Okay, get up and let's try this again. Move!" By now it was going on 0200. We got into our proper formations, and he seemed to be satisfied with our promptness.

"All right, Rangers; Alpha Company, you're in the barracks on the right, and Bravo on the left. Take your duffle bags, find a wall locker and bunk and get some rest, Rangers. 0500 formation right back here. BDUs, PT belt, and running shoes. You all have your five-mile run, so keep drinking water, Rangers. Platoon leaders, make sure you put together a fire guard roster for your barracks. Anybody got any questions before I release you, Rangers?"

Of course, in every military school, in every class, there's always one dumbass that raises their hand, and we had one right at that moment.

"Yeah, what do you got for me, Ranger?"

The dumbass's question was, "Sergeant, when do we draw linen for our bunks?" Usually, in most military schools, a set of linen consisted of a pillow, a pillowcase, a set of sheets, and two blankets. Everybody sighed out loud. We were all like, "What the fuck?"

The RI gave him a confused look, probably in disbelief that someone would ask such a thing in this course. Hell, we were appreciative of having a mattress to lie on at all.

"Ranger, who the fuck do you think I am—Martha fucking Stewart? Get back on your backs, Rangers. This night is not over!" We did another fifteen minutes of flutter kicks. At around 0230, zero day of Ranger School was finally over for us, twenty-two and a half hours after we signed in. I was Roster Number Five Zero, and we had sixty-one days to go before graduation.

RAP Week was a five-day pass-or-fail series of events that each student must complete successfully in order to actually begin Ranger School. These tasks consisted of day and night land navigation, a five-mile run, a two-man buddy run in combat equipment, a water confidence course, a bayonet assault course, an obstacle course, weapons and communications testing, more hand-to-hand combat classes, Airborne Refresher Day with a parachute jump, and finally, a fifteen-mile road march from Camp Rogers out to Camp Darby.

Our first formation was at 0500 back at the headquarters building. We wore BDUs, PT reflector belt, and running shoes. The RIs came out and took accountability of us by calling out our roster numbers. Lo and behold, a couple of students were not in formation. They must have left sometime during our full two and half hours of sleep. The RI that was on duty during the time that we bedded down came out and said to the other instructors that two had signed out about two hours ago, shortly after we had gone to our barracks.

"All right, Rangers, strip off your BDU tops, secure your PT belts around your waists and ground your two-quarts." We stretched out for about ten minutes before knocking out the five-mile run. The standard was to run it in formation at an eight-minute-mile pace—to be completed in forty minutes. We took off and did just that. The instructors kept us right at the pace. They must have done this a time or two. It was a pretty simple run to complete—if you were in great shape. If you made it this far on day one, you were just that—in prime physical condition.

We finished the run, fell back onto our two-quarts and BDU tops, and were told to stretch out on our own to keep our muscles from tightening up. Then we heard the good news. "Platoon leaders, march them to the chow hall, conduct the Ranger Creed, pull-ups, and get them inside for breakfast." We all cheered again, like someone had just told us we had won the lottery and were instant millionaires. There was a pattern beginning that we all quickly realized, and it became a standard for our class, and probably for every class before and after ours as well: when the RIs told us we were going to the dining facility, it was free game to cheer as loud as we could.

After chow, a quick shower, and clean BDUs, it was on the buses back to Main Post for TA-50 issue—our tactical gear, such as helmets, LCE items, and large rucksacks. Oh yeah, there was plenty more singing and grab-ass games from the Bat Boys on the way there. I looked at my Ranger buddy from Germany and said to him, "Well, the first RAP Week task is over, brother." Meaning the five-mile run. He high-fived me and replied, "Hell yeah, too easy, dude." That soon became our saying to one another after each mandatory task was complete—"Too easy."

When we got back to Camp Rogers, they had us secure our TA-50 in our wall lockers and hurry back out for formation. It was time to march back across the street for more hand-to-hand training and ass-smokings for the rest of the day and well into the night. We did get dinner chow in between. At this point, we were counting meals, and thus far, we'd eaten three meals in the past sixty hours.

The hand-to-hand combat classes were extensive and brutal at times. We were not allowed to "sugarcoat" any of the takedowns or body throws. This was the old hand-to-hand techniques, prior to the Brazilian-style Jiu Jitsu that became the Army combatives standard shortly afterward. As a matter of fact, we were told that we were one of the last classes that would get the twenty to twenty-five hours of the old-style combatives sessions in Ranger School. The new-style Jiu Jitsu combatives classes were more of a wrestling technique that emphasized choke holds and arm bar movements. Either way, they were long, extensive hours that went well into the night. When we finished training for the night and got back out in front of the headquarters, it was well after 0100 again.

"Rangers, put your LCEs and rucksacks together according to the standards posted on the bulletin board. Formation will be 0430, Rangers. BDUs, boots, patrol caps, rucksacks with a dry set of BDUs and boots inside one of your wet-weather bags. Make sure you have your reflective belts around your rucks, Rangers. Get to work on your equipment. PLs, when they're complete with their equipment, they can go nighty-night." There was no timeline or training schedule posted. We just went off whatever time and uniform they told us. Only the instructors knew what was next on the agenda. So, that made it a little more mind boggling—the not knowing. We had to make ourselves just go through each event as we were told to do so, because at the end of the day, we were just trying to make it out of this course successfully with a Ranger tab. Day one of RAP Week ended around 0200 again, and there were sixty days until graduation. Too easy.

Day two (actually day three if you count zero day) started out with a cool, brisk morning, and about a two-mile hike to Victory Pond. We figured it was going to be the dreaded Ranger School water confidence course because the RI had told us to pack a set of BDUs and boots in our rucks. I told Germany that I thought we were headed to the infamous water course, and he agreed. From here on out, I will refer to my new Ranger buddy as Germany, and not just for privacy purposes, but because I honestly forgot his damn name and roster number. Give me a break; it was a long time ago, and I've been through a lot, and have interacted with so many soldiers since then. Anyway, we looked at each other, and admitted a little nervousness, but convinced one another that it was a Band-Aid that simply needed to be ripped off. In other words, "Let's get this shit over with."

When we arrived at Victory Pond, we grounded our equipment in formation and moved over for a briefing and a demonstration by the instructors. The sun was just coming over the tree line in the distance, and it was still cool outside. After the demonstrations, they moved us over to draw life vests and then sent each of our two companies to the two separate events. The evaluations began immediately; they never wasted our time on this or any other event during RAP Week. I had to do the slide-for-life event first. We climbed up a seventy-foot metal ladder to the top and proceeded to a platform with an RI giving guidance on when to execute the task. I'll admit, when I got to the top, it seemed as if I had climbed more like two hundred feet, but that's probably because we were tired and hungry.

Anyway, the RI said, "All right, Ranger, move forward to the platform." Once I was there, he gave me the order, "Execute, Ranger." You had to jump up and a little bit forward to grab the bar, and once you did, away you went with a pretty decent speed down toward the water. The standard was, when you saw the RI below wave the red flag, you were to release from the bar and enter the water. It was more like a slam into the water because you were coming down so fast from so high up.

We then swam over to a ladder on the bank and got out of the water, just to hurry up and get into the line for the next event, which was the dreaded beam walk. This event was the one with all the horror stories. You climbed up a thirty-five-foot ladder. Once on top, you had to walk across a wooden beam that was about the width of a railroad tie. Halfway across the beam was a little platform that you had to step up and over, without using your hands at all. Once on the other side, you continued to walk the remainder of the beam until you got to a rope that was horizontal, still thirty-five feet in the air. You had to shimmy across the rope until you got to a two-foot-long, wooden Ranger tab, touch the tab, and then release your legs from the rope. Once suspended by your hands and arms, you had to ask the RI who was grading you for permission to drop into the water.

I made it across and made my request. "Roster Number Five Zero, request permission to drop, Sergeant!"

He replied, "Drop, Ranger!"

I released the rope and plunged into the frigid water.

If any student showed signs of fear of heights or hesitation to calmly go through either of these two events, they were dropped from the course. Fear of heights or water was definitely a showstopper in Ranger School, especially with Mountain and Florida Phases coming up, but we'll get into that later.

Once done, I reported to the RI, and he confirmed that I was a "go" on both events and said to go to my ruck and put on dry BDUs, T-shirt, socks, and boots. Again, it was bare-ass naked, changing in front of God and everybody. I got done before Germany. When he linked up with me over by our rucks, I asked him if he was good. He gave me a sarcastic look and said, "Ah, dude, too easy."

I replied, "Oh, fuck yeah it was—way too easy." The reality was that an hour ago we had both been nervous as fuck.

We got back to Camp Rogers, and it was only about 1000 hours. We were hoping they would march us to the chow hall, but that did not happen. No breakfast. Instead, we were told to secure our helmets, LCEs, and leather gloves. We emptied out our wet clothes and strung them up on the 550 cord we had outside our barracks in order to dry. We then formed back up on the street.

The instructors marched us down the road to the bayonet assault course. It was your typical training on using a bayonet attached to rubber ducks. They took us through the basic bayonet training on stabbing moves and butt strokes with our weapons. Once that was complete, each student ran the course himself. The only big thing I remember during this mandatory training was how hot it was outside and that we were covered with mud from head to toe after we were complete. I believe today bayonet training is no longer a part of RAP Week or Ranger School. Other than in Basic Training, I don't think the Army trains on it at all anymore. I don't see how you could, due to all the attachments one has on their individual weapon anyway. How the hell could you attach a bayonet with all the shit on your M-4?

Back outside our barracks we hosed off our equipment and got all the mud off everything. We hung up our wet equipment from the bayonet course and changed back into the now-dry BDUs that were hanging up from this morning. We formed back up with dry BDUs—not clean, but dry—and our two-quarts.

"It's chow time, Rangers!" Cheers and more cheers. We marched to the dining facility for our fourth meal in three days.

After chow, it was back across the street for another evening of beloved hand-to-hand combat training and ass-smokings. I remember they cut this session off earlier than normal. Come to find out, the special occasion was an earlier night for an earlier morning. Formation the next morning was around 0300 outside the building where we had initially filled out our green cards. Uniforms were going to be BDUs, LCEs, and patrol caps for land navigation. The RIs actually released us around 2330 for three and a half hours before the next day started. I remember taking a hot shower and getting into clean BDU bottoms and a T-shirt with clean, fresh socks for bed. No pillow, sheets, or blankets, just my poncho liner or what we call our "wooby," and I would roll up another set of BDUs for my pillow. Again, we simply appreciated being able to lie down for a few hours on a mattress. Fifty-nine days until graduation.

About three and a half hours later we were inside the same building we had started in. We lay on the floor with the maps we were issued, plotting out our points we had to find on the maps for day and night land navigation, the next mandatory event we had to pass to continue on in the course. The standard was to find seven out of nine points (if my memory serves me correctly) using a map and a compass. The course was to begin at 0500 and be completed by 0900, the logic being there would be two hours of darkness and then two hours of daylight to locate all nine points. We were allowed to have a red-lensed flashlight, only to be used to assist reading our map and to mark our point once we located it. If you were caught using it to navigate, or caught talking to another student, you were dropped from the course for integrity purposes. This was one of those tasks that would knock out a handful of students from Ranger School. I learned a long time ago during these land navigation tests to remain calm, trust in your compass, plotting techniques, and your 100-meter pace count and to definitely walk straight-line distance through whatever terrain you have to. Stay off the roads and firebreaks. If any student failed their first time, I believe they were allotted a second chance to retest.

Germany and I both received gos for the land-navigation event. We looked at each other before we got back on the buses to head back and said, "Too easy." He even gave me a "Pfft. Way too easy." One thing was for sure, my confidence was increasing more and more as these events came and went with success. However, I had to continuously remind and encourage myself that I was an experienced infantryman with twelve years of service, that I should have no problem passing these events with no excuses; however, I needed to remain humble, and not get cocky whatsoever.

When we got back to camp we were sent to breakfast, and then more training afterward. Each of the four platoons were split off, and we went with our assigned RIs. We went behind headquarters and were told to take a seat in the grass, and we received our first class on combat orders. The first one was a long, drawn-out class on writing a five-paragraph operations order. "Pull out your Ranger Handbooks and note-taking material, Rangers. This is a very important class that you are about to receive, and it is going to be your 'bread and butter' for the planning portions of every single mission you will go on during the duration of this course, Rangers. Therefore, it would behoove you to stay awake and pay attention to what you get from this block of instruction. If everybody starts falling asleep, Rangers, we'll just say fuck it, and take you over across the street and do some more hand-to-hand instead, so that you can wake your asses up. So, stand your asses up if you find yourselves falling asleep."

One thing I had noticed about Ranger School so far was that there wasn't a whole lot of screaming at the students. The RIs, for the most part, were calm and gave clear, concise instructions on every task we needed to complete. They told you the way it was, without bullshitting or sugarcoating anything. If you couldn't grasp it or meet the standards put forward, pack your bags because you were leaving and going back to your unit without a Ranger tab.

Lo and behold, within five minutes of our operations order class starting, everybody in our platoon was standing. Sleep deprivation was really starting to set in on all of us.

That evening was our final hand-to-hand session. It was four long, grueling hours of physical exhaustion. Throwing each other, punching one another, push-ups, flutter kicks, running around the pit, along with bear crawls and buddy carries until the early-morning hours. I was excited, though, because it being the last night of combatives training meant we were closer to getting through RAP Week and moving on to our first phase. Fifty-eight or fifty-seven days until graduation—I think. At this point, my classmates and I began to lose count. The days and nights were running together. "Just tell us the task we have to accomplish next in order to get to the next one after that" was the mentality.

Zero dark thirty the next morning started off with the two-mile buddy run in combat equipment, immediately followed by the infamous Malvesti Obstacle Course, also known as the "worm pit" obstacle course. It was called the worm pit because of the twenty-five-meter portion we had to crawl through with muddy water and knee-high barbed wire above our heads. I don't think I went through the run and obstacle course with Germany. I believe the RIs paired us up randomly with whoever was standing next to us before we were told to go at the beginning of the run. The run was conducted in BDUs, LCEs, and boots, with rubber ducks. I cannot remember what the time standard was for the run, or if there even was one. Once complete, we lined up at the beginning of the course, grounded our weapons and LCEs, stayed with the same buddy and began negotiating the first obstacle. The worm pit resulted in a familiar outcome: an ass-smoking while drenched with cold, muddy water. After completing the obstacle course, we were told to move back to the barracks, shower, get into dry uniforms, and look at the packing list for the next event, which was posted outside the headquarters.

That next event was a "fun-filled" day at the US Army Airborne School back on Main Post. After breakfast chow, we got on the buses for more singing and cheering from the Bat Boys. Hell, I was in such a good mood, I joined in the singing and grab-ass games too. Shit, we were about a day or two away from heading out to Darby Phase. The confidence was building up in all of us.

If you were Airborne qualified, you went through a day of basic airborne refresher (where we were headed). First thing the next day, we would complete a jump in order to ensure that we were all current and qualified Airborne certified before we entered any of the Ranger School phases because there were parachute assaults integrated within the upcoming training. I remember feeling as though it was a waste of time for me since I was a current, qualified jumpmaster from the 82nd Airborne Division. However, I went through the classes and the training without saying a word and did exactly what we were told. Too easy. I do remember I was made to exit the thirty-four-foot tower twice because the first time I exited I had my eyes closed—so the RI that was grading me said, "Unsatisfactory, Ranger, you had your eyes closed when you exited the paratroop door. Go back up the tower and exit again." My reply to him was "Roger that, Sergeant." I walked back up the steps of the tower and did it again with zero sarcasm or attitude. I knew how this "game" worked. If you expect to make it through these schools successfully, the number one thing you do not do is get into a pissing contest with those that evaluate and grade you.

We spent most of the day at Airborne School before heading back to Camp Rogers. Our jump time over Fryer Drop Zone the next morning was like 0800 or 0900. Once back at Rogers, we had extensive classes on demolitions, got to eat dinner chow at the mess hall, and then received more classes and hands-on training on communications and weapons disassembly and reassembly. After our Airborne operation in the morning, we were going to test on the M240B machine gun, the M249 squad automatic weapon (SAW), the AT-4 antitank weapon, the M-21A1 Claymore mine, filling out a range card on a machine gun position, and placing the SINGARS radio into operation. Almost sounded like a miniature Expert Infantryman Badge testing. Sounded like it was going to be a relatively easy day. For once, no obstacle course or long run or hand-to-hand combat session.

That evening before we could bed down, all the Airborne-qualified students had to rig our rucks and M-1950 weapons cases to jump. We were each issued a rubber duck to place inside instead of real weapons. The RIs went through and inspected each to ensure that they were properly rigged. We then went through sustained Airborne training, or prejump, which is mandatory training prior to any jump. All this was put out of the way so that in the morning all we had to do was get on the buses and head to the departure airfield on Main Post.

At zero dark thirty the next morning, we ate breakfast, got onto the buses with our rigged equipment, and headed to our first jump in Ranger School. Once inside the pack-shed, we drew our parachutes and reserves and were told to start donning them and our equipment. We were jumpmaster personnel inspected (JMPI) by the RIs and took a seat on the benches, waiting for the next block of instruction. It was "nighty-night" time as we sat and waited to load the C-130 aircraft. There were two chalks, or two aircraft, that we finally loaded when the sun came up. There was no wasting time. Once loaded into our seats, the pilots took off and headed straight for the drop zone. The nonjumpers were on drop zone details, to include parachute collection and part of the drop-zone safety teams. I exited the aircraft with no issues. I had a great daytime jump in sunny weather with no wind, and a soft landing. As a matter of fact, it was one of the easier mornings at Ranger School up to this point in RAP Week, which was almost over!

Back at Rogers, we proceeded with our weapons and communications hands-on testing. I remember running into two of the Benning RIs that I had been classmates with during ANCOC. They were both sitting down as I rotated through each testing station.

"Hey, Ranger, how's it going for ya so far?"

I was surprised to run into them; I knew they were RIs but didn't quite know what phase.

"Pretty good so far, Sergeants. Moving along day by day."

One of them replied to me with, "You know you're the only one left from our ANCOC class, right? So keep driving on, Ranger—you got this."

I said, "Thanks, Sergeant. I will."

The other RI gave me a "good luck" as I walked back to the next testing station. I remember feeling good after they gave me that few seconds of encouragement. After all, they knew what rank I was, and that I was older than most there as well.

After our testing was complete, we were filed into a set of bleachers and received a motivational briefing from the Ranger Training Brigade (RTB) commander and command sergeant major. They basically told us that it appeared those of us remaining, which was probably close to half of the approximate 200 that had started five days earlier, had successfully completed RAP Week. The last event would be the next evening, when we would conduct the final event to pass, which was the dreaded fifteen-mile foot march out to Camp Darby. I'm not going to sugarcoat it; they did not tell us anything we weren't already aware of. Receiving a motivational speech from the RTB leadership was mandatory, but we could have used that time to get more training on how to succeed in the upcoming initial phase. That final evening at Camp Rogers was spent packing our rucksacks according to the Darby packing list. I must say, after the rucks were completely packed, they were pretty damn heavy. We also spent the time getting our equipment put together according to the Ranger School standard operating procedures (SOPs). For example, our two-quart canteens and entrenching tools attached to our rucksacks, ammunition pouches and other items attached to our LCEs, and every piece of equipment being tied off with 550 cord, secured with the infamous Ranger School in-line bowline knot. The last day of RAP Week we received extensive classes on tactical movement formations, using hand-and-arm signals. Also, moving into and setting up a security perimeter and objective rally point. These were just as much part of a graded patrol as the mission itself. Movement into an objective rally point during combat operations is a detailed, step-by-step process where the squad or platoon sets up their final security area before moving on to their mission. It's the area where they finalize the plan, recamouflage themselves and equipment, and ground their rucksacks and equipment not needed for the mission itself. The assault element moves out of the objective rally point through a release point, where each Ranger is counted out. A small element remains back and pulls security at the objective rally point and also monitors the element conducting the mission through radio communications. Before moving out, the leader getting ready to move out will leave the leader staying back with a five-point contingency plan. This explains where they are going, what mission they will be doing when they get there, the estimated time they will be gone on the mission, what they will do if they run into enemy contact on the way, and actions to take if the objective rally point security gets attacked by the enemy.

All this sounds relatively easy, and for the most part it is. Except in Ranger School, they take away two elements that would make this process much easier—food and sleep. We practiced these tasks all day before moving out to Camp Darby that early evening.

We cleaned the barracks that we spent very minimal time in during the past few days, and loaded our duffle bags inside a container that would be transported to Darby. Like I said earlier, we only had a little over 100 students remaining from zero day. Students needing to recycle the Darby Phase would be integrated with our class once we organized squads after arriving to Camp Darby later that evening. We all drew actual weapons from the arms room (no more rubber ducks), to include machine guns and the tripods that go along with them. We were ordered to tie a piece of 550 cord from our weapons to our LCEs on our bodies. We were to never be caught by any instructor not having our weapons secured to our bodies at all times when moving on a tactical operation, from this point until the end of Ranger School. If you lost your weapon or any other sensitive item such as night vision, you would automatically be dropped from the course. So, having your weapon tied off to you was an insurance policy, especially under sleep deprivation.

We moved out right around dusk and headed out of Camp Rogers, on our way to Camp Darby. The standard was pretty simple: do not fall back too far or fall out completely. If a student does, they will be dropped from the course, no retest on the foot march. The cover of the Ranger Handbook we were issued on zero day had printed on it in bold lettering, "Not for the weak or fainthearted." They weren't bullshitting.

It was a typical pace for a tactical road march. Two columns, one on each side of the road, staggered formation. We stepped it out with a good pace, but not extremely fast. It was as comfortable as it could be, with a cool September evening. After a few hours of walking, we finally turned off the road and headed on a trail, which I had heard about from previous horror stories. It was a rocky, unending trail that led us uphill for at least a mile, right into Camp Darby. It was even darker out once we left the main road because the trail was in the thick Georgia woods. I remember falling on the son of a bitch several times, and getting more pissed off every time I did. That's all you heard on the way up: "Fuck!" We were already exhausted from the march itself, and now we were tripping over rocks and tree roots embedded into the thin trail. "When the fuck is this trail gonna end?" These were the shouts coming from the students. Then you would hear an RI shout out, "Shut the fuck up, Rangers. Quit the fucking crying and dry up your tears!"

We finally staggered into the camp like zombies. We formed up under a single light outside an old-looking Quonset hut and were told to stand by. I swear we must have been standing there forever. Nobody took off their rucks; we desperately wanted to but didn't dare because we hadn't been told to do so. Finally, after about a half hour or so, an RI came out of the hut.

"Rangers, when I call out your roster number, fall in to my right, your left."

He was putting us in our assigned squads for Darby Phase. We did lose a few more on the foot march out, I'm not quite sure how many. At this point, all I could think about was grounding my ruck and getting the fucking weight off my back. There was a formation of students off to the side that I assumed were the Darby recycles waiting for us to arrive. They too were integrated into the squads the instructor was forming.

After the squads were formed into thirteen-man elements, the RI sounded off with, "All right, Rangers, RAP Week has officially ended, and Darby Phase begins now. Ground your rucksacks at your feet and stand by for your instructors. We're about to issue your squad equipment. Do not sit down, and God forbid you fall asleep, Rangers. Stay your asses awake. We're not in the business of feeling sorry for your asses out here, Rangers." Again, they were calm with hardly any yelling or screaming. It was their tone and seriousness that had us concerned—and some a bit scared. At approximately 0200 hours, we began Darby Phase of Ranger School.

CHAPTER 11
DARBY PHASE

THE ISSUING OF our squad equipment seemed like it took forever, probably because it did. I really don't remember everything they signed over to us, just that it was a shitload of stuff. One item that I do remember for sure was the medical kit bag. That thing was big and bulky. It was a cylinder-shaped canvas carrier—real nice when it rained and got wet and added another ten pounds to our already sixty to eighty-pound rucksacks. Inside were typical medical supplies, such as gauze, bandages, small bottles of bleach for purifying river and stream water we drank, and a litter system for carrying the wounded. I want to say we were even issued laminated maps of the areas where we would be conducting our upcoming operations.

Anyway, this particular initial equipment issue was a long, drawn-out process that took at least two hours, I would estimate. The RI issuing it to us kept going inside the cadre hut and leaving us out there to inventory the equipment with his sheet he gave us. We were exhausted from the march and lack of sleep from the past six days. One thing was for sure; we knew we weren't going to sleep anytime soon, and it was well after 0200 in the morning—hell, maybe even after 0300. I remember saying to myself, "Damn, this Ranger School sleep thing really does suck." In reality, the exhaustion and tiredness I felt that first night at Darby was nothing compared to what was to come.

"All right, platoon leader, do your squad leaders have all their assigned equipment and has it been inventoried?" the RI came out and asked.

"Yes, Sergeant."

"Okay, PL, because you're signing my platoon hand receipt. Therefore, you had better check all your squads thoroughly, Ranger." We all stood there in the dark and were like, "Sign the shit so we can move on to sleep." That didn't happen either. He signed for the equipment, and then we distributed it among ourselves as evenly as we could figure.

The RI came out of the hut again and said, "Okay, PL, you got it all packed up yet?"

"Not quite yet, Sergeant."

"Well, PL, when you 'quite yet' get it packed in your rucks, I'll take you down to your new Darby home for the next couple of days. I'll be back out and check on you all in a few minutes, or whenever you decide to unfuck yourselves and get your equipment packed up, Rangers. We're on your time now." His "few minutes" meant about a half hour later.

We finally got our equipment packed up, and were standing around, falling asleep on our feet. He came back out and asked if everything was packed. When our platoon leader told him we were packed, the RI said, "Okay, Rangers, follow me."

We were under the impression that we were going to a barracks, like back on Camp Rogers. Those days were gone. Instead, we were taken to a pavilion area with a few tables underneath the overhead cover. "This is your planning bay area, Rangers. Get some rest, and, PL, I want everybody back up and outside the cadre building in two hours. Y'all got the Darby Queen in a couple hours, Rangers, so get some rest."

He didn't have to tell any of us twice. I pulled my wooby out of my ruck, laid down in the grass and went to sleep. We were too tired to worry about being sore from the foot march ahead of negotiating the biggest obstacle course in Ranger School, which was apparently going to take place in the next couple of hours.

Two hours later we were awakened by our platoon leader. I grabbed my personal hygiene kit out of my rucksack, brushed my teeth, quickly poured some water in my canteen cup, pulled out my little mirror, some soap, and a razor, and got to shaving—quickly. I put my hygiene kit back in my ruck along with my wooby, put on and tied up my boots, and I was ready to go. Not really. I was tired as hell and, just like everyone else, was in zombie mode. Germany and I walked toward the cadre shack, pulled out our one-quart canteens from our LCEs, and filled them up from the water buffalo near our formation area. I looked at him and asked, "You ready for the Darby Queen, dude?"

"Hell no," he replied.

Our feet were still chewed up from the foot march, but we were ready to get this over with. Now that it was daylight, I looked around the camp. It was old and gloomy looking. Seriously, this place looked as old as Ranger School itself. There were a few Quonset huts that were painted camouflage and some metal containers off to the left of our formation area. It was still kind of dark because this camp was in the middle of the Georgia woods. Small trails broke off and led down to each platoon's planning bay.

The RIs came out of the cadre hut and walked toward us. "PL, you got everyone? You up on all your weapons and equipment? Nobody quit last night, did they?"

The platoon leader replied, "Yes on personnel and equipment, and no on anybody quitting last night, Sergeant." It is difficult to refer to the timeline of two and a half hours ago as "last night," but that was becoming the norm in this place.

"All right, Rangers, I assume everybody has their canteens topped off, right? If not, there's a couple water buffalos on site, Rangers. Let's go; follow me." He led us down the hill on a firebreak that led out of the camp.

After about a twenty-minute walk, we were led into an open grassy area. "Okay, Rangers, ground your weapons, LCEs, and patrol caps, and gather around this map board. Welcome to the Darby Queen Obstacle Course, Rangers! This will be your first graded evaluation here at Darby Phase. If you do not negotiate an obstacle to standard, i.e., if you fall off or do not complete it in full, you will be given a second chance to complete it to standard. If you cannot, you will receive a minor-minus spot report, Rangers. If you choose to not attempt the obstacle at all or freeze up in the middle of negotiating the obstacle, you will receive a major-minus spot report, Rangers. Understood?"

We all replied, "Yes, Sergeant!"

"Okay, Rangers. Jog in place and remain moving at a double time throughout the entire course! First two Rangers, GO!"

Before I go any further, let me explain how the grading and evaluation factors work during each phase of Ranger School. Ways to recycle any of the three phases are as follow: Number one, if a student fails or no-gos their graded patrol, they have to have a go on the leadership position they are picked for. If there is time remaining in the phase, they may be afforded a second or even a third chance, depending on the size of the class. If it's a larger class that has to get graded on a leadership position, the student may only be afforded one chance for an evaluation. The patrols are broken down in two segments of grading within a twenty-four-hour period. The first half of the mission is the planning phase, and then a "change of mission" will be ordered, and the cadre will pick a new group of students to change leadership positions for the second portion, or the actions-on portion.

Number two, if a student receives three major-minus spot reports. If the student fails a mandatory test the first time, but gets a go the second chance, he receives a major-minus. If he fails the test or task twice, he automatically goes to a board of decision-makers for that phase to recycle. The board usually includes a company or battalion-level commander. Also, a student caught sleeping during a mission where it may be a safety issue or hinder the mission itself could earn himself a major-minus. Usually, it's at the RI's discretion. Three minor-minus spot reports equal one major-minus. Again, RI's discretion.

Last, if a student receives a low-rating peer evaluation at the end of each phase, they will more than likely get recycled in that phase. In other words, if your squad members do not think you're up to the job or not an asset to the squad, they may put you last or toward the bottom of the list on the peer evaluation. Again, the cadre will also be observing conduct within the squads themselves. No student or squad as a whole will get anything over on any of the RIs. Any student can recycle any of the phases as many times as it takes for them to pass and move on. During my time in the Army I'd known soldiers that spent six months to a year in Ranger School, prior to being there myself.

There are two ways of leaving Ranger School—actually three if you count successfully completing the course and graduating. One is voluntarily quitting, or what is known as LOM, lack of motivation. Any student can walk up to any cadre member and request to LOM anytime during the course. We'd already had plenty of them thus far. The second way to leave is receiving an SOR, serious observation report, from any of the cadre. To earn an SOR, the student has a definite integrity violation, such as lying to the RI; becoming hostile with a cadre member or a student; stealing from another student, to include food; and cheating or attempting to manipulate the system. Again, cadre's discretion. If a student has a negligent discharge with their weapon at any time during the course, they will be offered a "day-zero recycle." This means just that: in order to stay in Ranger School, you have to go all the way back to zero day and start all over with the Ranger PT test. I couldn't even imagine that, but it has happened, and it happened in my class at least one time.

Back to the Darby Queen. I started out moving up a hill, and when I began going over, it was a steep drop downhill. At the bottom of the hill was the first obstacle, which was the "belly-buster," a typical obstacle that is usually on any course in the military. You have to jump up onto a log, and then up again and over a higher log. When you come down, you are to land on your feet. Well, I landed on my back. I hit the obstacle with such momentum from running at it downhill that I went up and over and rolled right off the top log and came down about ten feet right on my back. I thought for sure the RI grading the obstacle was going to tell me to do it again. Instead, he called me over and said to me with a smirk on his face, "Get the fuck out of here, old man, and good luck to you." Lo and behold, it was another fellow ANCOC student who happened to be an RI at Fort Benning. "Thank you, Sergeant," I said as I ran to the next obstacle.

The Darby Queen Obstacle Course was the standard Army confidence course that is found at Basic Training, Air Assault School, and on most military installations. The difference here was that the obstacles were more spread out, making the student run up and down trails to get to them—a physical-fitness ass-smoking at each obstacle before you negotiated it.

I finished the course "almost successfully." I did earn myself a minor-minus spot report on one of the obstacles where I had to jump from tree stump to tree stump without touching the ground. I failed it twice and got a spot report. Honestly, I was glad it was over. My mentality was "Now let's get to patrolling and get on with this phase." I moved back up the hill to my equipment, grabbed a canteen, and slammed it down. My Ranger buddy, Germany, was already done with it too. He looked at me and asked, "Well, how'd you do?"

"I got a minor-minus, dude," I replied to him.

"Yeah, me too, man," he said.

"Which one?"

No shit, we both happened to get a spot report on the same damn, stupid little obstacle. We laughed and high-fived each other. "Too easy, brother!" The funny part was that we negotiated the high, difficult, even somewhat "scary" obstacles, but we couldn't get through this little one with one-foot-tall stumps. Give me a break!

"Way too fucking easy, dude. Darby Queen is like *George Washington*—history."

The next two days at Camp Darby were focused on cadre-led training and classes on planning and conducting a mission, down to the precise detail on how each squad-level combat operation would be graded for the next week and a half. The RIs set us up at each of the platoon's planning bays and went through extensive classes on how the planning phase should be conducted from beginning to end. Everything from the warning order and operations order, to the terrain-model briefing, to rehearsals on a tentative mission were explained to us. The operations order was embedded into our heads to the point where we simply had to fill in the blanks on the dry-erase boards or butcher-block paper when briefing our squads and fire teams. We did this well into the night and practiced missions until early the next morning. We stayed relatively close to the camp. The next day and night, we conducted a full planning phase, and an actions-on phase that was led by the RIs assigned to each thirteen-man squad. A Ranger squad consisted of the standard light infantry squad, which was a squad leader, two fire team leaders, two riflemen, two automatic riflemen, two grenadiers, and a four-man machine-gun crew consisting of a gunner, assistant gunner, ammunition bearer, and an antitank gunner.

The typical squad missions in Darby primarily consisted of movement to contact, react to a near ambush, far ambush, react to indirect fire, and conducting a reconnaissance on an enemy site. There was nothing really special or out of the ordinary when it came to conducting these operations in Ranger School. It was typical Field Manual 7-8 standards. The main things we had to take with us and learn were the step-by-step processes required to meet RTB (Ranger Training Brigade) standard, especially in the planning phases. The three graded leadership positions in Darby were squad leader, and

Alpha and Bravo Team leaders.

On the third morning at Camp Darby, it was on; playtime was over. We began our first graded combat patrols in Ranger School. We started at zero dark thirty with our first mission. I truly cannot remember what type of mission it was, but it was a long and drawn-out twenty-four hours—as were all days from here on out. We did about three or four days of graded patrols and then ended back at Camp Darby for a day of retraining on typical improvements that the cadre noticed on the patrols. This was a natural portion of the training calendar that was scheduled, and not an interruption of patrolling because we were "chewed up" or anything like that. Ranger School is set up so that the three phases are based off a "crawl, walk, run" concept. Our class was obviously in the crawl phase.

Germany and I had been placed into different squads, and he had already been graded on a mission and was quite confident that he was a go on it as well. I had yet to be called up for a leadership evaluation by this time. I remember asking Germany how it was being graded. He said it was just like going on a regular training mission back at your home base during a field exercise.

"Just treat it like that. Don't think about being graded, and you'll have no problem." Then he finished it off with, "Too easy." He and I broke out an MRE and devoured it as if it were our last meal and we were going to the electric chair the next day. I wished I could say it was "too easy" along with my Ranger buddy, but I had yet to be graded at this point.

The RI grading you gives you a quick after-action review right after your mission, when the squad is usually back into the objective rally point or patrol base. They'll give you "sustains and improvements" that you as the student need to work on. You can get the vibe during the AAR whether or not you are a go or no-go. If you receive the majority of "sustains" over "improvements," you're more than likely a go on your patrol. Technically, the RIs are not supposed to tell you whether you are a pass or fail until your final AAR when the phase is officially over—I say "technically."

Back out in the field, I finally heard my roster number called for a leadership position. "Roster Number Five Zero, Alpha Team leader. Let's go, Rangers. Get up here for your mission briefing." It was a movement to contact operation, and I was A Team leader for the planning phase and movement. You never know when your land navigation skills will be put to the test, and today was my time. I knew that the movement was going to be the main focus on my evaluation from the RI. Getting from point A to point B was going to be my primary responsibility, along with security as the squad's point man, of course. Failure to stay on azimuth and keep a precise pace count would cost not only me a passing grade, but the student being evaluated as the squad leader as well. Once we were briefed by the RI, I said to myself, *Okay, it's time to go to work.* I began planning the route to the grid coordinate that we were to move to, which turned out to be a three or four-kilometer movement from where we were, deep inside the southern Georgia woods.

During the terrain-model briefing, I explained the route, the distance, the azimuth on our heading, and that I would be identifying en-route rally points along the way as per SOP. During the rehearsals portion, we covered hand-and-arm signals and movement techniques, such as moving in a wedge and file formation in accordance with the terrain. Since this was a movement to contact, we knew that enemy contact was probable, if not imminent, so we prepared for that and did a battle drill for reacting to contact. The planning phase seemed to be perfect and went off without a hitch. It was time to recamo our faces and conduct final inspection checks on equipment, canteens, etc. I had my Ranger beads (each bead represents 1000 meters, and you slide them down the string as you land navigate) ready to go, tied off to my suspenders of my LCE, and my compass was attached to one of my front breast pockets. The squad took a knee, and we were silent from here on out. All we could hear were the birds above us and the crickets chirping in the thick wooded area. Everybody faced out for security. The Bravo Team leader and one of the gun crew members came up to the front and were prepared to count us out of our security perimeter. One of the RIs gave the squad leader a thumbs-up to go ahead and take off. He gave me the hand-and-arm signal to move out.

My first graded patrol in Ranger School went pretty smooth, I must say. I stayed on my azimuth, had good confidence in my pace count, and kept my head on a swivel during the whole movement. We were quiet, slow moving, but not too slow either. Eventually we came out of the wooded area, and I saw an open area ahead of us that seemed to be a couple hundred meters long. I gave the signal for halt and took a knee. The squad leader came up and asked me what was up. I showed him the open area and told him to prepare either for small arms contact, indirect fire, or both. We knew better than to go off azimuth and attempt to go around the open area. Murphy's Law would have us getting too far off course, and then the next thing you know, we would end up getting lost. *Lost*—a dirty word in Ranger School that no student ever wants to use. Make no mistake about it, at this point we were going on several days in the field, and everybody was already in zombie mode. The squad leader told me to stay on course and pick up the pace across the open area, and that we would spread out the formation as well. I told him, "Roger that." All of a sudden, here he came, the RI. As a matter of fact, it was the RI that was grading me specifically.

He took a knee beside me and pulled out his map. "Okay, Ranger, show me where you think we're at." I didn't even hesitate and pointed right to the edge of the open area.

"We're right here, Sergeant," I replied. He then asked, "Where do you think your end point is, Ranger?" He didn't say "objective" because it was a movement to contact and not an assault, ambush, or recon, or even a link-up point.

I said to him, "It's approximately two hundred meters just past that wood line, beyond this open area, Sergeant." I always preferred the word *approximate* instead of *about* because it sounded like you were more certain about your decision.

"Okay, Ranger, drive on." The RI then walked back to the rear of the formation. That meant that I was pretty much right on because we'd already noticed that if you were off course, they would give little hints like, "You might want to do a map check, Ranger, or check your compass and azimuth, Ranger." When they told you to "drive on," and left you alone, that pretty much meant you were good. I quickly got motivated, and my confidence shot through the roof. I turned around and gave the squad leader a thumbs-up, and he gave me the signal to move out.

As soon as the whole squad was in the open, we heard the loud whistling sound of indirect fire. Everybody sounded off with "Incoming!" We all hit the ground, facedown, and waited to hear the explosion. The squad leader gave us a distance and direction, and everyone got up and double-timed to that area. We encountered one more explosion and repeated the drill until we were back inside the woods on the other side of the open area.

One thing happened to me that I still remember to this day. Once we got to the edge of the wood line, out of the open area, I fell right into a fucking hole, up to my waist.

"Fuck!" I shouted.

The squad leader and another student grabbed my arms and pulled me out. I needed help because I only had about seventy or eighty fucking pounds on my back. I didn't have time to dwell on it; I just got out and had to continue moving. Once deeper inside the woods again, we halted and took a knee to get a head count before continuing movement.

One of the RIs came up and said, "All right, squad leader, change of mission." This meant our graded time was over and three different students would get called out for the leadership positions. The RI grading me came up and asked if I was all right or if I was injured. Apparently, he saw my fall into the hole. I think the hole was an old fighting position for training that hadn't been buried completely because I saw a couple sandbags on the sides as they pulled me out.

"No, I'm good, Sergeant."

Anyway, we changed leadership positions and received a new mission that took us well into the hours of darkness. I never did receive that first short AAR from the RI, probably because the next day we were heading back to camp to the end of the phase.

After our mission, we moved into a patrol base to link up with the other squads, so our whole platoon was together again. The other squads had not changed out leadership from the during their missions. Instead, they'd kept it going throughout the whole night. They were still being graded on patrol base activities—poor bastards. Hell, I even went around the perimeter and checked on guys to ensure they were awake and whispered that the same guys were still being graded. This was probably the hardest thing to do throughout Ranger School—to stay awake and active inside the patrol base at night, especially since everybody was exhausted. Oh yeah, the best part was that it had been raining on us for the past two hours straight.

As the sun was about to come up, I was wet and cold. The rain had stopped about an hour prior. I had the guy next to me cover down on security while I grabbed my ruck and fell back off the perimeter a little to change into dry BDUs. I took my ziplock bag out of one of my breast pockets. Inside, I had a notepad, mechanical pencil, and most importantly, my military ID card. I set it on the ground and changed my clothes. Before moving back to the perimeter, I forgot one thing—to put my ziplock bag into the dry uniform I had on. Instead, I left it lying there on the ground, like a freaking dumbass.

"All right, Rangers, change of mission! Secure your equipment! PL, once you got accountability of personnel and equipment, there's a firebreak over there. Get the platoon on it and we'll move you back to camp, Ranger. Roger that?"

"Hooah, Sergeant," the platoon leader replied. We got on the firebreak and marched about a mile back to Camp Darby. It wasn't until we got back to camp that I discovered I had left my ID card back at the patrol base. I didn't dare say anything. Again, you never say the words *lost* or *misplaced* in Ranger School. I knew that we were going to get an eight-hour refit break once we got back to Camp Rogers. I'd worry about a new ID card then, but for now, I was waiting to get my final-phase AAR from the Ranger instructor that had graded me.

As soon as we arrived at Camp Darby, the RIs wasted no time and sat us down in formation to begin our peer evaluations on one another within our squads. You went down the list of names and roster numbers and numbered each from one to thirteen or however many students you had in the squad. It was pretty quick and painless.

About a half hour later, the RIs started giving each student their final AARs for the entire phase. "Roster Number Five Zero!"

"Yes, Sergeant!"

"Let's go." He was sitting on a tree stump with a little stack of manila folders beside him. One of them had my roster number on it, and inside, I'm assuming, were my records during the course thus far. I stood in front of him at the position of parade rest. He started right off with the patrol I was graded on. He gave me "sustains" on my movement, land navigation skills, security, leadership, and technical and tactical proficiency. He gave me an "improve" on situational awareness because I had fallen into that hole. I simply said, "Roger that, Sergeant." He then told me that I was an overall go on my graded patrol.

He went over the other requirements to be able to move on, which were negative spot reports and peer evaluations. I had the one minor-minus spot report from the Darby Queen and had a pretty good peer evaluation of 80 percent or higher. I then heard the words I had been waiting for: "You are being recommended to move on to the Mountain Phase of Ranger School, Roster Number Five Zero. Any questions for me, Ranger?"

"No, Sergeant," I replied.

"Okay, move out."

I got back to the formation area and found Germany. He looked at me and asked, "So?" I gave him our standard answer, "Too easy."

He looked at me and said, "Oh, entirely too fucking easy."

The trucks pulled up, we loaded them, and we headed out of Camp Darby for the rest of our lives; well, most of us did. Others unfortunately were getting recycled and would have to stay there and start the phase all over again when the next class came staggering in from their fifteen-mile foot march.

Back at Camp Rogers, we unloaded our duffle bags and formed up for a briefing from the RIs. "Okay, Rangers, you're getting eight hours of mandatory refit time. A bus will be taking you to Main Post, to the big shoppette area. Once there, you can take a taxi anywhere on Main Post if you want to go anywhere else. Do not go off post, Rangers! I know y'all are gonna just worry about food, Rangers; we've been in your boots once before too! I suggest besides Burger King and Popeye's Chicken, y'all get your nasty uniforms washed at the laundromat. Get to the shoppette and buy yourselves items you may need, such as 550 cord, new socks, T-shirts, personal hygiene items, or whatever.

"Don't waste this eight hours, Rangers! Once I release you, go take a shower and get your nasty asses cleaned up, and put on your civilian clothes you brought. The bus will leave in about an hour. It will pick you up at the same spot it drops y'all off on Main Post at 1600. Be safe, Rangers, and don't get into trouble out there! Dismissed!" We all cheered and clapped.

On the bus, I told my Ranger buddy about what had happened to my ID card, and that I would have to go get a new one before I did anything else. I knew where we were getting dropped off, and I knew where the ID card facility was from there too. It was all in walking distance. We got dropped off, and I took my dirty clothes straight to the laundromat, which was right there in the shopping center area. After I got the washer going, me and Germany went over to the ID card place. I told him he didn't have to go with me because, shit, I knew he was as hungry as I was.

"Man, go get some food, dude. I'll take care of my ID card and catch back up to you in a few."

"Nope, we're in this shit together, brother."

I was like, "Okay, let's get this bullshit done."

It was a painless process. Hell, I'd just made it through the first phase of Ranger School. What could I complain about? It took about a half hour to get my new ID, and it was off to Burger King from there. One thing I wished I had worn with the jeans I was wearing—a fucking belt! My pants were a thirty-three-inch waist, and I was walking around holding them up with one hand like a fool. I had lost that much weight in the last sixteen days or so. I was about to eat a double whopper, large fries, and a large Coke. What the hell, let's throw in a side of chicken nuggets with it too. Something else we didn't realize: our stomachs were smaller, too, so we got full much quicker. Plus, we ate as if the world were ending that day.

After our clothes were clean, we took a cab back to Camp Rogers early. We weren't going to wait until 1600. Once we got back, I shaved my head in the latrine back in our barracks, put on a clean pair of BDUs, put the other clean uniforms back into my duffle bags, and went nighty-night, until it was time for formation later. Man, I was going to get about four straight hours of sleep—the most I'd had at one time since I'd been there.

After formation that early evening, our class received another surprise. I'd heard rumors but didn't know if it was true or not. We got a grilled hotdog meal, provided by the Benning RIs. It was fricking awesome. It was a tradition in Ranger School. Each student paid like five dollars for a hotdog, a bag of chips, a soda, and a candy bar. We thought we had died and gone to heaven. A Burger King meal for lunch and hotdogs for dinner! I must say, the Ranger instructors were pretty decent human beings and a bunch of great guys. We sat around and laughed and told stories about the Army and Darby Phase as we ate our chow on a back-patio area over by the Camp Rogers chow hall. The Benning RIs really let us be carefree for that evening before we left to go up north. However, I would soon find out in the upcoming phase that there was a small percentage of bad instructors at Ranger School, just as there is in any other military training environment. I was a drill sergeant for two years about a year prior to being there, and we had "shitbag" instructors there as well. I used to see it firsthand, and it really tested my patience.

The next morning at zero dark thirty, we cleaned the barracks, formed up with all our equipment, and got on the buses. We were headed on a four-hour drive up north to Dahlonega, Georgia, which was a small community in the Appalachian Mountains. It was the end of September and starting to get a little chilly outside. The Bat Boys were in full effect again. Those kids were sure full of energy. You would have thought that they had just come back from a vacation instead of completing a phase of Ranger School.

CHAPTER 12

MOUNTAIN PHASE
TWENTY TOUGHEST DAYS OF THE ARMY

WHEN WE ARRIVED at Camp Merrill, I got off the bus and was amazed at how beautiful the scenery surrounding the camp was. It was the first time I had ever seen this portion of the United States. Everything was so green, with the mountains and hills in the background. All the roads and buildings on Merrill seemed to be built into the hills. The closest I'd come to this type of scenery was when I'd been stationed at Fort Lewis, Washington.

Then reality set in. I quickly realized that, very soon, I would be humping up and down these hills while carrying heavy weight on my back. I shook my head and grabbed my bags and ruck from the bottom compartment of the bus.

About 100 of us came up from Benning. We lost count of how many were left from the original class on day zero because of those that were dropped, quit, or recycled. There were another eighty or so Mountain recycles waiting to integrate with us. So, we were back at two companies of trainees with the capacity of two full platoons each going into the phase.

The RIs came out and told us to form up in the platoons we were already assigned to from Benning. It started raining, so they gave us our barracks right off the bat and told the PLs to get us up there to ground our gear on a bunk and to hurry and get back down to formation. We got inside the barracks, and it was different from Camp Rogers. It appeared to be an updated-style barracks of two or three stories, open bays with latrines at the ends of them. If I'm not mistaken, the bunks weren't set up as double bunks, either. They were set up as single beds. Me and Germany found two bunks next to each other, threw our shit on them, and got back downstairs to formation.

We marched over to the 5th Ranger Training Battalion headquarters building and were told to take a seat across the street in a little open area, and to stand by for the battalion commander and command sergeant major's briefing. I can still see Camp Merrill in my mind as if it were yesterday.

I failed to mention earlier that each phase of Ranger School was run by 4th, 5th, and 6th Ranger Training Battalions—4th at Benning, 5th at Mountains, and 6th in Florida. They all fell under Ranger Training Brigade Command at Fort Benning.

The battalion commander came out and gave us his pep speech, which was pretty down-to-earth, with no bullshitting us students. "On behalf of myself and the command sergeant major, we would like to welcome each of you to Camp Merrill, Georgia, Rangers! Congratulations, first of all, on your successful completion of the Darby Phase of Ranger School. As you know, you will be upgraded to more responsibility during your time here at 5th RTB, where you will move from squad to platoon-size operations. As I'm sure you already are aware of, Rangers, Mountain Phase is where most students will recycle or will be dropped from the course, either voluntarily or forced out for some kind of violation of integrity. Reason being, you're going to receive less sleep, food, and the terrain is going to kick most of your asses, Rangers. Some of you to your breaking points, Rangers. Listen to your instructors, follow their lead, always do the right thing, even if it's maybe the hard way, follow the tactical standards of FM 7-8 and your Ranger Handbooks, and you will have no problem making it out of here successfully, Rangers!"

The RIs stepped back in front of us, and one of them explained the timeline of the Mountain Phase. "Today, Rangers, we're going to focus on getting you all in-processed into 5th RTB, starting with a thorough medical check by our medics, and then move you all over to your companies to ensure your packets are up to date and ready for evaluations. This next week will be focused on lower and upper basic mountaineering techniques. You will receive your lowers here at Camp Merrill, and then we will march up to Mt. Yonah for uppers training and testing, Rangers. So, we don't want you worrying about combat operations right now; you need to focus on mountaineering first, Rangers. One step at a time!"

Once we marched over to the medical station, we filed in when our roster numbers were called off, and each of us were personally checked by an Army medic from head to toe with a thorough screening. "Take off your boots, socks, and pull up your pant legs." They really paid close attention to your feet, ankles, shins, and knees. The medic went up feeling both my legs, up to my knees, and then squeezed on both of them.

"Owww," I said in a low tone—ensuring I did not yell or draw attention to myself.

"You have cellulitis in both knees," the medic said to me.

My heart immediately sank. "What does that mean? Does that mean I have to recycle or get hospitalized?" I caught myself going into panic mode. All I could think about was getting medically recycled or, even worse, medically dropped from the course.

He reassured me, "No, don't worry about it; it's in the beginning stages. I'm going to prescribe you an antibiotic that you'll take once a day for about the next ten days, and you should be good. You'll be able to continue on." I was so relieved to hear this.

Well, it was happening; my body was being affected by this school. We weren't just losing weight quickly; we were getting skin bacteria, too. Camp Darby really put more of a hurt on me than I had thought. *Oh well, suck it up and drive on.* I was happy to be able to keep going uninterrupted.

The medic then took out a needle and began pushing it into spots on my feet, and then squeezing out the puss. Apparently, I had blisters that were so thick I didn't even realize that they were blisters. I thought they were calluses forming, but the medic told me they were big blisters. So be it. "Fix me" was my mentality. I swear, going into that medical station was like taking your truck into Valvoline for maintenance so that you can get it back on the road for another three or five thousand miles. It was like a one-stop shop because when he was done examining me, he walked over, told the other medic behind a counter the prescription, and he handed me a small bottle with ten pills of antibiotics. I was then sent on my way. Too easy.

After our group was done with the medical screenings, they moved us over to our company headquarters for our records check and any more in-processing that we needed to complete for 5th RTB. We stood in formation in front of the small headquarters building, and off to the left of us was the rope corral. The corral was an area roped off by one main rope, with smaller pieces of rope, or sling ropes, draped over all around it for knot-tying practice and testing.

Now, I'll have to go back a few chapters and a few years prior to this point in my Ranger School experience. Remember the sergeant first class that I was in with at the beginning of Drill Sergeant School? Remember him quitting the school because he simply didn't want to be part of that world for two years? Well, here he came walking out of the headquarters hooch at Camp Merrill. He was a tall, lanky man, with a cocky look to him, especially in his eyes. He was wearing civilian shorts and a T-shirt with flip-flops on, and an old, worn-out John Deere hat. He appeared as if he had just woken up after his previous shift or something, because he was not in the best of moods. He had a big old dip of snuff in his mouth and a Styrofoam cup that he was spitting in. As he approached our formation, I said to him, "Hey, Sergeant, I remember you. What a small Army it is."

I think that was a mistake that I would come to regret in the next few days because he walked up to me and glared at me as if he was trying to remember who I was. He spit in his cup loud and with a purpose, and just shook his head and walked away from me. I think he had figured out who I was, which wasn't a bad thing in my mind at the time. Although I had absolutely nothing to do with him quitting Drill Sergeant School three years prior, I think he looked at me as part of a bad experience he'd had in the Army. *Oh well*, I said to myself. I remember having an "it is what it is" attitude about him at first. Within the next few days, however, I quickly realized he wasn't really feeling me being there or being in his presence at all.

After in-processing our records, we were told to file off and stand by a sling rope inside the corral. "Does everyone have a sling rope in front of them, Rangers? Go ahead and secure the rope and make your way back to formation." They had us sign for the sling ropes and then two steel carabiners, or what most grunts refer to as "D-rings." They then told us to go up to the barracks and secure our helmets, LCEs, and rucksacks, and be back downstairs in formation quickly. We had to strip the camouflage covers off our helmets and put a piece of masking tape in front and back of it with our roster numbers on them. Our other equipment was checked for proper configuration and tie-downs. We then went right into training for upcoming mountaineering techniques, starting with knot-tying. We sat in that corral practicing several different kinds of knots well into the night.

They marched us over to eat dinner chow at our new chow hall, with the same procedures as Camp Rogers. Six students went out front of the formation, and we sounded off with the Ranger Creed, knocked out our six pull-ups, and moved right into the chow line to get our food. I noticed by this time six pull-ups were almost impossible, at least for me, so I busted out as many as I could on my own and then had the guy behind me grab my ankles and assist me for the one or two I needed to finish in order to complete six. I wasn't alone on this physical difficulty, either. Our bodies were definitely losing strength as the days rolled on in this environment. Afterward, it was back in the rope corral tying knots under the lights until late into the darkness. Eventually, it was time to get to the barracks and sleep, with a little bit of fire guard in between.

The next morning in formation, the RIs had the recycles integrate into our two companies prior to reentering the chow hall for breakfast. All the rumors and urban legends of pancakes were real! Blueberry pancakes! Thick pancakes, too! I couldn't believe we were allowed to eat this. We were also fed eggs, bacon, sausage, you name it. I thought this was some kind of trick or something. Nope, "eat what you get" was the game plan. In reality, they were trying to get us fed for what was to come in the near future—a straight ten-day field exercise with minimal calories, hardly any sleep, and walking and maneuvering through terrain that is almost indescribable.

After chow, it was back at the rope-tying corral. "All right, Rangers, who thinks they're ready to be graded on their knot-tying?" Germany and I raised our hands, along with pretty much the rest of our platoon. I think we had to randomly tie two or three knots at the RI's discretion. He called out the specific knot, and we would then tie it to the rope on the corral with our issued sling rope. It was quick and painless, and an easy go. We formed back up, secured our rucks and moved in a file down a flight of stairs that were steep and long. The stairs ended and the path turned into a thin trail down the remainder of the high ground we were on, to an open valley area with trees and plenty of shade. It was the area of all "lowers" training activities. The area where we ended up, in the shade, was all about tying-techniques training and rappel preparations. To our right was an open area where the rappelling took place. We started right off with the basic rappel-seat configuration class on tying our sling rope into a standard "Swiss seat" around our waist. Once everyone in the platoon had that figured out pretty precisely, we moved into the proper configuration of a belay harness, with a figure-eight knot. We did these two configurations consistently to the point where we could do it in our sleep. The RIs, like during Darby, were pretty laid-back and precise on teaching us how to properly accomplish the task at hand. They were very professional and did all they could to ensure that everybody understood the "how-to" on rope tying and configuring the rappel seat and belay procedures. Obviously, before we could move over to the rappel station at the fifty-foot rock cliff, we had to certify on these two tasks.

Here he came, the Drill Sergeant School RI. From here on out, I'll simply refer to him as "DSS." My Swiss seat was already a go, graded by another RI. Now we had to rig up our belay harness with the figure-eight knot. Now, if my memory serves, we had to tie the belay rig with a figure-eight knot with the open loop on the end. The final pass-or-fail test on it was that when the loop was raised, if it went past your chin, then it was too long and a failing grade was given to the student. Anyway, DSS stopped in front of me as he was walking through the area grading us. He looked at me with a sinister expression.

"You ready for inspection, Ranger?"

"Yes, Sergeant," I confidently responded. He held and turned the rope in his hand as he inspected the knot. He then reached down and lifted vigorously on it, hard enough so that when he brought the loop up, it surpassed my chin. "Oh no, your belay rig is too long, Ranger. That's too bad. You are a no-go at this station."

He then pulled out a pad of blank spot reports and filled one out. I received my first major-minus spot report in Ranger School.

"Here you go, Ranger. I suggest you continue to train on the belay rig before you retest on this task. If you fail again, it will be an automatic board review to recycle this phase, Ranger."

As if I didn't already know this. I bit my tongue as hard as I could so that I did not mouth off to him. Now, I'm not that guy who's ever made excuses on my downfalls or failures, but this guy, no shit, was bound and determined to fail me on purpose, and he did. Why? Because I knew he had quit a school a few years back? Who the fuck cares? Apparently, he did, and had a chip on his shoulder for it, too. Oh yeah, there are real assholes in the Army.

As in any other training environment, a retest meant having a different instructor grading you. I received a go for my retest on the belay. However, it still stuck in my mind for the rest of that day, that I had a major-minus looming over me this early in the game. We still had rappels, rock climbing, and one of the roughest field problems in Ranger School to be graded on before we could even think about moving on to the next phase. One event, one day at a time is what I kept telling myself.

We did the rappels off the small cliff at lowers to certify in order to move on to uppers certifications on Mount Yonah. We did both a "Hollywood" rappel and a combat equipment rappel to be able to move on. *Hollywood* is military slang for conducting either a rappel or parachute jump in just your helmet; no combat equipment, such as rucksack, LCE, or weapon. Too easy! The next morning was more blueberry pancakes and then over to the arms room to draw weapons. The RIs put us on LMTVs (Army five-ton trucks) with all of our gear, and off to Mount Yonah for the next day and a half we went.

It was about a half hour to forty-five-minute ride on the back of the truck. When we got to the base of the mountain, we unloaded, threw our rucks on our backs, and up we went. The Ranger School tradition is foot-marching up Mount Yonah. As a matter of fact, a two-mile fast-paced foot march up that motherfucker.

"Let's go, Rangers, move your asses!"

I'd moved at high-speed paces on road marches in my day, but this shit was ridiculous! We hauled ass up the mountain—again, didn't seem like we were ever going to get there, but we eventually made it.

Once at the top, we marched into a small bivouac site and broke off into platoon formations. We grounded our gear and walked to the water buffalo to fill up our canteens. I admit, I was a little spent from that two-mile uphill hike. I slammed a canteen of water and filled it up again. Hydration was the key to success in Ranger School, especially in the final two weeks of Mountain Phase.

We walked down to the areas where we would be conducting our upcoming climbs and rappels. The RIs gave us some demonstrations and little tips on dos and don'ts for the next day's training and testing. They explained to us that the next day was going to consist of a half day doing climbing techniques, and the second half focusing on rappels. I remember standing on top of the area overlooking the view. I swear you could see the entire state of Georgia from up there. The worst part was actually looking down in front of us at the cliffs we would be rappelling off.

Germany looked at me and shook his head. "I don't know, man; this shit looks pretty high up and steep, dude." I replied with a "No shit. I don't know about this shit." I then told him that we shouldn't worry, that we would get through it like everything else up to this point.

When we got back to our bivouac site, we were allowed to break out an MRE and eat it at our leisure as if it were a dinner at a five-star restaurant. We all sat in our platoon area, shooting the shit and enjoying our MREs. Then we broke into the usual "MRE trade game" with the food.

"Who wants a cookie bar for cheese spread?"

"Right here! Right here!"

"Who's got a peanut butter for cheese?"

"Who wants a beef stew main meal for a chicken and rice?"

This went on the whole time we were breaking out our chow from our rucks. As a matter of fact, this trade game was the norm every time we had an opportunity to eat in a group like this in the field.

"Who wants my entire MRE? I'm not that hungry."

"Oh shit, right here, right here, man."

The response was, "Fuck you, I was just bullshitting, dude."

"No shit, who the fuck isn't hungry these days? I can't believe you fell for that shit!"

Everybody in the platoon just laughed. It was the best comradery experience you could ever have in Ranger School.

After dinner, the RIs wanted us to put on a little show for them. It was the opportunity for the students to put on skits to make fun of or imitate whatever and whomever. Imitate the RIs, each other, or the school itself. They gave us a heads-up, like about a half hour, for some of the students to put together a skit. It was something you commonly saw in Basic Training after two months with the same platoons and drill sergeants, not after about a month in Ranger School. I remember asking myself why they would have us do skits after only three days with these instructors, before we even had an opportunity to know them yet.

DSS was running the whole show. You could tell he was one of the senior RIs of 5th RTB, and he should have been. After all, this was apparently his second time as a Mountain Phase RI in his Army career. Who the fuck does two Ranger instructor assignments, especially in the same place, doing the same job? Apparently, someone whose career was pretty much wrapped up and who probably wanted to retire from the Army at Dahlonega, Georgia. After all, it was a beautiful, scenic area of the country.

These were the thoughts running through my head as I sat there looking at him, while he laughed and joked with a big dip of chew in his mouth. At this point, he wasn't my favorite person in the world, as I'm sure I obviously wasn't his.

So, the skit show went on, and it was minimal. The Bat Boys led the way in putting on the entertainment for the RIs. They actually did some pretty good skits and impressions, almost to the point of insult. That's what was funny with these kids; they didn't seem to give a shit about any of the pressures of Ranger School. Most of them just went by day to day, laughing off most of the events, and going through carefree.

The instructors split us up the next morning. One company of trainees went to the rappel side, and the other remained at the rock-climbing portion. Our company's first half of the day was spent conducting the rock-climbing training and eventually the climbing tests. Several lanes were marked off by numbers to do the testing. One Ranger student would do the climbing, and one would assist him with the belay. Each lane was approximately a thirty-five to forty-foot climb. Some appeared to be more difficult than others, but at the end of the day, having to go through it twice, I believe they were about the same. That's right, I failed my first rock-climb test of Mountain Phase. The RI claimed that I used my knees one too many times during my tested climb. You are only allowed to use your hands and feet to do the climbs. No other portion of your body can touch the rocks at all. The RIs would usually give you one or two warnings to "watch the knees." Of course, guess who I had grading me on my first climb? DSS himself. It was my never-ending luck during my time in the mountaineering portion.

"Stop! Come on down, Roster Number Five Zero." He ordered me to come down after I was damn near to the top of my climb. "Roster Number Five Zero, you failed to properly negotiate this climb due to unauthorized usage of your legs—primarily using your knees, Ranger. You are a no-go at this station. Initial here, Ranger."

I had just initialed my second major-minus spot report in Mountain Phase of Ranger School. One more and I would automatically have to go before the board at the end of the phase for, more than likely, a recycle determination. Now I was nervous that I would either fail the second climb or get another no-go on one of the rappel tests coming up next. As the moments ticked by, I continued to mind-fuck myself. I believe that was DSS's goal too. I wasn't feeling paranoid anymore with this guy. I was now thoroughly convinced he was out to fuck me on this phase. Again, the only benefit at this point was that I would be using a different lane, with a different RI for my retest on climbing.

Just like the belay retest a couple days prior, I received a go on my second climb. What was funny about it was that I climbed it in the same exact fashion as I had before—hands and feet, with hardly any contact between my knees and the rocks. But I kept asking myself, *Am I going to get this asshole again during one of my upcoming rappel tests?* Probably, because that seemed to be the pattern thus far with this guy.

Anyway, I didn't have time to dwell on it; I had to suck it up and drive on. Concentrate on the next task at hand. *That's how you're going to make it out of here, Nate,* I told myself.

That afternoon, we moved over to the rappel lanes. The first one that I got tested on was a Hollywood rappel. The scenery was intimidating to look at. We were pretty high up there on Mount Yonah, looking across the landscape of northern Georgia. The rappel went down an approximately seventy-foot cliff. About halfway down, the standard was to let go of your rope, lean back and get into a spread-eagle position. The point was to have total confidence in your belay man. It was the same standard as any other confidence-building test. If the student shows fear or reluctance to let go of the rope and lean back, they will be a failure at the task.

"Let go of the rope, Ranger!" This was being shouted from the RI at the top of the cliff and also the one at the bottom monitoring the belay man's actions.

"Ranger, if you reach for the rope again without being instructed to do so, you'll be a no-go. We will tell you when to grab the rope again. Okay, grab the rope, and continue with the remainder of the rappel, Ranger." These warnings echoed across the test site.

The second graded rappel was on the other side of the mountain, in more of a wooded portion. It was in full combat equipment, with LCE, weapon, and our rucksack with some weight in it, but not Ranger School combat operations' seventy to eighty pounds of weight. About halfway down the cliff, there was an open area with no rock at our feet, so it was a free-style rappel for the second half of it. I received a go on both rappels, and so did my Ranger buddy. We sat there sipping water from our canteens, happy that we were done with the first portion of Mountain Phase. For me, it came at a difficult cost of two major-minus spot reports, but it was time to move on and put it behind me. Thank God that DSS was not assigned to our company or platoon for the upcoming field-exercise grading. I believe he was assigned to the other, or maybe he was so senior that he was only assigned to the mountaineering portion of 5th RTB, if such a situation existed. Either way, I never saw my "old friend" DSS ever again.

The next three days back at Camp Merrill were nonstop tactical training, all at platoon level. We covered everything from writing and issuing platoon-level combat orders, to calling for fire, to medic training and calling in a nine-line MEDEVAC (medical evacuation), setting up and conducting machine-gun drills, and of course, platoon-level battle drills and patrol techniques—primarily platoon attack or raid, ambush, and conducting a reconnaissance (recon). We worked on our own internal platoon SOPs, such as our radio call signs, employment of our prisoner search, and aid and litter teams as well. This went on for three days straight, both day and night. By the time we were scheduled to move out for our upcoming ten-day field exercise, we were ready. The instructors even had a few hours set aside for tactical loading and unloading procedures of both the UH-60 Blackhawk and CH-47 Chinook helicopters.

We also had a little time here and there for fun during our MRE mealtimes at our planning bay. It was similar to the planning bays at Darby, an open wooden structure with metal roofing. Inside were a couple of butcher-block stands and a large sand table to construct a standard terrain model. Of course, once out in the field, the terrain models were never as detailed as they were back at the camp's planning bays. As a platoon, we had a pretty extensive terrain-model kit that was broken down in several ziplock bags and distributed among the squads. So, at any given time, any squad could break one out, and the leadership chosen could immediately begin constructing a terrain model. You had to have that shit ready to go, especially when you were out there for days, walking around like a zombie, hungry and tired, and not thinking so sharply.

"Who's got a cheese spread for a peanut butter packet?"

"Oh shit, right here, right here, man!"

"Who wants a pork patty for a beef stew?"

"Over here, man!"

"Who doesn't want their hot sauce?"

"Who wants a lemon pound cake?"

"Oh fuck! Right here, man, right here!"

"I got a cake for you; why don't you 'pound' it up your fuckin' ass?" The whole platoon laughed and giggled.

MRE time, for a short period, was our sanctuary away from the stresses of Ranger School. It was awesome. The comradery was tight among us. One unwritten rule in the military: if you want to bring any team together as a family, put them in a world of hurt together.

"Roster Number So-and-so!" an RI hollered out for my Ranger buddy, Germany.

"Yes, Sergeant!" he shouted back.

"Let's go. You got an emergency phone call from your unit, Ranger." I remember thinking, *Man, this can't be good when you get called and interrupted out in the woods in Ranger School.* Something very serious had to have happened back home or at his duty station in Germany. He was gone on the phone for about a half an hour. When he came back to the planning bay area, he and I walked off a little ways into the woods so that he could tell me what had happened. His six-year-old little girl had gotten hit by a car in the housing area he and his wife lived in. She had several broken bones and was in the hospital recovering. She was going to be fine and was going to heal back to 100 percent.

As he was telling me what happened, tears swelled in his eyes, and within seconds, he broke down crying. I put my arm around his shoulders and consoled him that his daughter was going to be fine and that she was safe and recovering. It didn't seem to help him because he insisted that he had to leave Ranger School and go back to Germany to be by her side. Now, as a father myself with two young toddlers at home (both of whom were born while I was on drill sergeant duty), I felt his pain, and anger as well. I had to ask him if his wife had asked him to come home and be with them. He had said no, that he just felt it was the right thing to do. That if he stayed in school, it might look selfish. I had to give him a reality check really quick because he was very serious about walking over to the RI and saying the three dreaded letters to him—LOM.

"Hey, man, what are you saying?" I asked him. "You're not seriously thinking about leaving, are you? Hey, man, she's going to be all right and she's going to recover just fine. You leaving and going back to her now will not change what happened. Instead, she will continue to recover like she is going to under professional medical supervision anyway, and you will be going back to your unit as somebody who quit Ranger School. You know you're in a long-range surveillance unit, which means if you quit this course, you'll have to leave and go into one of the mechanized infantry units down the street." I had to break it down to him in the details of the reality he would face if he quit and went home now.

He replied as he wiped up his tears, "No, man, I should probably leave because that's the right thing to do. It's not about me and Ranger School. It's about my daughter, man."

I came back with, "Okay, I understand, but what are you going to do for her now that you can't do a month from now when we're out of here? That's right, dude; we are halfway done with this shit. You know the truth. You won't admit it, though, so I'll say it for you. If you leave now, you'll never come back, and you know it. You know how bad it really does suck here, and you wouldn't come back. I wouldn't blame you because I don't honestly think that I would come back either."

Germany finished wiping his tears and the snot off his face and said to me, "You're right, brother—you're absolutely right. Okay, I'm good now. Let's get back to the platoon. We gotta prep for the field tomorrow. Thanks, man."

I said, "No problem, brother. I'm here for ya. Now let's get this field problem over with and get the fuck on to Florida and get this shit over with, right? Too easy, huh?"

He looked at me with a shit-eating grin on his face. "Way too fuckin' easy." We walked out of the woods together and never brought up the subject again.

■ ■ ■

"Incoming!" the entire platoon shouted out and got down to the ground. The platoon leader shouted back a distance and direction in response. "Twelve o'clock! One hundred meters!" We were all running uphill, panting and gasping for air in full combat equipment, with the heaviest rucks one could imagine. The next whistling sound echoed through the misty wooded area. "Incoming!"

After the explosion went off, the platoon leader sounded off again with, "Twelve o'clock! One hundred meters!" This went on and was repeated for approximately a half hour straight. Before this we had unloaded from the trucks at our debarkation point in the valley below us. It was uphill movement at a double time as we reacted to indirect fire. I guess we didn't move fast enough and with enough purpose for the RIs. Their most effective way for getting our platoon to move was to start throwing the artillery simulators.

When the indirect fire ceased, the platoon moved into a security halt. Accountability of personnel and equipment was priority first and foremost. The RIs designated at least two "casualties" along the way. One was walking wounded with minimal wounds, the other critical with a sucking chest wound. The medical evacuation (MEDEVAC) procedures started right away. This is how our field exercise began as soon as our feet touched ground out there after leaving Camp Merrill. I was glad I wasn't part of this initial leadership team being evaluated because it was pretty chaotic—just like combat, confusing and chaotic.

There was no simulation on the MEDEVAC, either. The platoon sergeant (PSG) and the medic found a nearby open area on the map, and two of us moved our wounded guy toward it with a security team attached. The medic and RTO, overseen by the PSG, called in a standard nine-line MEDEVAC. No shit, within about ten minutes, a Blackhawk helicopter landed, and we carried him to it and loaded him on. This was an actual MEDEVAC taking place right here in this school—the only simulations were the wounds. I was impressed, and we were all made aware very quickly that we were not going to bullshit our way through this training exercise. Our radios, along with procedures, were being truthfully utilized up here, and were not to be taken for granted. There was not going to be any "checking the block," at least not for this field-training initiation portion.

The RI that was out with us for the MEDEVAC procedures told the student to get off the bird and go back with our group to the platoon area. His wound was "cured," and he was told to "Charlie Mike" (continue mission) with the rest of us. The procedures went off without a hitch, and I told myself that the PSG being evaluated would definitely receive a go for this mission. Anyway, this was how the first hour kicked off for our ten-day field exercise, and the instructors had all of our attention right off the bat.

Our first actual mission that we were to be conducting before the "indirect fire interruption" was a movement to contact, and to establish a patrol base, if memory serves me correctly. One thing is for sure: we moved all day and all night. By the time we did our leadership changeover, the platoon was already spent from moving up and down hills for hours upon hours. From here on out, the graded leadership positions were platoon leader, platoon sergeant, and the four squad leader positions. Everything else was assigned by the student leadership, or volunteered, but not graded, such as the team leader positions, RTO (radio telephone operator), platoon medic, and forward observer (FO). The bottom line was that everybody needed to do their jobs, volunteer, and give it all they had in order to take care of those that were being graded. Failure for just one student to do their assigned task, no matter what it may be, could result in mission failure. In this case, it probably would result in a failed grade for the other leadership positions. Everybody watched each other and got to know who was lazy and who tried to give it their all most or all of the time. I say most of the time because everybody gets exhausted and reaches their limit at times. To say not everybody falls asleep before, during, or after a mission is simply not true. Anyone can accidentally fall asleep in Ranger School—everyone is a human being.

We conducted patrol-base activities all night and well into the next morning as the sun was coming up. The first day of the field exercise was behind us, but we felt like we had already been out there for days, if not a week. We got hit by small arms fire once or twice on the movement, conducted hasty attacks, and moved on. Once we established our platoon patrol base, the enemy hit us at least once there as well. It was pretty much nonstop, as expected. The Ranger School enemy or opposing force (OPFOR) was made up of infantrymen assigned to that particular training battalion. I suppose it would be a pretty decent assignment for a junior enlisted soldier. They remained under the complete guidance and control of the RIs, and timely coordination with them was essential for our missions getting underway.

■ ■ ■

"What the fuck, Rangers? Why the fuck isn't anybody moving? You're getting hit by the enemy, and nobody is doing shit! What the fuck?"

The enemy had hit us very early in the morning, before sunlight, but who was counting days and keeping timelines by now, anyway?

"Rangers, I swear to God, if somebody doesn't start taking charge of this gaggle fuck, I'm gonna start throwing Arty Sims on this perimeter!" *Arty Sims*, or artillery simulators, were used on us if we were not "motivated" enough or simply not moving fast enough for the RI's standard. At the end of the day, they were absolutely correct, in that we were showing lack of motivation. After all, we were smoked and pretty much out of it for that initial forty-eight hours of the Mountain field exercise. When the instructors threatened to hurt grades if the platoon did not react appropriately to combat situations, you knew they meant business.

"PL, if you don't start making a decision and this platoon does not react to the enemy, every leadership position will fail this mission."

I remember thinking, *What mission?* We were technically on the same leadership positions from the day prior; there had been no official changeover of leadership yet.

As soon as the threats came down from the instructors, leadership started making quick and fast decisions, and we maneuvered on the enemy with every weapons capability we had. We pretty much lit up the tree line, and the platoon leader flanked a squad to maneuver and destroy the two OPFOR that were harassing us. Again, it went right by the book.

"Hey, Rangers, keep fucking around and thinking this is some kind of game out here, and you all are going to be very disappointed with the end result! Do not fuck around and hesitate again, Rangers, because you're fucking too tired and think somebody else is going to do your job for you again!"

We had received another eye-opener on just how serious these guys were on this training. By the way, we were a nation at war by this time, on two different fronts in the Middle East, too. So no shit the instructors were being serious about this, and I thought about how I was headed to Iraq to link up with my unit right after I got out of this school.

Once back at the patrol base and accountability was conducted, it was time for water resupply, and this shit was for real. Each squad was tasked to have at least one guy with an empty duffle bag to move out with the other squads' detail personnel to collect each squad's canteens and move out with a security team to move down whatever high ground we were on and go to the nearest creek and fill up the canteens with fresh water. In the hills of northern Georgia, low ground always had some sort of natural water source. After filling up each squad's canteens, we would enter back into our patrol base and put one drop of bleach in the one-quarts, and two drops in the two-quarts. Each student had their canteens marked with their roster numbers so that we could easily identify our own. Too easy. Yeah, there were no water buffalos in the field in Ranger School during combat operations evaluations, at least not in Mountain Phase.

After a routine morning check by the school medics on each of us in the platoon, it was on. "Roster Number Five Zero—platoon sergeant!" I'll be damned; I received a planning phase platoon sergeant position relatively quick in the Mountain Phase. I was actually feeling pretty lucky because for the most part, I was still very coherent and not exactly in zombie mode yet. Not to mention, planning phase graded positions were an advantage too; you, as a student, had daylight. Usually when they called a changeover on you during actions-on phase, it was during hours of darkness. In the Infantry during combat operations, very seldom will any assault mission be planned to be executed during daylight hours.

So, I felt lucky. However, my game face was definitely on and no bullshitting. I got very serious, of course; who didn't when your roster number was called at any time for a graded position in this environment? Germany wished me good luck as I walked over to receive our operations order from the RIs, who had just changed out their shifts too. I believe their shifts in the field were twenty-four hours on, forty-eight hours off. That could have varied as well. Depending on the mission or personnel count, it could have been twelve or twenty-four off. All I remember is it was twenty-four seven for us. I looked at my Ranger buddy and said, "I got this shit, dude."

"Let's go, Rangers. Get up here and get your briefing. We're burning daylight. We got everybody here?" They would always verify our roster numbers with our positions and make sure we understood completely before we received our mission briefing. It was an ambush mission on an enemy vehicle patrol, with approximately a four-kilometer movement. So we knew that meant we were going to get "hit" along the way, either by indirect fire, or personnel, or both. After the RI issued us our warning order, we immediately began planning the mission, the movement, and of course, the timeline.

Once complete, along with the medic and forward observer, I began constructing the terrain model while the platoon leader and squad leaders wrote the operations order. Like I said earlier, by now we pretty much had this shit down to a science. However, never underestimate Murphy's Law when it comes to any military operation. Contingency planning is critical. This also included me as the platoon sergeant being prepared to take over as the platoon leader at any time from here on out until our mission was over or until my evaluation time was complete.

After issuing the operations order, going over the terrain model, and rehearsals on the mission itself, it was time to move out. I'll admit, I was nervous, because you never know what you were going to run into in this school. Taking this thing one step at a time was my goal, and getting it right was crucial if I was ever going to make it out of this phase.

It was around 0900 in the morning and relatively cold out. We could see our breath. Mornings like these, we just wanted to get moving in order to warm up a bit. Boy, did we end up "warming up" by the time this shit was over.

I moved up to the release point with the medic and took a knee. It was fucking silent as all get-out. All you could hear was the sound of radio squelch and the chirping of crickets. I looked at my fingers and got disgusted by my cracked fingertips, caused by lack of vitamins and nutrition. We all saw our bodies deteriorating from lack of food and nutrition. I didn't think about my fingertips too long because the platoon was getting ready to move up in a file so the medic and I could count them out of the perimeter, one at a time. When Germany walked past us, I swatted him on the ass as I counted him. He turned and gave me the finger. Once everybody was out, I confirmed the count with the medic. Then my RI evaluator walked up and asked what I counted, and I confidently gave him my number.

"Are you sure?" he asked.

"Yes, Sergeant," I replied—confidently again. They always tried to make you second-guess yourself, but I had it right. He actually was cool and admitted I was right, that he just wanted to make sure I was alert. He shot the shit with me a little bit on the movement. Those guys, I'm sure, got bored a lot doing these missions time after time, cycle after cycle, and year after year.

About a klick into the movement, we got hit with small arms fire from the front of our formation. A *klick* is military slang for a kilometer. The platoon leader moved up to the front and assessed the situation. The weapons squad leader moved up and took control of the lead machine gun. The lead squad became the support by fire, and I quickly moved up with the rear gun and oversaw the support element while the platoon leader moved back and grabbed the second squad in the movement, which became the assault element. He swiftly took them around and flanked. Once he got the assault squad in position, we shifted fire toward the opposite direction they were assaulting from. Once they got close enough to the three or four enemy personnel, I ordered the support by fire to lift fire, and then called the confirmation of the lift to the platoon leader so that he could proceed with the assault through the objective. Pretty textbook stuff.

Once they were through the assault and killed the enemy, we consolidated and reorganized around the objective. The platoon leader called in the ACE (ammunition, casualties, and equipment) report with the number of enemy killed in action. Luckily, the RIs assessed no casualties from our platoon. I'd say it went without a hitch. We recovered our rucks, I counted everybody out, and we moved out to continue the mission. My evaluator walked up to me once we started walking again and gave me a little encouragement.

"Hey, good job back there, Ranger. You're looking good; keep it up." Without telling me, because they're supposed to wait until the end of the phase, he pretty much told me I was a go. We hadn't had changeover yet, and I wasn't going to get ahead of myself, but man, I was feeling motivated and excited that I might be receiving a go for my combat patrol in the Mountain Phase.

After about three hours of movement through the massive hills, we finally got close to our grid for the objective rally point and went into a security halt. We then heard the magic words from one of the RIs, "Change of mission, Rangers." They called out the roster numbers for the leadership changeovers. Germany got picked to be one of the squad leaders for the actions-on portion of our ambush patrol. After we turned over equipment to the changeovers, I went back to a squad to be a rifleman for the remainder of the mission. My evaluator came up to me once everything got calm and took a knee next to me while I was pulling security.

"Hey, Ranger, you looked good, and I have no issues with your performance today. Keep it up, Ranger." That was it. Without my receiving an official pass or fail grade, he pretty much hinted that I would be receiving a go on my patrol.

"Roger that, Sergeant," I said with enthusiasm. I was done with my grades in Mountain Phase. If I could have, I would have gotten up and started doing backflips around our security halt! All I had to do now, for the rest of this exercise, was keep motivated, help the platoon with anything they needed help with to get the next guys through, and I would make it out of this phase successfully. I could even work off one if not both of the spot reports I had gotten from DSS in the mountaineering portion earlier. Damn! That seemed like a year ago by this time. For the next couple of missions, I volunteered to be team leader, carry one of the machine guns, you name it. I was so stoked!

The remainder of the mission was successful as well. I believe all graded positions received a go, to include my buddy Germany. After it was over and we received our AAR, Germany came up to me, took a knee, and said the magic words. "Too easy, brother."

I replied, "Way too easy, Ranger buddy. I'm starting to believe that we're going to make it out of here."

We had a mission the next day where I volunteered to carry one of the M240B machine guns—heavy son of bitch. It was one of those movements where we had to climb a huge, steep-ass hill. This thing was so steep that it could have been considered a cliff. When we approached the base, we noticed there were ropes already secured to the top of it, so obviously it was a requirement for each platoon to climb up this thing.

Oh boy, I said to myself as I looked up at this steep son of a bitch. I had the gun slung around the front of me with my eighty-pound rucksack on my back, and my LCE weighed at least twenty-five or thirty pounds with all my ammunition and water.

I grabbed the rope and started pulling myself up, concentrating on putting one foot in front of the other. It probably took us about half an hour to get to the top, but it seemed like two fucking hours. When we got to the top, the battalion commander and command sergeant major were waiting to greet us. "Good job. Keep it up, Rangers," the commander said to us.

■ ■ ■

A couple more days and missions later, we were in the patrol base. The sun was just coming up, and it was freezing. This phase had become an uphill struggle for me, and my worries were back on again. I'll explain because it could happen to any student this far in.

It was my turn to get off the perimeter, get to the center of the patrol base, and begin weapon maintenance on my M-4. I took my weapon apart and started cleaning it. While I was at it, I took a main meal out of my ruck and ate it in like thirty seconds. I ate it like I was going to prison. I was so hungry and tired.

After I put my weapon back together, I locked and loaded and went back to the perimeter to pull security. The medics were conducting their checks on the students prior to us receiving our next mission. The RI that had graded me on my patrol a couple of days prior approached me, and, of course, I had fallen asleep.

"Hey, Ranger, how you doing?"

"Oh shit! I'm good, Sergeant, just fighting this sleep monster that keeps crawling on my back."

"All right, Ranger, keep your ass awake. I know it sucks."

"Roger, Sergeant," I replied.

He then said, "Ranger, pull your charging handle back so I can check your chamber."

They did this to ensure that we remained locked and loaded at all times during combat operations.

I pulled it back and said, "See? I'm good, Sergeant. Always ready."

"Okay, you're good, Ranger." As he started walking away, he came back and approached me again. This is when my world seemed to come crashing down, and the stress level went back up. "Ranger, look at your safety selection lever, and tell me what's wrong with this picture."

I had left my weapon on fire after cleaning it and hadn't done my functions check like I've been taught and been teaching as an NCO for fucking years.

"Oh shit, Sergeant, I just literally got done cleaning my weapon and because I'm so smoked, I didn't do a proper functions check and left it on fire, Sergeant. I know I fucked-up." I tried to talk my way out of this nightmare that I had created for myself.

The RI was writing me a major-minus spot report.

"Oh no, please no, Sergeant; this will be my third one this phase."

"Ranger, sign here that you are receiving a major-minus spot report for having your weapon off safety within the patrol base."

I signed it as I continued to plead with him, but it wasn't working.

"Ranger, I don't want to hear any more of your shit. Think what would happen if you had a negligent discharge. You know the alternative from there, right?"

"Yes, Sergeant." The alternative would be an automatic day-zero recycle or go home. I don't think I would have been able to handle it at that point. I would have had problems even passing the PT test with the state my body was in.

So, three-quarters complete with Ranger School Mountain Phase, I received my third major-minus spot report, and my entire world collapsed in on me. I knew what I needed to do. Now I had no choice but to work off at least one of these before the end of the field exercise, or I would be facing an automatic board for phase recycle. What a dumbass I was and how I could make such a boneheaded mistake kept running through my head.

When the platoon received our mission and new leadership was assigned, I knew what I had to do. I volunteered to be the forward observer (FO) and carry one of the radios. It was a chance to hopefully receive a positive spot report, which would cancel out one of my negatives. As a matter of fact, I'd probably have to have a radio on my back as an FO or RTO the remainder of Mountain Phase. I was pretty confident that I could do it and pull it off. After all, we still had about three days remaining in the field.

As we moved out of the perimeter, I stayed close to the platoon leader, along with the RTO. About a kilometer into the movement, we got hit with indirect fire. After the platoon leader got us out of the area and onto higher ground, the RI informed him that the indirect was coming in from a hilltop to our east, so we started plotting it on our map. I called in a fire mission according to the standard format that we carried on us. The RI was taking a knee next to me and the platoon leader, observing me the whole time.

"All right, PL, the enemy on hilltop such-and-such is neutralized—continue mission."

The platoon leader replied, "Roger, Sergeant." Once we started moving again, I thought, *Man, I hope that was it. All I needed for a major plus.* Unfortunately, it didn't come. I would just have to keep driving on until it happened. I had to remain positive and focused on our missions.

After another mission of being FO, I honestly quit worrying about it and simply focused on completing this phase, which was a near reality for us, and hoping that the board members would waiver me from being recycled in Mountains. I could not "wish" anything positive from these instructors. It was either going to happen or it wasn't.

I volunteered to be a team leader for one of the guys that got picked to be a squad leader. He was nervous and a younger soldier. I was going to do anything to help him out and help him receive a go. It was an ambush patrol, and we were to be set in by midnight, I think. We were all in zombie mode with only one more twenty-four- hour mission after this one. When we got to the objective area and after we were set up waiting for the enemy vehicle, I moved up and down the line, making sure that everyone was as awake and as alert as humanly possible.

When the vehicle approached, we engaged. The momentum was definitely not there; aggressiveness from the platoon as a whole was almost nonexistent. The RIs were pissed off and yelling out, "PL, this platoon better start getting aggressive on this fucking target!"

The firing of our weapons just didn't seem to be there. It was like *pop, pop, pop*. The M240Bs seemed to be jammed. The enemy dismounted and moved in on us, and the RIs did not assess any of them casualties, due to the nonaggressiveness our platoon was showing. Finally, one of the guns kicked in and started firing, and then one of the SAW guns started firing as well. At this point they began assessing the enemy as killed. The platoon leader ordered the assault element to move through the objective and get across the firebreak. As I came across, one of the bad guys jumped out from behind the vehicle, so I hollered out, "Close kill, close kill!" We were not allowed to fire blanks too close to them, especially at point-blank range, due to safety issues. We made it across the ambush area, and the platoon leader designated our LOA (limit of advance). "LOA, LOA!"

Afterward we conducted an enemy prisoner of war search and a search and aid litter for our casualties, and there were a couple of them. The less motivated the students were on missions, the more casualties the RIs assessed. And they were pretty pissed off after this particular mission. Once our left- and right-side security linked back up with the rest of us, we went into our AAR, which turned into a complete ass-chewing. As I remember it, they even put us in the front leaning rest position while they were yelling at us.

"PL, that was weak as hell, and completely unacceptable! Rangers, you've been out here nine days now. You're hungry, tired, and your minds are all jacked up—I got it! We've been through it too, Rangers, or we wouldn't be here ourselves! You guys have a little over twenty-four hours left out here, so suck it up and drive on, Rangers! All right, on your feet, men. PL, get us back to your fucking objective rally point."

Wow, I didn't know if he was a go or a no-go. I thought I was nervous for having three spot reports under my belt, but this guy was possibly looking at a patrol failure. If he went down, I wondered what that meant for the platoon sergeant and the squad leaders.

For the final assault mission the next day, I volunteered again to carry a radio, this time to change it up a bit and be the platoon RTO. It was a mission that I won't ever forget. I believe I ended up getting targeted by the RIs. I'll explain.

The mission scenario was that the enemy had kidnapped one of our platoon members and was holding him captive. We were to plan and execute a raid on the complex in order to rescue him. It was the culminating mission of Mountain Phase. I remember it being pretty realistic as well. You could hear the enemy over loudspeakers give a speech over and over on how we Americans just "need to let it go" and get out of their territory. That bullshit echoed through the hills as we got closer to the objective. It actually was pretty eerie to listen to. Our minds were already playing tricks on us.

We moved into our objective rally point right at dusk and conducted our final mission preparations—recamouflaging, taking off our patrol caps, putting on our helmets, putting on night vision, etc. The sounds of the speaker system grew louder and louder. I remember this so vividly. Our objective rally point was on top of a huge hill (of course they were all huge hills), and the objective was at the bottom. It felt like we were a mile up from it. I remember busting my ass on the way down at least twice because of the weight of our rucks, especially carrying a radio on top of it, with the extra batteries too.

The raid was successful, and we got our Ranger back. Prior to our platoon AAR, we obviously had to go back up the hill to recover our rucksacks. Well, of course, me and the FO already had ours on. So I walked up to one of the RIs, who was a captain, and probably the company commander. I respectfully asked him if me and the FO could wait for the platoon at the AAR site since we already had our equipment on us.

He said, real sarcastically, "No, Ranger, you move your asses back up there with your platoon. You move with your platoon at all times."

"Yes, sir," I replied.

So, as we started heading up the hill, the FO said to me in a real low tone, "Hey, man, fuck this. Let's just hide out down here and wait for them to come back down the hill. Nobody's even going to know we're here."

I said, "No, man, we better do what we're told. I'm not fucking around with this place."

"Yeah, you're right about that. We've come too far to get into trouble."

So up the hill we went with the platoon. When we got up there, the captain was sitting down in our objective rally point, waiting on us. When I walked past him, he grabbed my leg and said, "Sit down next to me, Ranger. I want to talk to you."

I said, "Yes, sir, what's up?"

"So, you thought you were going to try to trick us and stay down there, huh?"

"No, sir. It was mentioned, but we quickly decided to do what you told us and here we are—on top of the hill with the rest of the platoon like you ordered."

"Okay, Ranger. I can't argue with that, but you better watch your ass. I got my eyes on you. What's your roster number?"

"Five Zero, sir."

"Okay. Get out of here and head back down with the platoon."

"Roger that, sir."

At that point, I really wasn't concerned about it. I mean, after all, we did what the fuck he told us to do. Furthermore, I wasn't even the guy that had suggested it, but I wasn't going to dime out the FO. That was the fucking problem with this place: others would in a heartbeat. It was a dog-eat-dog world in Ranger School. There were a few in each platoon that would dime out others to save their own asses. Either way, it wasn't me, but the problem with this whole thing was that this captain thought it was. I found out in the next three hours that it wasn't forgotten or going away after all.

After about two hours of sleep, the new RIs that were changing over came out to us. You could always tell they were in the area because you could smell them, as they were fresh and clean. I mean, you could literally smell soap and even deodorant.

"Where's Roster Number Five Zero?"

"Here, Sergeant."

"Get up here, Ranger."

"Moving, Sergeant," I replied. It was a staff sergeant that I pretty much thought was a great guy up until this point. I approached him. "Yes, Sergeant."

"You know what, Ranger? You almost got your ass SOR'd this morning. You know that?" Then he repeated himself with a sarcastic look in his eye that I will never forget. "Yeah, did you hear what I said? You almost got yourself fucking SOR'd, Ranger. I think you'd better watch your ass from here on out."

I simply replied back to him with, "Yes, Sergeant." I didn't say anything else to him or mention doing what we were told or anything. I'm not stupid. I know what the fuck he was trying to get me to do. He was fishing for me to smart off back to him so that he could get me on a serious observation report, which, again, would mean automatic board to get released from school for an integrity violation. Nope. I wasn't falling for his bullshit. I simply kept my mouth shut and moved back with the platoon. I thought, *If I ever see that piece of shit back out in the Army, I'm going to fuck him up.* He was a dumpy-looking bastard. Back in the Army he probably wouldn't add up to shit. Oh yeah, some Ranger instructors were shitbags too. Not too many, but there were a couple hiding out in RTB for their NCO careers—like DSS back at Merrill.

Our final mission was a movement back to Camp Merrill and out of this godforsaken field exercise. It was basically just a planning phase with a movement. I'm sure it was also to provide a last chance for some of the students who still needed a go in Mountain to get a passing grade. The senior RI on site was a sergeant first class, and he began calling out roster numbers and duty positions. "Roster Number Five Zero—platoon sergeant!"

I said to myself, *What the fuck? I know I already got a passing grade because the RI who evaluated me damn near told me I did.*

Okay, now I was worried again because I knew there were guys in this platoon that still needed a passing grade in order to get out of here. What I thought was transpiring looked more and more to be the case. They were targeting me. They were going to put me on this patrol as a graded platoon sergeant position, where I would receive a no-go at the end, mark my word. I knew the system all too well, but I kept it to myself, and kept my mouth shut. We were probably going to get hit one last time—too easy. You really couldn't fuck this up, but they were the ones with the gradebooks.

Without getting into the details of our movement, which was pretty basic and routine, we did get hit by small arms fire from a couple of opposing forces. We fought through them, defeated them, and there were no casualties on our end. After consolidation and reorganization, the medic and I counted the platoon out, the count was perfect, and we continued movement. After about a kilometer or so, the RIs told us "change of mission," and we would be moving the rest of the way back on a road in road-march formation. At that point I knew we were done with the field, and we would be back in society soon. Thank God! However—and most people wouldn't believe this, but it happened—some poor bastard in the platoon had a negligent discharge with his weapon just before we entered back into camp. I shit you not!

Pow! His M-4 went off, and the RIs immediately stopped the formation.

"All right, Rangers, who the fuck was it? Raise your hand." It came from the front of the formation, but they couldn't exactly pinpoint what student it was. He raised his hand reluctantly but did so in good faith and without sugarcoating it.

"Here, Sergeant," he said.

"All right, Ranger, you know what that means when we get back."

"Roger, Sergeant," he said disappointedly. I actually felt for him because he was a great kid and I believe he was smooth sailing up until this point. I looked down on my weapon and made sure the damn thing was on safe. Man, we were done too.

When we got back into Camp Merrill, I remember thinking how great it looked after the past ten days. I also remember wondering whether or not I was going to be recycled. At this point I was so hungry and tired, I just wanted something to eat and four hours of sleep. The RI that had evaluated me on that final movement came up to me as we were still walking in and told me that he would give me my AAR later after we turned in weapons and got cleaned up.

"Sounds good, Sergeant," I said to him. Actually, I wasn't worried about all that shit back there anymore. Hell, I was going to take a hot shower after ten days and get a hot meal.

After we thoroughly cleaned our weapons and equipment for two hours, we were finally authorized to turn them back in to the arms room. "Okay, Rangers, get up to the barracks, wash your nasty asses, and get into clean BDUs and boots."

Normally we would have run for the showers, but none of us

had the energy to run. I wish there was a scale in those barracks. I would have loved to find out how much I weighed at that point. One thing about the latrine in the barracks at Camp Merrill that I didn't mention earlier: The stalls had mostly 187th Parachute Infantry Regiment graffiti drawn all over them. So, I pulled out my ink pin. I drew a picture of the 82nd Airborne Division insignia with my regiment below it. Too easy.

We formed up outside after we got cleaned up and were marched to the company headquarters where we conducted our peer evaluations, and yes, it was time for hotdogs again! This time we were authorized two hotdogs, a bag of chips, a candy bar, and a soda to wash it down with. Again, I ate that shit like it was my last meal. Damn, they were the best hotdogs I ever ate in my entire life!

My state of bliss soon came to another crashing halt. Real calmly the RI approached me after I threw my paper plate away. "Okay, Ranger, I have your AAR from the last movement done now."

"Roger, Sergeant," I replied.

"Okay, Roster Number Five Zero, your performance on the mission was substandard. Overall you are a no-go, Ranger." Yep, my instincts were right on! Those motherfuckers were targeting me. All because of that fucking captain after that final mission.

Again, I kept my mouth shut, and simply replied, "Roger, Sergeant." In the back of my mind I knew that I already had my go on patrols, so that bullshit he'd just pulled on me was irrelevant. You only need ONE fucking passing grade on combat patrols in Ranger School. He was attempting to strike a negative reaction from me so that he could SOR me for disrespect or some shit. I had a go on patrols, and I was pretty sure I was going to peer good again. The only thing I had to worry about were those fucking major-minus spot reports.

Afterward it was time for us to receive our final phase counseling. Of course, guess who got to be the RI that counseled me? Yep, the captain himself. Joy! I took a seat in front of his desk, and I couldn't wait to hear what was about to come next.

"Okay, Roster Number Five Zero, you have a passing score on your graded patrol. You scored an 89 percent on peer evaluations. With that, you pass on evals. However, you have a total of three major-minus spot reports that you were unable to work off. Therefore, I will be recommending that you recycle Mountain Phase of Ranger School. Any questions?"

"No, sir."

"Okay then, tomorrow morning after chow, you will report to the battalion commander, upon which he will determine whether or not you will be recycled or able to move on to the final phase. Again, any questions?"

"No, sir."

"Okay, you're dismissed."

I stood up, saluted him and replied, "Rangers lead the way, sir." He didn't even reply with the proper response of "All the way." His return salute was half-ass too. This guy was a real piece of work, I'm not kidding. I said to myself as I walked back to the barracks, *Whatever, it is what it is. I'll find out my fate tomorrow morning, I guess.* I knew the reality of how this worked. If the battalion commander decided that I would recycle, I knew I was never going to make it out of Mountains. When the next phase began, they would no-go me on every test starting with mountaineering again. I got back to the barracks and went to bed. Was this going to be my last night in these barracks, or was I going to have to start all over again? I'd worry about it tomorrow. I was too fucking tired to give a shit now. I had a mattress to sleep on, for Christ's sake.

The next morning after chow, I walked over to the 5th RTB headquarters and stood outside the door. The captain came out and told me to go inside and report to the battalion commander. He did not remain in; instead he went back to the company—thank God. I walked in, stood in front of the commander and rendered a sharp hand salute.

"Sir, Roster Number Five Zero reporting as ordered, sir!"

He returned the salute and replied, "At ease, Ranger."

He had my file in front of him and was looking it over.

"Okay, Ranger, your file says you passed patrols and received a high peer evaluation, but that you have three major-minus spot reports. Did you make an attempt to work those off in the field?" The command sergeant major was standing off to the side. He looked really familiar too, like he had come from my brigade back at Bragg. Wow, that place seemed like a hundred years ago.

"Yes sir, I did. I volunteered all the time to be the RTO, FO, and team leader after I was complete with my patrol. I just never could receive a positive spot report for whatever reason, sir." I was getting very nervous.

"Ranger, what are your spot reports exactly for?"

"Sir, I received one for getting a no-go on my initial belay test, one for a no-go on my initial rock climb, and my final one was during the field exercise. I had my weapon on fire while in the patrol base, sir."

"It says here that you're an E-7, huh?"

"Yes, sir."

"I can see the first two spot reports, but that third one is ridiculous, especially for a senior NCO. What the hell was your weapon doing on fire in the patrol base for, anyway?"

"I had just gotten done cleaning my weapon and didn't do a functions check after I put it back together, sir. I was just tired and smoked, sir, but no excuse."

He then went into my duty station. "Where are you stationed at, Ranger?"

"Fort Bragg, sir."

"What unit?"

"3-505, sir."

He then looked at the sergeant major. "The 505th. Aren't they currently deployed, Ranger?"

"Yes, sir, they've been in Iraq for about two months now."

"Okay, Ranger, so what you're telling me is, that there's a platoon over in combat right now without their platoon sergeant?"

"Yes sir. Immediately after graduation from here, I will be linking up with them over there." I started getting a vibe and a strong feeling that I was going to make it out of there.

He looked back over to the command sergeant major and asked, "What do you think, Sergeant Major?"

He replied, "Well, sir, under these circumstances, I think we can overlook and waive the spot reports." I started feeling motivated and confident again.

"Okay, Roster Number Five Zero, I'm going to let you move on to Florida Phase this afternoon. Remember, you being a senior NCO, the instructors are looking at you to be an example, so no more mistakes like leaving your weapon on fire. Had you had a discharge, I wouldn't be able to do anything for you—you know that, right?"

"Yes, sir. I understand, sir."

"Okay, Ranger. Get out of here and go link back up with your company. I believe they're preparing for the jump into Florida as we speak. Also, good luck and go get down there in Florida, and get back to your platoon in Iraq."

"Thank you so much, sir." I turned toward the command sergeant major. "Thank you, Sergeant Major." I snapped to the position of attention and rendered another sharp hand salute. "Rangers lead the way, sir!"

"All the way," he replied as he returned the salute. I did a right face, stepped off with my left foot and marched out of his office and the headquarters. Once outside, I threw my arms in the air, looked up in the sky and verbally thanked God.

CHAPTER 13

FLORIDA PHASE
ZOMBIE MODE

AFTER LEAVING THE 5th RTB headquarters, I ran with excitement to link up with the company, which was conducting sustained airborne training, or prejump, down in the landing zone, just on the other side of camp. I sprinted down there with so much enthusiasm because the battalion commander had approved me for getting out of this godforsaken environment of Camp Merrill and Dahlonega, Georgia. I first had to report back to the captain that had the issue with me and let him know that I would be leaving and jumping into Florida with the other sixty or so students that made it out of Mountain Phase. I couldn't wait to look him in his face and tell him the commander's decision.

I approached him down on the landing zone, saluted him and told him my good news.

"Okay, Ranger, fall in the group. We're about to start prejump." Surprisingly, there was no attitude or sarcasm from him.

"Yes, sir," I replied, and then I moved out. I believed he was over it, and so was I. I found Germany.

"You get to come with us, brother?" he asked.

I replied with, "You know it! You know I ain't leaving my Ranger buddy." We all moved out and gathered in somewhat of a circle around the RI jumpmaster that was about to give us prejump. I looked around for the asshole staff sergeant that had thrown the term *SOR* in my face in the field, and I spotted him walking around. He saw me looking at him too. He didn't say anything to me, nor did I to him. I simply wanted to get out of there and begin a new slate in the final phase.

After prejump, mock door training, and parachute-landing fall practices, we collected our duffle bags stacked up in the parking lot outside of the barracks. We loaded them onto a cargo truck that was headed down to Camp Rudder in Florida. We then rigged our rucks or ALICE packs to jump and began painting our faces and necks. We loaded a bus and were taken to an airfield right outside the camp. We were so happy to be rolling out of there. The Bat Boys started singing their songs like the old days, and hell, me and Germany even joined in.

When we got to the airfield, we secured a main and reserve parachute. We didn't have actual weapons on us, obviously, so they had the M1950 carrying cases with two-by-fours in them to simulate the weapons, as they had in Benning during RAP Week. The RIs immediately had us don our parachutes, so me and Germany helped each other rig up. It was called "buddy-rigging." Afterward, they began the jumpmaster personnel inspections, or JMPI. I was so motivated, I even asked if they needed help JMPIing the chalk, as I was a current and qualified jumpmaster. I knew the answer was going to be no, being a student myself, but I asked anyway. You can never have enough help; trust me. I don't think that my "buddy" the staff sergeant was jumpmaster qualified; he couldn't touch any of us during the inspections.

After the chalk was JMPI'd, we sat on the ground and waited for the aircraft to arrive, which was a C-130. If I remember correctly, only our chalk was jumping; there were only about sixty jump-qualified students getting out of this phase. The rest (maybe about twenty) that were not jump certified would be trucked or bused down with our duffle bags. I sat there thinking of the poor bastard that'd had that negligent discharge the day prior. He was probably getting ready to be bused back down to Benning to either be day-zero recycled or go home.

We loaded up the bird in reverse chalk order. Once seated, we were going to be in flight for about an hour, maybe an hour and a half. We sat down and it was nighty-night time for us.

We were awakened by the jump command, "Twenty minutes!" Then, "Ten minutes!" We then went into the ten-minute sequence before exiting the aircraft. The primary jumpmaster and his assistant on the other door gave all the jump commands, and us jumpers sounded off by echoing them. I remember thinking how relaxing it was to be "Joe Jumper" and not have the stresses of jumpmaster duty like I had so many times back at Bragg. Again, that world seemed so distant in my memory.

Germany was in front of me. He turned around and said, "Have a good jump, Ranger buddy!"

"You too, brother!"

Then we both said it simultaneously: "Waaay too easy!"

I heard the final jump command "Go!" As we moved toward the door, my heart started really racing, as it always does. I handed off my static line to the safety, turned in to the paratroop door, and exited. As I was blown through the air by the initial blast from the aircraft, I counted. "One thousand, two thousand, three thousand, four thousand!" My parachute opened and I floated down over sunny Florida, thinking, *Mountain Phase is* now *officially over!*

After a pretty soft landing, I removed myself from the parachute harness and "policed" up my equipment. I swear, it had to have been at least twenty or twenty-five degrees warmer than Georgia! Ahhh, man, if felt so good. I carried my parachute, reserve, ruck and my M1950 weapons case off the drop zone, turned it into a crew that was at the leading edge, and was told to form up.

We were at Eglin Air Force Base in the northwest corner of the panhandle of Florida. We got on a bus that took us over to Camp

Rudder, which was on the other side of the base and home of the 6th Ranger Training Battalion. I was nervous. Number one, about simply going to a new phase, but two, about whether I was going to have to put up with biased instructors like I had just encountered in the previous phase.

There's nothing you can do about it. You're here now, so just take it one day, one task at a time, and you'll get out of here. And absolutely ZERO fucking minus spot reports. You have a "clean slate" down here. This is what I told myself on the bus ride into our new camp.

When the bus pulled into Camp Rudder, it stopped and let us off in front of our barracks, a three-story building painted in Army light tan. Across the street were the two small company headquarters buildings. Down a little farther was the chow hall, which was next to 6th RTB headquarters, and across the street from that was the Gator Lounge, the little Camp Rudder bar and pub.

There was already a formation of recycles standing by, as there had been for the first two phases. We got off the buses, and the senior RI, a sergeant first class, was standing there waiting on us.

"Go ahead and form up, Rangers. We're still waiting on your duffle bags to show up from up north. They should be arriving anytime now." After about a half an hour, I heard, "Roster Number Five Zero, where you at?"

I sounded off with, "Here, Sergeant!" I ran up to the senior, stopped and went to parade rest. I worried what this was going to be all about. I hoped and prayed that all that drama from the Mountains wasn't going to follow me down here with these Florida Phase RIs. If it did, I'd definitely be screwed.

"We have to change your companies. You're now going to be in Bravo Company for this phase, okay?"

"Yes, Sergeant, but may I ask why?"

I was waiting for him to say, "No you may not, Ranger," but he didn't. Instead, he pulled me off to the side away from the formation and explained. "Hey, look, these are mostly recycles. We know what rank you are and what your duty position is back at Bragg. We're going to need your help with this group of students. They're mostly struggling. I'm actually putting you in a squad that has the most recycles from the platoon in it, so they're going to need your help in order for them to get out of here. So we expect your support and your help with them, Ranger, all right?"

"No problem, Sergeant. I'll do my best to help them."

He then asked me, "How's it going in that Panther Brigade back at Bragg, anyway?" I thought, *Wow, this guy really does know everything about me.*

I responded with, "Well, Sergeant, they're currently deployed to Iraq right now, and when I make it out of here, I'll be linking up with them over there." I made a point to emphasize the fact that I was linking up with them in Iraq as soon as I could graduate from this place—in case he didn't know, but he did. That was a good thing.

"Yeah, that's what I heard," he replied. "I was in 2 Panther before I got down here a couple of years ago."

"Oh, Airborne," I said.

I went back in front of the formation. I was relieved that, one, I wasn't going to be targeted by these RIs, and two, they counted on me to help out with my platoon and squad while we were going through this phase. What a fucking relief! At that point I felt so motivated again. After we got our bags and put our stuff up in the barracks, I ran into Germany, and explained to him why I had to leave our company and platoon—that I wasn't in trouble or anything like that. He congratulated me, shook my hand, and we wished each other luck.

"I'll see you when we get done with this shit, man," he said to me.

"Yep, later, brother. Good luck to you." If I remember correctly, the other company, or simply two platoons, were on the floor below ours. When we all got back downstairs, we formed up and went over to the company headquarters building and began receiving our platoon equipment. Same procedure as before. Equipment draw, which included medic bag, VS-17 panels, a couple of AT-4 anti-tank weapons, etc. Each of us also drew another sling rope and set of D-rings as well.

As it had the first two times, equipment draw and accountability of it all took about two hours. It wasn't that dramatic of an event this time, as it had been in Darby and Mountains. I also noticed that for some reason the RIs seemed more hands-off down here thus far. My new platoon seemed to be a bunch of good guys, and the same with my new squad. I remember feeling so at ease with everything down in Florida.

After we put our equipment up in the barracks, it was time for our first meal at Camp Rudder! We were starving (as usual). We hadn't eaten; at least, I hadn't eaten since breakfast up at Camp Merrill that morning before the jump. The chow hall was pretty awesome, and they fed us great too. Just like the other two phases, while we were training in camp we only ate two meals per day out of the chow halls. Usually breakfast and dinner.

For the next five days at Camp Rudder we performed some pretty long, drawn-out training, and had some really interesting classes. The first class was actually in the classroom. It was on the wildlife that we might encounter there in the swamp phase of Ranger School. This RI brought in this big-ass rattlesnake. It was the largest eastern diamondback I had ever seen in my entire life, and I had been to plenty of zoos across the country by this time. I couldn't believe how huge this thing was, and the RI just carried it around the classroom like it was a garter snake. Of course, there were some students that couldn't keep their eyes open during the class. The RI would tap them on the shoulder and tell them to wake up, and when they did, he'd have the rattlesnake's head next to them. It would scare the living shit out of them. One guy actually jumped up so startled that he fell over. Of course, we all laughed our asses off. Good times.

They also brought in an alligator and some lizards. The alligator was just a baby, and another RI was handling it as well. Another snake they showed us that we definitely would and did encounter was the little pygmy rattler. When we got out to the field exercise, we found one or two under students' rucksacks throughout the ten days. That's why when you are out there, you always look under your ruck. At night you look under it with a red-lensed flashlight—always. I remember saying to myself, *I'll be damned if I'm going to leave Ranger School because of a fucking snake bite. The hell with my health; I want to finish this shit and get my tab.* They also warned us about the wild boar that were in the area, but hell, they were in every phase of Ranger School, not just Florida.

One class we pretty much used an entire day and half the night on was setting up and crossing a rope bridge—not a bridge that you could walk across, but simply a rope from one anchor point to another, in order to safely get a platoon across a river. During the upcoming combat-operations portion of the phase, there would be two missions that would have a river crossing where we would have to utilize this technique.

The class started with the RIs from our platoon demonstrating everything from beginning to end. First portion was learning how to properly configure and tie off our ropes around our chests and how to properly snap link into the main rope. We practiced until we all had it down, and then they came through and inspected each of us to ensure we did it correctly. After they demonstrated actually tying off the main rope and then simulated swimming across a large river and tying it off on the other end, they had us do it ourselves. Everyone in the platoon had to tie off until we all had it figured out. Same standard; the RI would verify each of us did it correctly without error. Each of us would then simulate swimming across and securing the rope on the other end. Then each in the platoon would snap into it and cross by holding on to and shimmying across the rope until we all got to the other side. Accountability of personnel (as always) was a must. Once on the other side, the platoon sergeant, along with the medic, would count each individual until the entire platoon safely crossed. For training on this task while on camp, we did this from one tree to another that was about thirty feet away.

It was imperative that each individual got this down to a science because it was known as a critical task. I believe in 1995 a few students had died during a swamp river-crossing mission due to hypothermia. So everybody took this shit very seriously. We practiced this all day and most of the night. The RIs even had us doing it as a timed competition among platoons. We had it down pat. It brought more comradery to our platoon as well.

I got to know my platoon a lot better as the days went by, and they were good to work with. We asked each other what we did back in the Army, and what each other's rank was. It's kind of how everybody operated in Ranger School, at least in my class. Come to find out most if not all of my squad were second lieutenants in the Army National Guard. We all had something in common; they had just graduated from the Infantry Officer Basic Course prior to being here, as I had from the Advanced Noncommissioned Officer Course. Great bunch of guys—or so I thought, but I'll get into that later on.

Another good class was one on loading on and off and conducting boat operations. They trucked us out to a nearby lake and gave their demonstration and class. There was definitely an orchestrated, coordinated method of positioning on these zodiac watercraft. It wasn't simply "Everybody just get on and start paddling." Each craft carried a squad. There were set positions, to include the machine gunner up front on the bow of the boat. All our rucks were in the middle. Each Ranger, except the gunner, sat up with one leg inside the boat and the other outside in the water, as each paddled it through the water. It looked all intimidating and high-speed, but it was an ass-smoker after you'd been paddling for six or seven hours. Again, during combat operations, there were three total boat movements, two of which had the river crossings integrated in them. Like I said, a total ass-smoker.

We spent like half a day on that, and it was back to camp doing tactical-rehearsals training. Pretty common in each phase. We rehearsed movement techniques, room-clearing techniques by fire team and squads, more rope-bridge rehearsals, you name it. This preparation for the field exercise went on for the first five or six days after our arrival at Camp Rudder. We'd eat about two meals a day and get about three to four hours of sleep per night. Pretty standard for all three of the camps while we stayed on them prior to the field. You'd still lose weight because you were constantly training and doing some kind of activity outside all the time. So you felt hungry all the time as well. By now, our bodies and minds were pretty much used to it.

Speaking of feeling hungry, for our last day in camp before heading out to the field, we didn't get breakfast in the chow hall. You would have thought someone killed my dog. I'm not kidding, we were depressed. Of course, we were already starving, tired, and had slight attitudes because we knew the dreaded ten-day field problem was coming up within twenty-four hours. I believe they were preparing us and putting us in starvation mode before we received our operations order for our first mission. Honestly, I was looking forward to it, because it was our last field exercise of Ranger School. Once we knocked that out, we were done and going back to Benning for graduation. We could do this—too easy.

Yeah right . . .

The next morning, it was time to get our faces painted, get all our equipment, and get outside. We would not see these barracks again for the next ten days. There definitely wasn't any mess hall chow today either, but we had already figured that. Instead, we marched out of Camp Rudder to our platoon planning bay area, and it began.

"All right, Rangers, listen up for your roster numbers and duty positions. You all know how this works by now. Roster Number So-and-so, platoon leader. Roster Number Five Zero, platoon sergeant!" He then called the four squad leader positions out. It was the same grading system as in the Mountains. The platoon leader, platoon sergeant, and four squad leaders. Everything else, such as team leader, medic, RTO, or FO, were extras and volunteer positions in order to help out and maybe try to receive a plus spot report. I was excited to get my graded patrol out of the way right off the bat, especially before I ended up in zombie mode like I knew I was going to be in the next couple of days. I figured that the RIs got mine out of the way first so I could concentrate on helping the others in the squad during the rest of the field exercise, as had been mentioned to me when I first got to Florida by the senior RI. One thing was for sure, though; I was not going to fuck this up. I was going to do everything by the book and correctly. Remaining motivated would be my state of mind for this entire field problem.

We received our warning order from one of the RIs and went back to our platoon and immediately began the planning phase of our mission, which was a platoon raid on a small enemy complex. We also had a vehicle movement to our drop-off point. So I had to add a vehicle movement on our annex portion of our platoon operations order. The platoon sergeant is always responsible for writing this portion of the operations order, and then overseeing the loading and unloading of each vehicle to ensure proper accountability. After we dismounted the trucks, we would have a five-kilometer movement on foot to our objective. The terrain looked relatively dry for this mission—thank the Lord.

After I handed the platoon leader my written portion of the operations order, I went over with the medic and FO and began constructing the terrain model. Same standard as described earlier. We issued the order to the platoon and conducted rehearsals on movement techniques and actions on the objective. Once all this was complete, we loaded the LMTVs and moved out to conduct our first mission of Florida, or what was called the swamp phase.

We dismounted the vehicles, and the platoon leader directed what direction we needed to move out. I checked all the vehicles to ensure no student remained on, having perhaps fallen asleep, and ensured nobody had left any equipment. I gave a thumbs-up to the platoon leader, went to the front of the platoon, took a knee, and the medic and I counted everybody out for our movement toward our objective.

About a kilometer into the movement, we got hit with enemy small arms fire to our front. Everybody immediately got down, took off our rucks and waited for the platoon leader's directions. The lead squad got on line and began returning fire as per standard operating procedure. The platoon leader moved up in order to assess the situation. He quickly made the decision to have the lead squad maneuver up and conduct a frontal assault by fire team. Apparently, it was two enemy personnel, and it seemed to be the fastest way to destroy them, instead of conducting a flanking movement. The two fire teams conducted three- to five-second rushes while one team supported the other. Once one team was set, the other would move up. They did this until they assaulted through the bad guys and killed them. We then consolidated and reorganized, searched the dead bodies, sent up the report, and continued the mission. The RIs did not assess any friendly casualties. It was pretty quick and to the standard.

After about another three and half kilometers, we went into our security halt, and moved into our objective rally point. I thought it went relatively smooth and without any issues or hiccups. It was still daylight, so we were moving a little bit ahead of schedule, and that was a good thing. The mentality in Ranger School was the faster you complete your mission, the more sleep you may be able to get.

"All right, Rangers, listen up," one of the RIs sounded off. It was leadership changeover. After he gave out the new positions, he said, "Okay, you guys go ahead and switch out your equipment and get yourselves squared away." It was pretty standard procedure, and we were all used to how this worked by this point. Nothing came as a surprise—yet.

The RIs took former leadership off to the side and gave us our after-action reviews individually. My instructor gave me pretty much all good remarks, but I was still nervous. I mean, it was natural in this environment to want to know if you passed or failed.

I asked, "So, Sergeant, what do you think—"

He quickly cut me off. "Hey, Ranger, did I tell you that you needed to improve on anything?"

"No, Sergeant."

"Okay then, that should tell you all you want to know. Now, you help your squad out because they're going to need all the help they can get, you hear me?"

"Roger, Sergeant, and I will," I replied. Fuck yes! It happened again! Without telling me whether I officially passed, he pretty much hinted that I was a go. I said to myself, *That's it! I did it! I just got a go in Florida phase.* I was so stoked and pumped up. I promised myself that I was going to bust my ass to help my squad and the rest of the platoon out. I would volunteer to help wherever they needed me from now until this field exercise was over—and I did.

I went back to the platoon and asked if any of the squad leaders needed a team leader or anything else.

"No, we're good; thanks, man. You just got done with your graded patrol. Take a break and just be a rifleman in your squad. Maybe next mission, brother."

This is what the new platoon leader told me in front of the squad leaders.

"Okay, just let me know how I can help."

They were good guys, and we were taking care of each other, but in the next couple of days, it got really rough. However, that was to be expected. After all, we were in the "run phase" of this program, and we knew it was going to be the hardest.

A couple of days and a couple of complete twenty-four-hour missions later, it was time to knock out our first mission that had a boat movement, major swamp movement by foot, and a river crossing to boot. We were so hungry and tired. It was going to be another platoon raid on a small enemy complex. Most of our missions during this phase were raids, with extremely long movements to each objective. Also, by this point in Ranger School, we all started noticing something else. There was a strong, odd odor in the air, but I had heard about this throughout the years prior to making it to this course myself. The odor was ammonia, and it got stronger the closer we got to one another. It was the smell of our muscle tissue burning in our bodies. After the body burns most of its fatty tissue, and there's no more to burn or very little left, it begins burning muscle. The smell is literally the stench of ammonia. So be it; suck it up and drive on. We had to get through this next tough mission.

After the operations order and rehearsals, we loaded trucks and headed toward the river. We got to the riverbank, secured one zodiac watercraft per squad, and began loading them. Each zodiac had an RI on board, sitting on a little fold-out stool in the back of the boat. RIs with their little folding chairs were a pretty common sight, and they usually carried them on the back of their LCEs each mission. Also, it was common down in Florida to see them moving with walking sticks too. The walking sticks were nicely carved out, usually with some kind of design on the top.

We began moving down the river, and as we did, everybody was quiet and remained tactical. I remember thinking, *Now, this is some real Ranger high-speed shit.* After about two hours of paddling, it started to suck. It was kind of funny, because as we moved in silence, you could hear stomachs growling. Then, as we went around this particular corner, one of the funniest, most memorable comments and moments happened during my time in Ranger School. There was an older guy in a small boat fishing. With him he had a small chihuahua sitting up and staring at us as we paddled by.

"You boys in the Navy?" he asked.

The Ranger behind me replied, "No, we're in the Army."

Then it happened. The guy in front of me looked at the man and asked with a real strong Southern accent, "Hey—what you gonna do with that dog?" Everybody on our boat quickly turned toward the older man and waited for his response. He never offered one. We went about our business and continued paddling on. About a minute later, when we were away from him, the RI busted out in laughter.

"Rangers, do you all realize what the fuck you just asked that old man?"

"Roger, Sergeant. We wanted to eat his fucking dog."

I swear we would have in a heartbeat. One thing you realize in this school is that human beings are animals too, and you will eat anything when you're literally starving.

After about six hours of moving down the river, we arrived at our debarkation point and would move the rest of the way on foot to our objective. It was probably around 1300 or 1400, and we would not see dry land again until well after dark. We remained in waist and chest-deep swamp water this entire movement until we got to the river we had to cross. Everybody fell down periodically from tripping over tree roots that we could not see under the water. These swamp movements were definitely the worst of any phase. I'd rather have been moving through the mountains again. At least we could see what we were stepping on or through.

The guy in front of me turned and told me, "Hey, dude, I just shit my pants, so move out of the way." I didn't care at this point because I just wanted this movement to be over with and couldn't wait to see dry land again. By now, nobody would have a solid shit anyway. I know I didn't.

After about four or five hours, we made it to the river. Since we'd been submerged in water, the only sign we were at the river was that it was a wide-open area. We wanted to get across it before it got dark, and we were cutting it really close, as it was dusk already. We didn't waste any time at all. The rope man swam across the river with a security guy. There was a boat standing by with instructors and medical personnel aboard for safety purposes. Remember what I mentioned earlier about the students that had died out here about seven years prior. The cadre took no chances with our safety, especially since it was late October, and the temperature was a lot cooler.

Once the rope was secured and tied off to the anchor points, we tied our sling ropes and secured them around our chests. We made sure our wet-weather bags were tied up completely inside our rucks, in order to ensure our gear inside would remain dry while we crossed. We all went one at a time, snapped into the rope, and began shimmying across the river. Man, it was deep, and those eighty-pound rucks weighted us down. The goal was to get across as quickly as possible, get out of the river, and get counted out by the platoon sergeant. Once we all got across and were counted, we moved into a security halt on a nearby area of higher ground. Finally, we had made it to dry land!

Once in the security halt, the RIs made us all change into dry uniforms in order to prevent hypothermia because the temperature was dropping, as it was already completely dark. They then called off the next chain of command for the actions-on portion of our raid mission. We were smoked, especially after six hours on the river and that bullshit five-hour movement through the swamp. We definitely were not looking forward to doing that again. At this point, I don't think any of us knew what day we were on or how many days we had left of this field exercise. I'm pretty sure the previous leadership had all gotten gos on the planning and the two major movements because everything seemed to go pretty smoothly with the land navigation and the river crossing. I can't say the same for the actions-on leadership that night. Our first river-crossing swamp movement was a failed mission for the actual raid portion. I'll explain.

Once the equipment was turned over, the platoon leader told the RIs we were prepared to move out. The platoon sergeant counted us out, and we began moving again. I think we had like a three or four-klick movement. We didn't get too far, and we were already heading off course from our azimuth we were supposed to be on. The assigned platoon leader for this portion did not correct the direction we were moving, and the RI had to correct him. I'm not going to sugarcoat it; we were all walking zombies at this point.

"PL, what azimuth are you supposed to be on?"

"Such-and-such degrees, Sergeant."

"Well, are you fucking aware that you're not even close to that right now?" He halted the patrol, got with the point man, and checked his compass, trying to get him straight. I walked up to the platoon leader and asked if he wanted me to take over as the Alpha Team leader and take point. He came back like an ass and told me no, that he wanted to keep his buddy up there.

"Okay, roger that," I told him. I think they were lieutenant buddies, and I was all right with that. It wasn't my patrol. I tried—right? Anyway, we started moving again, and within a matter of minutes, we were off azimuth again.

"That's it, PL, stop! Everybody just fucking stop! That's the third time we've run off course, Rangers! PL, this is your last chance to get this platoon moving in the right fucking direction. I'm going to tell you that right now." I would have taken that as a hint that maybe it was time to find a new point man, but I knew what he was doing. It was his Ranger buddy, and he didn't want to offend him. In this place, you had to do what you had to do sometimes for the good of the mission, or it was going to cost you and the rest of the leadership. For this mission, it did just that.

We went off course again for the fourth time, and the RIs had enough. "Stop, Rangers! Just stop! This is a failed mission, PL. Your platoon has failed to move in the correct direction four times now, and you didn't do shit about it. Rangers, give me a patrol base right here. PL, once you're properly set in, put them to sleep."

I remember feeling bad, but I had offered to help and was pretty much told to fuck off. Once in my position on the perimeter, I pulled my poncho liner out of my ruck and pulled out my wet boots and uniform from the previous movement to dry out. I used my field jacket liner as my pillow on my kidney pad on my ruck, threw my wooby on top of me, and it was nighty-night time. Yeah, I felt bad because I had just watched all the leadership get a no-go. I felt bad for about thirty seconds and then fell asleep. It was about 0100 in the morning. Our hit time on the objective was supposed to have been an hour prior, but we hadn't moved more than a klick and a half before they finally stopped us. Welcome to the reality of Florida Phase.

About four hours later, the instructors woke us up. We could smell the fresh soap and deodorant, so it must have been their RI changeover. "Let's go, Rangers. Get around, conduct personal hygiene, and recamo your faces. The medics will be around to check on you all. The same leadership will remain in place." I remember thinking that it was cool that they were going to get another patrol—this time planning.

"PL, you're not getting your next mission until this afternoon. This morning the platoon has a survival class."

After the medics checked us, we packed up our gear, and the RIs led us out to a nearby firebreak. We walked down it for about an hour and got to our destination around 0900. "Ground your gear in formation, Rangers, and get into the bleachers."

It was an outdoor classroom setting—a set of bleachers with an overhead cover. Pretty standard to see throughout all three phases. It resembled a planning bay for field operations. Off to the side was a wild boar hanging on a wooden structure. It had been already gutted and cleaned, and looked like it was ready to cook and eat. We were so excited because we thought we were going to be able to eat it. That is what we all thought during this entire first class.

We received a full block of instruction on how to gut and clean the boar, but like any other class in Ranger School, it was hard to keep our eyes open. The thought of being able to eat this thing kept most of us awake and excited to be there, doing something other than walking through the woods or the swamps. When the block of instruction was over, the RI giving us the class gave us all some very disappointing news.

"You won't be able to eat any of this, Rangers! About ten years ago you could have, but now the Army says we have to feed you domesticated animals for this class."

The whole platoon at the same time cried out, "Awwww."

Another RI walked out in front of us with a chicken in his arms, and he was petting it. "This is the domesticated animal that you will be eating today, Rangers! It is a nice chicken. Plump and very lively, Rangers! One thing about this animal that makes it very easy to kill, Rangers, is that it's head will come off relatively easy!" He then grabbed the chicken's head as he was petting it and ripped it clear off and threw it over our heads.

"Oh shit!" we all cried out. It was a shocking moment that we weren't expecting. He then placed the chicken, as it was still kicking, upside down in a coffee can to allow the blood to drain out of it. It lay in the coffee can kicking back and forth for about fifteen seconds before it finally stopped. Now I learned where that *running around like a chicken with its head cut off* phrase came from. He then gave us the class on how to properly clean it.

Once that class was complete, the instructors gave each squad a live chicken, and it was time to go to work. Each squad received the chicken, about three coffee cans, a five-gallon container of water, and a bunch of carrots and sticks of celery. It was awesome; the RIs actually brought us carrots and celery to go with our chicken! This was heaven!

I grabbed the chicken, secured its legs with my hand, put my boot on its neck and pulled up, popping its head off like a dandelion. Then I placed it upside down in one of our coffee cans. Once it was dead, we wasted no time. We began cleaning it, ripped off its feathers and chopped it up. Other squad members chopped up the vegetables. We were going to make ourselves some homemade chicken soup, goddamn it! We set the three coffee cans over our little fire and boiled the pieces of chicken and the vegetables in the water. We made sure it was cooked thoroughly enough, and then everybody got our canteen cups and an MRE spoon out and went to town. Everybody in our twelve or thirteen-man squad got an even cupful. I took out some hot sauce and a salt packet and had myself a nice cup of hot, fresh, chicken soup. It was awesome, and we starving grown men didn't even fight over the chow like I thought we would. There was good comradery among our squad. We talked about what the RIs were going to do with that wild hog. We knew they were going to have a cookout with it, and that it wouldn't go to waste. Man, we wished we could have been a part of that one. Anyway, we ate our canteen cups of chicken soup like it was our last meal.

After the little "treat" of our survival class, it was back to combat missions and the bullshit. It was time for an operations order, planning, rehearsals, and a long-ass movement with another raid mission. Like I said earlier, the instructors had left in the same leadership that had the failed mission last night, which was pretty cool. They all got another chance, and we were going to pull together to help them be successful. Especially now that we'd had four hours of sleep and food in our stomachs! We were motivated to get going with the realization that we were closer to getting out of this field exercise. I believe we did the mission with no issues, and the leadership were probably all gos.

The next day's mission was our second boat swamp-movement river-crossing mission. This time they added a helicopter insertion along with it. We were dreading it after we received the order. We had it in our minds that this was going to be the ass-smoker of all ass-smokers. Come to find out, it wasn't as long or grueling a movement by boat or foot as the first water mission had been. The boat movement was about two hours, and the swamp movement was about another two hours. We knocked out the river crossing with no issues. This mission got started a lot earlier than the first one did too. We were on the river in our zodiacs as the sun was coming up, and we were across the river by around 1700 hours. Once on dry land again, we changed into dry uniforms and headed for our landing zone to get picked up by the birds. Once at the LZ, the RIs did the leadership changeover, and we were to conduct another raid on an enemy complex after landing. At this point, I was so weak that I could no longer put my rucksack on over my head and slide my arms through the shoulder straps, like I had up until Florida Phase. Now, I had to sit on the ground and lean back and slide my arms through the straps, tighten them down and have another Ranger pull me to my feet.

Once the choppers landed, we boarded and buckled ourselves in. We were on UH-60 Blackhawks, and I will never forget what came next. I had heard rumors about this in the past but had kind of forgotten up until this point because we were so smoked. The pilots brought each of us a bag of McDonald's. In each bag, we had quarter pounders, fries, and a Snickers candy bar. You would have thought we all died and went to heaven. In fact, I remember almost seventeen years later that my Snickers candy bar was in the yellow wrapper, which meant it was a Snickers with almonds. That is how vividly I remember this meal.

The pilots told us we had to eat it all before we took off. Shit, they didn't have to worry about that! We ate that meal like someone was going to try to take it from us. This meal from the pilots was a Ranger School 6th RTB tradition that dated back to the sixties. I'll explain. This particular flight unit had a helicopter crash back then, and a platoon of Ranger students were in the area and came to their rescue. They ended up saving and pulling the pilots from the crash site. So, it is a tradition that the pilots pay back each Ranger class with a meal in appreciation. That's a true story.

After a couple more days and a couple of missions, we were almost done with the field exercise. We were on our final mission of Florida Phase, and our final twenty-four hours out in that shit. This was the final, biggest mission of Ranger School, a long movement into a hasty defensive position. From there, we were to move out and conduct a vehicle movement, a boat movement across the Gulf of Mexico (about a mile or so), land on Santa Rosa Island, conduct a raid on the enemy headquarters compound, and, finally, conduct a helicopter extraction. At this point, being at our end and so tired and hungry, I was glad my leadership graded position was over—or was it? One of the most shocking and depressing moments of my experience in Ranger School was about to happen.

After we walked all day and arrived at our patrol base location, we were to dig hasty fighting positions and partner up with another student for security. Once we got ours dug and were set in, I pulled out an MRE and began chowing that son of a bitch down, like it was my last meal on death row in San Quentin. It was dark by this time. I got done with my main meal, and started pulling security so that my Ranger buddy could eat his.

We were waiting to hear the changeover roster numbers for the actions-on leadership change. The RI began calling out the numbers for our final mission. "Roster Number Five Zero—platoon sergeant!"

I looked at my partner and said, "Wow, it sounded like he said Roster Number Five Zero."

He replied with a sad tone, "Ah, he did, brother."

"What the fuck?" I immediately started feeling sorry for myself and got sick to my stomach.

"Let's go, Rangers. Get up here and get your changeover!" Since it was dark, he sounded off with our roster numbers to ensure we were all there. I mean, it was dark as shit. You couldn't see two feet in front of you.

"Roster Number Five Zero."

"Here, Sergeant."

"Don't sound so sad, Ranger. It's your final mission." He then pulled me off to the side. He explained to me, though I pretty much already knew the deal, "Hey, listen, Five Zero, the PL is going to need your help to get him through this. He already has a failure this class, and as I'm sure you already know, these guys are mostly recycles. So we need you to help get him through, Ranger."

"Yes, Sergeant," I assured him.

"All right then, get your equipment changed over and get everybody prepared for move out."

"Yes, Sergeant."

Damn it, I said to myself. Man, this was a vehicle and boat movement across the fucking ocean (at least a mile), the mission itself, and then a helicopter extraction to boot. I had my work cut out for me. Arrive at the cutting edge of battle by air, land, and sea, right?

Okay, Nate, suck it up and quit feeling sorry for yourself, motherfucker, I told myself. *You have a job to do, so make it happen and you'll be out of here once and for all.*

When the LMTVs pulled up, we got everybody loaded up, and I got accountability and let the platoon leader know we were good to go. He gave the report up to the RI, and we moved out for our final mission of Army Ranger School.

After about a half-hour drive, we got to the beach. Each squad unloaded our zodiacs off a parked trailer that was there waiting for us. I got accountability of the platoon, reported it, and we began loading the boats. I was very careful and paid close attention to detail. After all, it was dark (very dark), and I was at my end, both physically and mentally—we all were. I'm sure that's just the way Ranger School wanted us at this point.

We paddled to the island. This was actually a battalion mission with each company having their own mission and section of the compound to assault. Our platoon's portion was to clear and secure the first two buildings. The boat movement actually didn't take as long as I thought it would. A mile and a half or so doesn't take long to get across. The water was pretty calm, believe it or not. I was impressed by how smooth this operation was going thus far, but it wasn't going to be smooth for long.

We landed on the beach and began our assault on the first building. We set up a support by fire on one of the larger sand dunes, and then, once set, the platoon leader took up the first squad and went to enter the building. At this point, we weren't taking fire and seemed to have the element of surprise, so we did not open up with the guns as the initial squad moved up. Once they got close enough, the enemy began shooting at them. We opened up on the building to the left, while they moved around to the entrance of the target building on the right. Once inside, the next squad moved up to enter the building. I left with them because we started getting casualties within our platoon, and I needed to establish a casualty collection point. When the second squad entered the building, I asked what room was secured first. I marked it as the casualty collection point with a red cross made with red chemical lights.

It happened so fast that by the time we were in the building, it was secured but chaotic with screaming. There were already enemy prisoners being guarded, and while the medic was triaging the couple of casualties we had, I called up the third squad and told support by fire to collapse and enter the building. The next building needed to be assaulted; we were starting to bunch up inside Building One.

The platoon leader was fucking around with the prisoners and worried about our casualties that the medic was tending to. I told him, "Hey, PL, you need to take the next squad and begin your assault on Building Two!" He wasn't moving. I commanded, "Second and third squads to line up and prepare to take Building Two! Weapons squad will secure outside and the couple rooms in here! Let's go, sir. You need to move out with the assault element on the next building. We're losing our momentum, goddamn it!"

The RI was standing there just watching and observing our situation.

I then commanded, "Second squad, begin your assault on Building Two! PL, you need to follow and command them!" He was still so worried about the casualties and prisoners. I was getting more pissed off by the second. I walked over to him, grabbed him by the back of his LCE, picked him up, and practically threw him out the fucking door after the assault element.

Second and third squads cleared the second building and took another two casualties. The medic and I went over and picked them up and brought them back to the casualty collection point in Building One. Each squad gave their reports over the radio. I walked back to the second building and grabbed the few other "enemy soldiers" they had captured and brought them back with a couple guys to watch them from the third squad. We consolidated and reorganized, called in the MEDEVAC for our casualties, and the walking wounded were simply going to fly out with us. Our portion of the objective was secured.

The senior RI that overwatched our platoon sounded off with, "Change of mission, Rangers! PL and platoon sergeant, get accountability of all equipment and form them up out back."

"Roger, Sergeant, WILCO!" *WILCO* is radio lingo for "will comply." That was pretty much it for our last mission, other than the flight out back to Camp Rudder.

"Okay, Rangers, somebody get your platoon out on the road behind this village and move them down until you get to the clearing. Once there, stand by for us to link up with you all."

"Roger, Sergeant," we replied. He came back over to me and told me to stand by, that he wanted to talk with me on the way out there one-on-one. I remember thinking, *Now what?*

"Yes, Sergeant," I replied to him.

The platoon headed out to the open beach area down the road. Once they left, me and the senior instructor took off about ten minutes behind them. He just wanted to shoot the shit with me, because he too had been assigned to my regiment back at Bragg prior to coming to 6th RTB.

"Hey, good job back there, Ranger. You did a strong job."

"Ah shit, I thought I was in trouble for being a little rough on the platoon leader during the assault. How did he do, by the way?"

"He'll probably pass, thanks to you getting him out of that first building. I'm telling you, if he hadn't gotten out of there, he would have been a no-go."

"All right, that's good. I don't want to see him fail, especially since I was assigned to help him pass." He was a good instructor and was cool with me. After all, realistically he knew what rank I was. It wasn't favoritism, either. I believe I did a good job during this phase and helped out as much as I could. Anyway, we finally linked up with the rest of the platoon as the sun was coming over the ocean.

"Okay, Rangers. Everybody go ahead and relax. You all did a

pretty good job last night. Sit back against your rucks and enjoy the view. It's going to be a little bit before the birds arrive, Rangers."

I sat there on the white sand beach, leaning up against my ruck. We all simply stared out at the ocean as the sun rose. The seagulls flew overhead, and waves crashed against the shore. It was one of the most peaceful scenes and moments of my life. I was in a state of euphoria as I stared out on this beautiful moment.

It's over. It's all over. No more worrying about getting through this school. No more dick-measuring contests back in my unit at Bragg. These were the thoughts running through my head. I also wondered how my Ranger buddy, Germany, had done during this phase. I was sure he'd done just fine.

Two CH-47 Chinook helicopters landed behind us on the other side of the small road.

"All right, Rangers, everybody police up your equipment and load up the aircraft. We're headed back to Rudder!" We all cheered and clapped, got our shit on, got into two single-file lines, and boarded the aircraft.

Once back on Camp Rudder, we all marched over to our classroom, the same one where we had received the animal class prior to heading out to the field. We grounded all our equipment except for our weapons and went inside the classroom to conduct our squad peer evaluations. After every phase, that was the very first event they had us complete prior to anything else. The logic being they wanted all events to still be fresh in our minds.

"All right, Rangers, you know the deal by now. Be honest with yourselves and with your squads when filling out your peer ratings—and stay awake. Wake up back there, Ranger!" We were smoked, and it was difficult to keep our eyes open. All we cared about was getting our end-of-phase hotdog meals.

After we were done with our peer ratings, we went outside, secured our equipment and were told to head back to the barracks to get cleaned up. We got showered up and put on fresh BDUs out of our duffle bags. That hot shower after coming out of this ten-day field maneuver was the best, as expected. We got back outside the barracks and formed up with our weapons. We were told to begin cleaning our squad and platoon equipment and not to worry about our weapons yet; that would be later. Man, we just kept thinking about our hotdog dinner.

That afternoon, the RIs started calling us into our company headquarters to receive our final-phase after-actions reviews while we were cleaning our equipment outside.

"Roster Number Five Zero, come on in, Ranger." I went running across the road and into the building. I was feeling so good, nothing like I had felt when I was about to receive my final review in the Mountains. I knew I had two gos during my combat patrols, no spot reports, and I was sure I was going to get a high peer rating, especially after helping out as much as I had.

"Have a seat, Ranger." It was the sergeant first class that had graded me on the final patrol from the 82nd. "Okay, you got two passing grades on patrols, zero negative spot reports." I noticed he didn't mention peer evaluations yet. "You got peered last, Ranger. You will be boarded by the company commander first thing tomorrow morning."

I looked at him with the biggest look of confusion. "What the fuck, Sergeant? What's this shit all about?"

"I guess they got pissed off at how you were up their asses on that final mission. Again, I'm guessing."

I sat there in such disbelief and disgust with those motherfuckers. I just put my head down, crossed my arms, and began shaking my head. All I could think about was going back outside and beating the hell out of every single one of those buddy-fuckers. He began to reassure me. "I'm going to talk to the senior instructor after this and then we're going to talk to the CO. We're going to explain what exactly happened, and that we both believe that they tried to fuck you in order to save their own asses on the peer evals. I wouldn't worry too much about it tonight or lose any sleep over it. I think you're going to be all right, Ranger."

I'm sure he could tell how pissed I was because then he added, "Also, DO NOT go back to those guys and start any shit with them whatsoever, like I know you want to. I can see it in your eyes. Don't worry, Ranger, I'd be pissed too. You're one of the only enlisted in the squad, and they tried to peer you last. We were with your platoon the entire field problem, off and on, and you did a good job, like you were asked in the beginning of the phase. Now, I'm not going to sit here and guarantee you that you won't get recycled, but I think you'll be all right. Now, you go start any shit with them after this, you sure as shit will get into trouble and not only recycled, but probably even worse than that. So, keep your head cool and just ignore them. Okay, Ranger?"

I looked at him and, still shaking my head, replied, "Roger, Sergeant." I then got up and walked out.

I didn't go back to my squad and platoon. Instead, I went straight to the barracks and paced around our bay in disbelief, talking to myself. How the hell could they have done this to me? I mean, the platoon leader had gotten a go because of *my* actions. How did I know for sure? Because the fucking RI had *told* me to my face that he was going to be all right. And to think, I was actually worried for the little prick.

This was the reality of Ranger School. Not only do the students have to worry about meeting the standard on all the tasks, but the *real* worry is getting on the bad side of the instructors and your student peers. First, I had to worry about not getting out of Mountain Phase for pissing off those couple of asshole RIs at the end, and now I had to worry about getting out of Florida because of this handful of National Guard lieutenants. Why? Because I hurt their feelings on the final mission? I guess I yelled at them too much to do their fucking jobs, right?

Okay, Nate, shake it off, and get your ass outside. Don't say a fucking word to those fuckheads. Just finish cleaning the equipment and get the shit turned in, and then you can go enjoy your hotdogs.

When I got back outside and linked back up with the squad, nobody said shit to me, but I waited for it. I was going to keep my cool, just like the RI warned me to. As a matter of fact, none of those cowards would even look at me. The RIs continued to call more students inside to give them their AARs. I remained as quiet and professional as I could be under the circumstances.

After we turned in our platoon equipment, I walked over to the other company and linked up with Germany. He had gotten an overall go in the phase, and Ranger School as a whole. I was happy for him, but I would have been happier if I had known what my future was going to be. All I knew was that if I had to recycle this phase, it was going to be the end of me. It was the worst ass-smoking I took in the entire course and definitely throughout my twenty years in the Army. I'm not exaggerating, either.

At this point, I simply stayed with my Ranger buddy the remainder of the night and stayed away from that platoon and fucked-up squad of mine. I told him the story about what I had to deal with, and he couldn't believe it. He then told me not to worry about, that the RIs were going to "have my back."

I said, "Yeah, you're right. Let's get our hotdog meal." We got three hotdogs, a bag of chips, and a candy bar this time!

They fed us outside the Gator Lounge, on the patio. The RIs even let us go inside and have a couple of beers. It was heaven on earth. I think I had three beers. Although I could have stayed in there all night, I figured I'd better cut myself off and leave the lounge. Surprisingly, the instructors were pretty much hands off the rest of that night. I left, went back up to the barracks, and went to sleep. I had a busy morning ahead of me.

The next morning at around 0500, we were downstairs in formation. We marched over to the mess hall, sounded off with the Ranger Creed, and knocked out our pull-ups. Well, sort of. We were all pretty weak, so we all helped each other out by lifting one another's legs so that we could knock out six. It was our last breakfast and meal all together at the Camp Rudder dining facility. Scrambled eggs, hash browns, and sausage, with some pancakes to boot! Damn, that was awesome food!

After breakfast, we were to draw our weapons from the arms room and begin cleaning them. That was our entire task for that day until it was time to leave and fly back to Fort Benning, Georgia. Our duffle bags and rucksacks were already packed, and our uniforms were washed and cleaned. I had a little task before cleaning weapons. Actually, so did my entire squad. The senior RI came out of the headquarters and called for me and then told the entire squad to march over on their own and stand by outside until he came out and got them.

I went inside and reported to the company commander. I stopped in front of his desk, conducted a left face, saluted him and sounded off with, "Sir, Roster Number Five Zero reporting as ordered, sir!"

He returned the salute and replied, "At ease, Ranger. Roster Number Five Zero, do you know why you are before this board this morning?"

"Yes, sir."

"It says here that your squad peered you low. Do you have any reason why they would, Ranger?"

"Yes, sir, I believe they're upset with me because on Santa Rosa Island, I was yelling at the platoon leader to go after and lead the assault element on the raid. For whatever reason, sir, he refused to do anything. I finally physically grabbed his LCE and pushed him out to follow them, sir. Had he not gone with them, I was going to take over his duties as platoon leader and put the weapons squad leader in charge of the casualty collection point and the prisoner guards in order to oversee the completion of our mission, sir."

The CO came back with, "Okay, Ranger, that's pretty much what Sergeant So-and-so [the RI] told me happened out there. You pretty much helped Roster Number So-and-so receive a passing grade. Okay, Sergeant, call in Roster Number Five Zero's squad."

When the squad filed in, they were instructed by the captain to stand directly behind me.

"Okay, Five Zero, you're going to turn around and your squad is going to tell you why each one of them peered you last."

"Roger, sir," I replied. I did an about-face and stood at the position of attention. The CO ordered me to stand at ease. He then asked the squad to raise their hands if they would follow me in combat and if they believed I was tactically and technically proficient. I couldn't wait for this reaction. As I thought, every hand in the squad went up. Starting from the left, each member was to tell me their reasoning for their decision.

The first student went ahead. "I peered you last because you became out of control on the final objective and physically put your hands on Roster Number So-and-so, and I believe that was unnecessary."

"Roster Five Zero, go ahead and respond to your classmate, Ranger," the commander ordered.

I looked at him very humbly and said, "I understand your frustration, but it was combat, number one. Number two, had I not forced him to follow and lead the assault element, he definitely would have been a no-go on the mission. That's why I did what I did." He just nodded, almost in agreement.

The next member of the squad said to me, "I peered you last because, well, I mean, well, somebody has to be last."

The commander slammed his fist down on his desk and began yelling at the top of his voice.

"What the fuck kind of answer is that, Ranger? Somebody has to be fucking last? That is not a legitimate reason under any circumstance to peer anybody in this fucking school last!"

He was pissed!

"Roster Number Five Zero, turn around and face me!"

I did an about-face.

"Ranger, I think I know what's going on here. I've seen this kind of shit before. You're going back to Fort Benning this afternoon with the rest of the class to graduate in a couple of days. You are dismissed, Ranger, and good luck to you."

I saluted him and said, "Rangers lead the way, sir!"

He returned the salute and replied, "All the way!"

I conducted a left face and marched out of his hooch. He didn't even wait for me to fully leave before he began yelling at the squad. When I got outside, the senior instructor was waiting on me.

"Remain cool, and don't do anything that's going to keep you here, Ranger. Good job and congratulations." I shook his hand and thanked him—"Roger, Sergeant"—and moved out to clean our weapons.

When the squad came out and linked back up with the platoon, which was about a half hour later, it was pretty quiet at first. I couldn't hold back anymore and had to say my piece—but did it calmly.

"Your little plot against me backfired on your sorry asses, didn't it?"

They didn't say shit back to me.

I finished by telling them, "This is the last thing I'm going to say to you shitbags. Don't ever let me catch you out there in the real Army after this school. It ain't gonna be pretty, boys. I'm done with y'all." There, I had said my piece to their sorry faces. Hell, I don't even think but a couple of them even left. I believe the majority of them were recycled again.

Like Forrest Gump would say, "That's all I have to say about that."

After we turned in our weapons for the final time, we went upstairs and got our duffle bags. We came back downstairs with our gear, and I walked right back to my original company and platoon. I didn't even ask; I just did it. Fuck it. Nobody said shit, either. I was back with my platoon from Darby and Mountains again. It was like a little reunion. We all sat down on our bags and waited on the buses to take us to the airfield. Once there, two C-130s were waiting to fly us back to Fort Benning. We loaded, and by early evening, we were back at Camp Rogers where it started and would end in the next couple of days after equipment turn-in and out-processing.

We graduated at Victory Pond, and it was an awesome ceremony. My old buddy and boss, Tim from the Trail, and his wife came to the graduation. He was stationed at Fort Rucker, Alabama, which really wasn't that far away of a drive from Fort Benning. I was so relieved to have finally graduated from this course that had been a monkey on my back for years.

After eating a great meal at Golden Corral, I said my goodbyes to Tim and Germany. I drove back to Fort Bragg, North Carolina. About three weeks later, I linked up with my battalion in Iraq. However, there was one thing I had to do first—link up and go visit my old platoon sergeant and mentor: First Sergeant P.

He was the first sergeant at the time of Headquarters Company of the 82nd Airborne itself, which was a pretty prestigious first sergeant position—probably the biggest in the whole damn division. He had already made the E-9 selection list and was getting ready to PCS to the Sergeant Major's Academy, which was the final NCO academy in the US Army.

He gave me a big hug when he saw me walk into his office at his company. He looked at my newly sewn Ranger tab on my left shoulder. It was the first time he actually treated me like a peer and not one of his subordinates. He wished me luck on my upcoming deployment to Operation Iraqi Freedom and told me to be very careful. I gave him one last hug. That was the last time I ever saw one of the biggest mentors that I had in my twenty years in the Army.

**SERGEANT FIRST CLASS AUGI.
FRESH OUT OF US ARMY RANGER SCHOOL**

CHAPTER 14

IRAQ
JUST SOUTH OF BAHGDAD

THE MOST IMPORTANT individuals in combat are your medics and surgeons. Thank you, God, for these individuals; that's no bullcrap. Our battalion in the 505th Parachute Infantry Regiment, 82nd Airborne Division, was headquartered in Mahmudiyah, Iraq, at Forward Operating Base (FOB) Saint Michael. It was named Saint Michael after an enemy mortar round landed on the roof of the chicken processing factory that our battalion cleaned and began housing our companies in while we, along with engineers, were building the back forty of the rest of the FOB. The mortar round was a dud and did not explode. If it had detonated, it would have killed dozens, if not more, of the paratroopers in our battalion. The name quickly became *Saint Michael, Protector of Paratroopers*, right after that miracle.

I arrived with about three other soldiers coming in from Fort Bragg, and there he was, Command Sergeant Major Z, waiting for our LMTV to arrive at the battalion headquarters building. I jumped off the back of the truck, and he grabbed a hold of me, gave me a little hug, and looked directly at my left shoulder to see me newly sewn Ranger tab. "All right Sergeant A. I have a platoon for you in Alpha Company, like I promised. Let me introduce you to your new company first sergeant and commander." He then asked, "How did they treat you in school?"

I replied with, "Very good Sergeant Major—no issues at all." I didn't mention all the drama, because it happens in every class, and it wasn't worth wasting my breath over it. That chapter of my life was over, and I had bigger things to dwell on—like combat.

This area of Iraq became known to Coalition Forces as the "triangle of death." The triangle, formed by the cities of Yusufiyah to the northwest, Latifiyah to the south, and Mahmudiyah to the east, held the fastest routes from Baghdad southward to the Shiite shrines in Najaf and Karbala. The major terrain feature of the triangle of death was the Euphrates River, which bordered the triangle to the southwest. The terrain was mostly farmland but was sliced by many irrigation ditches. These areas were also surrounded by hundreds of rural villages as well.

My platoon and I had just finished a daily patrol in a neighborhood in Latifiyah. It was my company's primary sector of responsibility (Alpha Company). We were out conducting routine "knock and talks" with the local Iraqis, going house to house. We would ask the homeowners questions, such as if they had any information or concerns about any enemy activity within these neighborhoods. We would get the homeowners' names, ask them how many members were in their households, and if they had any weapons. We would also take a picture of them with their addresses.

Occasionally, we would come across a home where the owner would not open the door but would move the curtains, so we knew they were home, and immediately they became suspected of hiding something—usually weapons or bomb-making material. We would have to kick in their doors and search their homes. We'd have to blow the hinges off the door with a twelve-gauge shotgun and occasionally would find heavy weapon systems, take the two or three military-aged males from the home, zip-tie their hands behind their backs, and put sandbags over their heads. We would then take them back to the base with us and turn them over to our military intelligence interrogators.

One time, we found a Russian machine gun in a couch. Seriously. They had the springs torn out of it with a thin sheet of wood over it and had the cushions on top of that. Pretty sneaky, but we knew they were hiding something because they wouldn't open their door. We searched the small home and didn't find anything until I told one of my team leaders to take the fucking cushions off the couch, and low and behold, there it was. The owner tried to tell us he didn't know how it got there. He soon had a sandbag over his head and was heading back to FOB Saint Michael with us.

It wasn't always bad. I mean, we tried to make it as humanly fun as we could when we were in these villages. We passed out candy to the kids. Sometimes we'd even pull out dollar bills and give each one of these kids a dollar. Normally, we had about three or four kids that would just be hanging around our vehicles. The next thing you know, in a matter of ten minutes, the entire village's children would storm around us. "Mista, mista, mista," they'd say with their hands out for a dollar. The Iraqi locals always referred to us as "Mista." It wasn't bad; we didn't mind. Usually, we had someone with a portable CD player with some small speakers hooked up to them. We'd put them on the roof of the vehicles and play some current music at the time, like Jay-Z or the Black-Eyed Peas. We would clap our hands, and the kids would have a ball. We also had brand-new soccer balls we'd pass out to them, and they would go apeshit.

Soon, the short moments of fun would end, and it would be time to head back and remember we were in a war. "Time to head back, gentlemen. Let's go," I would have to tell my soldiers. It was hard to leave good moments like this, primarily because we all had families and children back home that we wished we could play with. In reality, though, we did not get too attached to these locals. The Sunni insurgency would figure out a way to kill them and their families if they got the word that they were getting too close to the Americans. It was as simple as that. It was black and white, with no gray area. Our

Iraqi interpreters were simply trying to earn a paycheck to feed and take care of their families. Unfortunately, they had to start leaving them. The bad guys started killing them off in their homes and killing their wives, too. So we ended up having them living on our base so that they could be protected and better hidden. Those insurgents were fucking savages—fact. Like the old Metallica song—"Sad but True."

Those rides back to base were pretty stressful because you just hoped to make it back without getting hit with an IED (improvised explosive device) or rocket-propelled grenade or simply getting ambushed with small arms fire, especially when driving through the congested crowds of downtown Mahmudiyah itself. I always feared someone lobbing a grenade inside our vehicle. That's why I always had my M-4 outside the window of my door, telling everyone, "Get the fuck back." This was about six to eight months before we started getting up-armored vehicles over there. Whenever our convoy would get downtown in those streets and our speeds dropped to ten miles per hour, our standard procedure was to dismount the vehicles and walk alongside the vehicles. This was with the exception of the drivers and gunners on top of each Humvee, of course.

One mission was to conduct a raid on a small complex. It was a battalion mission, and our company was the main effort. Delta Company was to secure the intersections that surrounded this small compound of about two or three houses, out in the middle of nowhere. Bravo Company was to have our internal support and security as well. Charlie Company was back pulling FOB security, which included manning the entrance gate. This was back when battalions were responsible for manning their own guard posts internally. Now, they usually have a separate unit pull the security. My last tour in Iraq, we had the Ugandan Army pulling the security on our FOB.

Anyway, we convoyed out to this little village around 0230, with a hit time of 0330 or something like that. It was only a few miles away. Our mission was to secure and capture two bad guys that were affiliated with Al Qaeda, and they were to be found within this compound. Delta Company led out first in order to get into their positions and block all the entrances into the compound. Once we arrived, each platoon in our company dismounted their vehicles. Usually, we would have at least two soldiers, such as the driver and another guy for security, to stay with each truck and guard them.

As we approached our assigned houses, we lined up by squads and began our entry procedures. I would move up with the initial breach squad, knock on the door and holler out, "Open up! Coalition Forces!" I immediately heard a female screaming inside the house. After about ten seconds, I gave the hand-and-arm signal to forcefully breach. We did this usually by kicking the door in after checking for wires around it. Once inside, we began clearing room by room. They didn't know we were coming because we always traveled with our vehicle headlights off. We had this shit down to a science.

Once cleared, we separated women and children and collected up the military-aged males and took them outside. We made them get on their knees with their heads down along the side of the home. Of course, we would put a couple of guys on them for security. The two males we got from our house were the targets we were after, which meant our platoon was responsible for securing them and taking them back to our base. They were positively identified as the targets from the Military Intelligence guy we had with us. We zip-tied their hands, put sandbags over their heads, and took them to our vehicles. Our platoon leader called it in to the company commander that we had them. He, in turn, called it in to the battalion commander, who was on site as well.

I went back inside with our interpreter and informed the females that we were taking these men back with us for an undetermined amount of time. A couple of them started crying and even screaming at us. I didn't care; they shouldn't have been trying to mortar and rocket our fucking FOB or blow up our fucking vehicles daily. "Let's go," I told the interpreter. "All blue elements, load up, separate the prisoners in two separate vehicles, and prepare to move out." Once the battalion commander gave the order, we moved off the complex and headed back to FOB Saint Michael. Again, I hoped that we wouldn't get hit with an IED on the way back.

Once back, I ordered the squads to lock and clear their weapons, and they reported back that they were all green. I told them to drop me off at the detention center on the back forty of the FOB. I then took the prisoners myself into the tent where we had cells built for them. I ordered the platoon to fill up the vehicles at the fuel point, unload all the equipment, and go eat chow. The sun was just coming up.

I entered the tent and turned the prisoners over to the guards in the inside. It smelled so disgusting in there, to the point that I will never forget it. The prisoners were kept in there for no more than about forty-eight to seventy-two hours. Then, after their interrogation process, they would get sent to bigger, actual prisons or even Guantanamo. I didn't really give two shits. Our job was to capture them from the battlefield. What they did with them afterward wasn't my concern.

When I walked into the door of the tent, one of the guards, a young Black soldier, hollered out, "Oh shit! Motherfuckin' Sergeant Augi's up in this motherfucker! Goddamn!"

The other guard said, "Man, Sergeant Augi's motherfuckin' *Clint Eastwood* up in this motherfucka!"

I said back to them, "I don't want to hear all the bullshit, gentlemen. Just take these two motherfuckers. Where's the sign-in sheet?" We had to annotate target numbers that the battalion provided (bad guys were marked by a target number), mission number, location of capture, and date and time. Once they got them in separate cells, they cut off the zip-ties and removed the sandbags from their heads.

"Man, Big Sarge, you da man up in this motherfucker!" the first guard said.

I just shook my head and said, "I'm going to get me some scrambled eggs and sausage. Did you boys get something to eat?"

"Oh, yeah, Big Sarge, we had an MRE when we first got on duty out here because the chow hall wasn't open yet."

"Okay, have a good one out here, and be careful."

"Thanks, Big Sarge!" the soldier said.

When I got to the mess hall, I ate my breakfast. When I left, I got two to-go containers for the two guards anyway. I loaded them up with eggs, bacon, some hash browns, and pancakes. I put two or three packets of butter, syrup, and salt and pepper in my cargo pockets for them, too. I even grabbed a bottle of Texas Pete hot sauce for them, because you cannot eat military scrambled eggs without it. It was our unwritten rule. I took it back to the detention center for them. When I walked in, you would have thought I had given them a million dollars apiece.

"Goddamn, Big Sarge. You da man! Thanks, Big Sarge!"

I turned around and said, "You gentlemen have a good day. You need anything else? Do you have enough ammunition?"

As they were choking down their food, they both shook their heads and replied, "Naw, we good, Big Sarge. Thanks, man."

"Okay, goodnight. I'm going to bed." It was about 0800.

"Goodnight, Big Sarge!" I believe their duty was twelve hours on and twelve hours off. It was a shitty detail to work.

A couple of days later, our platoon's mission was to patrol around the "Ammunition Depot," which was in between the route of Latifiyah and Yusafiyha. The Depot was an old Saddam Hussein Iraqi Army major ammunition supply point out in the middle of nowhere. There was no ammo out there anymore by this time. One of our battalion's missions was to patrol through it every now and then to ensure nobody was trying to steal the copper pipes that were embedded throughout the facility. They used the copper pipes for high-dollar sale that would eventually or could eventually be used to make bombs. One of our missions was obviously to stop and prevent it. Every now and again, we would encounter a couple or a few people that were out there trying to retrieve the copper, and we would have to deal with them.

We pulled up as we witnessed three dudes out there. By the way, they knew they were not authorized to be out there. That place was known to be off-limits for the locals—big time. We were a distance from them, maybe about three hundred meters or so. One of them began to fire at us. Too easy. "Light those motherfuckers up!" I gave the order to my M240B machine-gunner that was on my vehicle, and he did. All three went down immediately. That shit was so loud, too. There are no earplugs in combat, my friends. I mean, there are, but when you have to command and control with a radio, it makes it very difficult to use them. Therefore, I never wore them, and many others did not, either.

We didn't fuck around. I ordered three-hundred-sixty–degree security from the vehicles as we approached the bodies. I had my medic assess the bodies. Two were dead and one was still breathing but badly wounded. I called in the situation report to battalion headquarters. Simultaneously, I ordered two soldiers to grab the wounded guy and put him in the back of my Humvee. We were going to take him back to the FOB for medical attention because he was still alive. Yes, we took care of enemy wounded, too, because we were not savages, no matter what they did to us. We were not murderers; we were soldiers.

The Latifiyah police would pick up the two bodies while we were medically evacuating the live guy. We secured their one AK-47 that they were shooting at us with also. The bad guy in the back of my vehicle wasn't looking too good, obviously. He called out to me as I lit up a cigarette. "Mista, mista." He gave me the international hand signal for *give me a cigarette*, the two fingers to the mouth symbol. So I reached in my ammo pouch and pulled out my American pack of Marlboro Reds and handed him one. I then pulled out my lighter and lit it for him as well.

One of the privates in the back of the vehicle yelled at me, "Hey, Sergeant, fuck that shit. Don't give that motherfucker a goddamn cigarette! Fuck him!"

My anger level went to full capacity instantly. "You shut the fuck up, you little piece of shit! You don't fucking tell me what the fuck I'm going to do or not do, you little motherfucker! This guy's going to be dead by the time we even get back. So if I want to give a dying man his last cigarette, that's my business, you fucking shitbag! Don't *ever* question me again, fuck-stick! You hear me?"

He replied calmly, "Yes, Sergeant."

I still remember that exchange with that young man. I mean, I am Catholic. What was wrong with me giving a dying man his last cigarette? I hope he enjoyed it. I had my platoon medic with him and asked him, "Doc, is there anything you can do for him to keep him alive?" He looked me in the eyes and shook his head. The guy had five or six 7.62-millimeter bullet holes in his chest and abdomen. He was bleeding profusely. I looked back at my doc and nodded my head in response. He was dead in the back of my vehicle before we approached the outskirts of Latifiyah, which was about three miles up the road. The back of my Humvee was full of his blood. That's okay, though. I knew just the right person who was going to clean it up. Quite often to this day, I have dreams of him asking me for that last cigarette.

When we arrived back to Saint Michael, I had my driver take us straight to the battalion aid station to drop off the body. When we pulled up, the first sergeant was out front. I had two soldiers carry the man inside as I stayed out with the first sergeant. "So what happened out there?" he asked me. I told him that we pulled up to the ammo depot and they started shooting at us, and I ended it quickly. He then asked me for a cigarette, and I gave him one.

The soldiers came back out of the aid station, and I told Staff Sergeant K, my weapons squad leader, to take the vehicle back down after they filled it up with fuel and that I wanted Private So-and-so to clean the back of it. "He will get two five-gallon jugs of water, a bottle of bleach, and a broom and clean the back of my vehicle. When I get back down there, I want him and you to show me, so I can inspect it. Tell that little motherfucker the next time he questions me, I'm going to fuck his ass up!"

Staff Sergeant K replied, "Roger, Sergeant." The first Sergeant asked me what had happened, and I told him about the cigarette episode. He just shook his head and laughed a little.

While standing there talking with the first sergeant, two Humvees came barreling into the area. The lead vehicle's windshield was shattered, so we immediately suspected an IED attack. "Help us! Somebody help us!" one of the soldiers inside shouted.

I ran over immediately. "What can I do?"

"Grab him! Is this your aid station?"

I replied, "Yeah, man, this is it! Let's get him inside!" It was an MP unit with their wounded guy from an IED attack that they had just got hit by up the road on ASR Jackson, about a mile north. ASR means "ammunition supply route." Our military named this one Jackson, but it was a four-lane highway that ran straight up to Baghdad.

I reached my hands in the shoulder areas of his IBA (body armor) and pulled him up. One of the MPs grabbed his legs, and we carried him inside the aid station, where we had at least two surgeons. I remember when I was carrying him inside that he coughed hard, and blood came splattering out of his mouth, getting on my face and on the IBA I still had on. We put him on a gurney, and I rolled him on his side to prevent him from choking on his own blood. "Doc, Doc! He just got hit outside the wire!" I hollered. One of the surgeons came out and rolled him inside their operating room. I left the aid station, told the first sergeant goodbye, and headed down to the living area tents on our FOB. When I got down there, the first thing I did was inspect the back of my vehicle to ensure it was clean. Staff Sergeant K walked up to me and asked if I needed to see the private that had run his mouth off to me. I said no. I decided to let it go and that I just didn't want to see any more blood that day. Who knew? The evening was still young . . .

I got into my shorts and towel and walked to the shower trailer, still with this MP's blood on my neck and face. When I got into the shower, I realized the only thing we had accomplished that day was that me and my platoon had killed three people and some bad guys had tried to kill a platoon of American soldiers. I just stood under the hot water, letting it run over my body, and shook my head. I may even have cried a little bit, but I won't admit that to you. I remember telling myself, *You better hurry up and dry off and get back to your tent behind the Hesco* (the barriers around the base) *before the bad guys start launching their nightly mortar rounds at us.* It was almost dark out and creepy. Sometimes combat is a motherfucker.

The next day, I walked up there and asked if the MP had made it. They said he had and that he was going to Landstuhl, Germany, for medical evacuation. That was great news. At least something positive had come from that day. Anyway, my truck was spotless. I mean, you could have eaten off the bed of that vehicle.

One evening, we had just returned back to the FOB around 1900 from one of the knock and talk patrols down in Latifiyah. After we arrived, we headed to the mess hall for dinner chow. We had to eat our dinner before our nightly mortar round attack was attempted from the bad guys. The reason I say "attempted" is because they couldn't hit shit. Yeah, those fuckers would launch between four to six rounds at us every night there for a while until we conducted a battalion raid on the nearby village outside of our FOB. That shit ended really quick after snatching up several of those motherfuckers and bringing them back to our detention facility.

Anyway, I got my tray of food, and on my way to sit down with my squad leaders, I was stopped by my first sergeant, and he introduced me to our new Battalion EOD sergeant. EOD stands for "explosive ordinance disposal," a pretty big deal in Iraq and the entire Global War on Terrorism. He was a young staff sergeant and seemed to be a very eager young man to go out and get into the fight, as we all were on a daily basis. I sat down with them and introduced myself to him. "How you doing, Sergeant? I'm Sergeant Aguinaga, but I go by Sergeant Augi, because 'Aguinaga' has too many syllables in it, and motherfuckers always mispronounce it anyways."

"I'm doing good, Sergeant," Staff Sergeant O replied back as we shook hands.

"When did you get in?" I asked.

"I got in this morning and can't wait to get out there and go to work, Sergeant."

"Don't worry, you'll get your chance and real fucking soon, I guarantee it. You got your work cut out for you over in this motherfucker."

"Yeah, so I've been hearing." We sat and talked about what was going on back in the States and ate our dinner together.

When I was done eating, I stood up and shook his hand. "All right, Sergeant, have a great night. Don't get hit by one of these mortars that'll get launched at us soon." He looked at me with a surprised look in his eyes. I then said to him, "Don't worry, those stupid fucks can't hit shit anyway. However, I ain't standing around outside waiting to become one of their lucky hits, either. You know what I'm sayin'?"

He started laughing. "I hear you, Sergeant Augi."

"Okay, have a good one, and I'm sure I'll be seeing you both in here and out in sector too." That was the last time I saw that young man alive.

The next day, our platoon's mission was to pull security around a school in the town of Yusufiyah, which was Charlie Company's main sector of responsibility. Our platoon got tasked with assisting one of their platoons with the security mission. Charlie Company had been helping the school by delivering supplies, such as paper, pens, notebooks, etc. Some bad guys had threatened the teachers that if they accepted another pencil or piece of paper from the Americans, they were going to kill them and possibly blow up the school. The teachers were not intimidated, and we definitely were not, either. Our mentality was, "Bring it, motherfuckers, if you want some of this." It was a bad town, too. Out of all the towns of our battalion's responsibility, that was the worst. During our time there in Iraq, we had conducted several battalion-sized missions in that town.

The day was relatively quiet, with no activity. Our two platoons pulled security around the school, and by the end of the day, around 1700, we got a radio call from battalion headquarters telling us to return to base. I gave my platoon the safety convoy brief and the order of movement back to the FOB. It was a considerably longer movement since it was the farthest city away. At the end of my briefing, I told them when we got back to the FOB that we needed to watch the next episode of *24*. We were on a *24* kick during that time. Overall, it was a very calm, easy day. All we had to do was get back to Saint Michael, eat dinner, and watch our show. Little did I know, it was going to be an evening I will never forget and that continues to haunt me in my sleep to this day.

The sun was about to go down as we turned onto ASR Jackson to begin heading north toward Mahmudiyah and then to our base. Not too long after we made the turn, it came—the worst radio call we could have ever received. "Alpha Blue Seven, this is Three Panther Three November over." I'm not sure as I write this why our platoon leader was not with us that day, but he was back at the FOB knocking out administrative work he had to do, no big deal. It was actually common that he didn't go out with us on every single mission. There were times I stayed back to take care of admin shit back at our command post as well.

"Three Panther Three November, this is Alpha Blue Seven, go ahead over," I said.

"Roger, Alpha Blue Seven, you have a change of mission, break. You will proceed just north of the oil refinery on ASR Jackson and conduct a roadblock on both north and southbound traffic, break. There has been an IED explosion with one friendly KIA from Three Panther. How copy over?"

My first reaction was, *What the fuck? Doesn't Hadji know he's fucking my shit up tonight? That we're supposed to have an easy night and watch the next episode of 24?* Then it hit me like a bolt of thunder: *Fuck. Did he say KIA from our battalion?* KIA is the worst nomenclature that there is in the military. It stands for "killed in action," for those who did not know. "Three Panther Three November, roger, WILCO, we're in route to that location. Will notify when we arrive on site, over."

"Alpha Blue Seven, roger out."

I then looked at my driver and said, "Fuck..."

I got on my platoon's internal radio and ordered, "All Blue elements, this is Blue Seven over."

They all replied:

"This is Blue one, over."

"Blue Two, over."

"This is Blue Three, over."

"Blue Four, over."

"Roger, we have a change of mission. We will proceed northbound on ASR Jackson, just north of the oil refinery, break. There's been an explosion, possible IED, with one friendly KIA. Identity unknown at this time, break. Once on scene, our mission is to conduct a blockade on both north and southbound lanes until further notice. How copy over?"

All four squad leaders responded in order. We picked up our convoy speed to get to the scene, which was about ten miles up the road. Once there on the obvious site, there was a military police element with two of their vehicles pulling security, a medical vehicle, and a couple of EOD guys as well. We maneuvered our five vehicles to close off traffic on both north and southbound lanes of ASR Jackson around the scene. My guys dismounted as per standard operating procedure. I pulled up near the MPs, called in to our battalion operations in order to notify them that we had arrived on scene and had the roadblock executed. I walked over to the EOD soldier with Staff Sergeant K, my weapons squad leader. "What the fuck happened, Sergeant?"

He looked at me with tears in his eyes, and I could tell he was so shaken up. "It was Staff Sergeant O, Sergeant Augi."

I replied in utter shock, "Staff Sergeant O?"

"Yes, Sergeant." He then broke down in tears.

I screamed out, "Goddamn it!" I turned around, pulled out my pack of cigarettes, and immediately lit one up. It was the new EOD guy that I had just had dinner with the night before.

So standard procedure is whenever an IED has been identified or suggested by the locals, the battalion sends out one of the two EOD teams with a security force to the scene to investigate it. Once they have identified the explosive device, they will detonate it. Once detonated, one of them must go up and confirm its destruction in order to declare the area is clear of danger. On his first mission in Iraq, Staff Sergeant O, as the team's noncommissioned officer in charge, went up to the small crater to confirm destruction of the IED. When he approached it, the enemy, who apparently had eyes on them, detonated a secondary IED, blowing him all over ASR Jackson. It was an overhead IED that was mounted on the walkway overpass just above the staff sergeant. It had been the first time our battalion had encountered such an IED and, more disturbingly, this tactic by any bad guy thus far. Those motherfuckers always studied and figured out our tactics, techniques, and procedures, hence why we had to adjust and modify them constantly. This was a continuous problem during the US's eight-year involvement in Iraq.

Staff Sergeant K walked up to me and asked me for a cigarette, and I gave him one. As we were facing the medics' vehicle, we both watched a scene we will never forget. I haven't, anyway, and I'm sure neither has he. One of the medics had Staff Sergeant O's torso in his arms and threw it up and over into the back of their Humvee, like it was a bale of hay. His torso was charred, with no head, arms, or legs. Staff Sergeant K and I both turned around very quickly. "What the fuck!" I cried out.

"I wish I hadn't seen that shit," K said to me.

"No fucking shit," I responded.

One of the medics walked up to me. "Sergeant Augi, can you give us a few guys to help look for other remains, please?"

"You got it, buddy," I replied. I got on my radio. "All Blue elements, listen up. I need one guy per squad to come to my location, over." They all responded and sent their soldiers over to me. I also got my medic, forward observer, and my radio operator as well. Once they were all around me, I gave them the order they didn't quite want to hear. "All right, listen up. Put your tac lights on and begin searching the area in pairs. We got other parts of Staff Sergeant O to look for."

"Ah, man," one of the soldiers replied to me.

"Hey, I know it sucks, but let's get this shit over with so we can get the fuck out of here, you hear me?"

"Roger, Sergeant," they replied.

"Okay, move out, and let's get this shit done."

I told K that I had just eaten dinner with O last night and that he was the new EOD NCOIC. He was young, too. I thought to myself, *Now he's lying in pieces in the back of that vehicle over there*. Other shit kept running through my head as well, such as whether or not we were going to find out who the fuck had done this and go after his sorry ass. I was willing to bet the answer was definitely yes.

As I was standing there thinking about all this shit, one of my soldiers walked up to me. He was trying to hand me something. "Here you go, Sergeant Augi." As I looked down at what he had in his hand, I almost shit my pants. It was a piece of Staff Sergeant O's jawbone.

"Oh shit, what the fuck? Son—get that fucking shit out of my face." After I took a deep breath, I realized I didn't give clear enough instructions on what to do with his body parts after they found them. "Go over there and give it to the medics, son," I told him.

"Roger, Sergeant."

After about half an hour of searching, I told them to go back to their squad leaders and follow their instructions. I walked over to the medics and told them that we were done searching, and they concurred. After a couple of minutes, they were done packing up the rest of his remains and with the two MP vehicles, they took off and headed back to FOB Saint Michael. I called in to the battalion to inform them of their departure, and they instructed me to stand by and await the Mahmudiyah Fire Department, which was bringing out a fire truck to spray off the road.

It seemed like it took forever, but eventually, the fire department showed up on the site and sprayed off the road on all four lanes. Once they were complete, I called back to headquarters again and gave them the update on the situation on the site. We were finally given the change of mission and were ordered to return to base. Thank Christ. At approximately 2300, I gave another convoy safety briefing to my platoon, then we loaded up the vehicles and finally headed back to Saint Michael. Our assholes were puckered pretty tight on the way back. We were still about ten miles away from base and safety. After what we had just witnessed, we were all on edge on that ride back, and for the next few times outside the wire, as well. Don't get me wrong, we always maintained a high status of alertness, but that night, understandably, was a little scarier.

When we got back to the FOB, we locked and cleared our weapons and drove straight to the fuel point to fill up all our vehicles. When we got there, I got out and walked straight to the battalion operations shop (S-3). I signed my patrol back in with the time. As I did, I realized that what was to be a routine ten- or twelve-hour day had ended up being a sickening eighteen-hour day with the loss of one of our soldiers. After I left battalion headquarters, I walked over to my company and briefed our commander on the day's events.

We got back to our tents, unloaded the trucks, and nobody said shit to each other. There was no episode or two of *24*. Instead, there was a night of sadness and silence. I walked over to the shower trailers, took a shower, shaved, and when I got back to the tent, I told the guys to turn off the lights and go to sleep. To this day, sixteen years later, that night is the last thing I think about when I go to bed and the first thing I think about when I wake up. Every so often, I dream about it in between. My nightmare often finishes with a kid handing me half a jawbone and saying, "Here you go, Sergeant Augi . . ."

The next day around 1600, our battalion conducted Staff Sergeant O's memorial service outside the battalion headquarters. One night you're having dinner with somebody you just met, and the next night you're picking up pieces of his body that were blown up across an entire highway. In April 2004, our battalion redeployed back to Fort Bragg after we were relieved and handed off our sectors to a Marine Corps battalion.

When I was a kid in high school, I wanted to be war veteran. I especially wished I could have gone back in time a couple of decades and be a Vietnam War veteran. After my first tour in Iraq, I said to myself, *Be careful what you wish for.*

CHAPTER 15

POLITICS ESCALATING IN OUR MILITARY

DURING OUR OPERATION Iraqi Freedom deployment, my annual evaluation timeline came up. I was curious how the rating scheme was going to work. Since my arrival in the battalion, nobody had really had ninety days to be my rater or senior rater. So I did the best I could with the timelines and put nonrated time for the five months I had spent at Fort Benning. I gave my rough copy to the first sergeant. He played around with it a little bit and turned it into Command Sergeant Major Z for his review and approval before we went final on it.

A couple days later, it came back to the company from the command sergeant major with red ink all over it. The first sergeant handed it back to me, told me to fix it according to the edits, and get it back to him for signatures. When I got back to our tent, I sat down and started going over what the command sergeant major had written or changed on it.

I'll be damned! The damn NCO evaluation report had "mysteriously" changed from a change of rate evaluation to an annual platoon sergeant evaluation. He had put me back on track to the same rated timeline with my peers. All that bullshit time before I left for school had become part of this timeline! I was stoked and very appreciative of this command sergeant major after all. The next time I ran into him on the FOB, I approached him and said, "Hey, Sergeant Major, thanks a lot for—"

He cut me off and said, "No problem, Sergeant A. I knew you were serious about going to Ranger School. Why do you think I put you back in a line company before you left? If I would have just put you into the S-3 shop, you wouldn't have had your mind in the game before you went to Benning."

Wow, that blew my mind. I hold this man and my former platoon sergeant as the two primary individuals that got me promoted to E-8 years down the road. Yeah, I'm responsible for my own accomplishments and drives for success, but without them pushing me to the "no shit get-there mode," I may have chosen an easier path in the Infantry.

People have asked me how we coped with our experiences in Operation Iraqi Freedom when we got back home afterward. I'm not going to lie; it was great to be home and out of the shit, but it had changed me. You look at things differently than you did before you went over there. I treated certain aspects of life as if making the wrong simple choice could cost me or those around me our lives.

For example, and I will not dwell on it too hard now, but driving down Yadkin Road to pick up my BDUs from the cleaners, I can remember avoiding every small pothole or discoloration of the pavement where one may have been patched up. In my state of mind, just coming home, for all I knew, it could have been an IED because they may have brought that technical knowhow back here. So I avoided driving over rough edges on the roads.

One afternoon, my wife and I were walking out of the PX. On our way to the vehicle, we saw a toy still in its package lying in the parking lot. It must have fallen out of someone else's cart. The wife saw it, said "Oh, look," and started approaching it. I began hollering at her to get away from it. "Don't touch it! It's gonna fucking blow! Stay away from it!" She and others in the parking lot just stared at me in disbelief. That was a quiet ride home. PTSD? Probably, but back in those days, you didn't mention that shit unless you wanted to lose your duty position in a rifle platoon or company. There was no going to mental health for evaluation unless you wanted a new job passing out basketballs in the gym.

After the battalion got back off block leave from the deployment, it was back to going a hundred miles per hour on Ardennes Street again. One of the very first training events that was priority for the battalion was to get everyone out of an aircraft at eight hundred feet above ground level ASAP, and we did. Our S-3 Air had a large-package jump set up for us in a heartbeat. I mean, it was Fort Bragg, right?

All the jumpmasters in the battalion were already refresher certified before we left Iraq. The Division sent over Black Hats to Iraq to give units jumpmaster refreshment within sixty days of re-deploying back to Bragg. We were ready to go. I was primary jumpmaster and my chalk was a C-17 (the Cadillac). As a matter of fact, I think for the rest of this chapter—or perhaps the entire book—just consider me a primary jumpmaster from here on out. I swear, after about a year of it, I just wanted to be "Joe Jumper" with zero responsibilities just once.

My assistant jumpmaster was another platoon sergeant from our company. Remember "John Rambo," the demonstrator squad leader from the infamous trench live-fire? He made the E-7 list while we were in Iraq and was put into our company about two months after I got there. As a matter of fact, I'll just refer to him as Sergeant First Class Rambo for the remainder of this chapter.

The initial rumor was that command was going to let everyone conduct a Hollywood jump since they had been gone for over eight months on deployment. Hell no, not around here. We got back and hit the road running. It was combat equipment, nighttime, the whole nine yards. There were also brand-new paratroopers just in from Benning assigned to each company. Some had been waiting for us to return, the rest came while we were on block leave.

We started our Airborne timeline to standard with conducting final manifest on Lindsey Field. That is usually a pain in the ass because you're trying to get a hundred jumpers in reverse chalk order, because we load the aircraft from rear to front. It's like herding sheep to ensure they get from point A to point B, because it's all about making station time on the aircraft.

Manifest was actually easier than it had been when I first got into Division because each jumper just had to hold out their ID cards to get them scanned by the S-1 staff that walked by them as they were in chalk order. Their names and social security numbers automatically came up electronically. They then would go inside and print each chalk off and gave the required copies to the primary jumpmaster, pilot, and so on. Back in the day, the safeties had to hand jam that shit with a clipboard and a pen. This definitely saved us time. Once complete, I gave sustained airborne training and then had them conduct four parachute landing falls off the three-foot platform in all four directions. Once that was complete, we had them fall back in on their equipment and wait for the cattle trucks to take us to Pope Air Force Base.

"All current and qualified jumpmasters, please come up here and see me!" I shouted out inside the rigging facility once we arrived at Green Ramp. Within each chalk, there were usually at least two jumpmasters from other units that were jumping with us. One time, I got so lucky, I think I had like five. The point was to have them help us with the jumpmaster personnel inspection portion after the troops rigged up their parachutes and equipment. Normally, by Division standard, they would wear a yellow arm band on their right arm in order to be identified as a jumpmaster, but not part of the jumpmaster crew for the chalk. The arms bands were reversible, red on one side and yellow on the other.

Loading a C-17, like I said before, was easy as pie. The paratroopers basically walked on, stopped at their seats, pushed the seat down, sat down, and buckled themselves up. On the C-130s and the old C-141s, the seats were canvas and were in sections of about five or six feet long. The troopers had to cram into them, hip to hip, and there was no aisle space or walk path in between outboard and inboard rows. The safeties simply walked on top of our rucks positioned on our legs when they moved from the rear to front of the aircraft.

The smell of jet fuel filled the airfield as we loaded and met our station time. The jumpmasters would then get a briefing from the pilots about their confirmation of drop zone, flight path to get there, and approximate time of flight, which was usually like an hour, as before. Once that was complete, the jumpmasters sat down next to the number one jumper and sat back and closed our eyes to take a little break. A break of both mind and body. The Airborne timeline is exhausting, but once on the aircraft, it's almost over.

After about forty minutes of flight, the Air Force loadmaster walked over to me and gave me a twenty-minute warning. I stood up, along with Rambo on the other door. We both turned toward the jumpers and simultaneously sounded off with and gave the hand-and-arm signal for "Twenty minutes!"

The jumpers are supposed to repeat all jump commands back to the jumpmasters. We both sat back down and stood by. The loadmaster looked at me and gave me the ten-minute warning. I signaled over to Rambo. We both stood up, hooked up our static lines to the outboard anchor line cables, turned toward the skins of the aircraft and gave the command, "Ten minutes!"

We looked at each other to ensure we were in sync and gave the next jump command, "Get ready! Outboard personnel stand up!"

Once they were on their feet, we said, "In-board personnel stand up! Hook up! Check static lines—last two jumpers turn toward the skin of the aircraft, second to the last jumper, check the last jumper's static line! Check equipment! Sound off for equipment check!"

All jumpers tapped the jumper in front of them, simultaneously sounding off with "Okay!"

Once it got all the way back up to the number one jumper, the number one jumper pointed with his fingers and thumb extended and joined at me and sounded off with, "All okay, jumpmaster!"

I then inspected my universal static line snap hook, turned again toward the skin of the aircraft, looked over my left shoulder, and ordered, "Number one jumper, check my static line!"

After ensuring there was no excess static line dangling, he then tapped me and said, "Okay, jumpmaster!"

Then we waited for the aircraft to slow down, which it did. The loadmasters approached each paratroop door, reached down, unlocked the hatches, and pulled up the doors until they locked into the upright positions. That screeching wind immediately broke through the aircraft and took over almost all the rest of the sound onboard. The loadmasters then pointed at me and sounded off with, "Army your door!" I handed my static line to the safety and sounded off with, "Safety, control my static line!"

I then moved directly into the doorway and reached up to check the locking device on the door, pulling on the handle and using my index finger to follow it over and inspect the locking pin. Then I slid my hand outside the door and traced it all the way to the floor and around the parachute platform, to ensure there were no sharp edges that would cut or fray any static line. I then repeated this in the opposite direction, all the way back up. I then grabbed the side handle on the doorway, stepped onto the parachute platform, and looked to the rear of the aircraft to ensure there were no other obstructions that would injure any of the jumpers, such as another low-flying aircraft.

Behind us were the other C-17s, flying in chalk order formation. The lights of Fayetteville were straight ahead in the distance as we approached the drop zone. Still standing in the doorway, I was waiting to hit our one-minute reference point. The loadmaster tapped my shoulder and showed me his index finger, which meant one minute from drop. I turned my head toward the number one jumper and showed him my index finger for the warning. He then raised his hand and passed it back. At thirty seconds, I stepped out on the paratroop platform again and looked back outside the aircraft to the rear, came back inside, and looked at the assistant jumpmaster. We both gave each other a thumbs-up. We then both gave the command to each door of jumpers, "Stand by!"

I then extended my hand opened and the safety handed me my static line back. The number one jumper moved up and stood in the doorway. I stood behind him, and with the safety to my left, he was prepared to receive static lines. I stood staring at the red light above the door. Once it turned green, I gave the final jump command, "Go!"

Once all forty-nine jumpers exited on my door, I handed the safety my static line for the final time, then slightly turned to ensure that Rambo exited. Once he did, I looked up to ensure the light was still green and exited the aircraft myself.

The wind speed of the aircraft blasted me away from it. I counted, "One thousand, two thousand, three thousand, four thousand." I felt the initial shock of my parachute, then floated down peacefully. The sky became silent with the aircraft flying away from the drop zone. I lowered my equipment, made sure my feet and knees were together and that my knees were slightly bent. I had a soft, comfortable landing. Once on the ground, I always said to myself, *Another JM duty and jump out of the way.* Once a jumpmaster exits the aircraft, his duties are officially over.

Since we had jumped on Sicily and had no follow-on tactical mission, the assembly plan was to bring the parachutes up to and drop them off in front of the bleachers. Once we were all accounted for at the bleachers, we got in the cattle trucks that were already prepositioned there and went back to the battalion. Once back, we wiped down the weapons, turned them into the arms room, and were released with a late first call for the next day: no PT, show up in BDUs for the first formation at 1300.

We'd had some big changes within in our company. Both the company commander and the first sergeant were leaving close to each other. Our new commander was a great guy coming in from the S-3 shop and our new first sergeant was coming from 2 Panther scout platoon. I didn't know who he was, and he didn't look familiar. We also received a new platoon sergeant that had recently PCS'd to Fort Bragg from Fort Benning. All three rifle platoons received new platoon leaders as well. So actually, the only two remaining senior leaders that had deployed to Iraq were me and Rambo. Obviously these changes did not occur in the same week, but they did within about six weeks, it seemed like. My new platoon leader was a great guy, too, and eventually proved to be an excellent rifle platoon leader. I was shocked to find out that he had been branch detailed from military intelligence to infantry.

One evening I was awakened at home by the phone. It was a week night around 0100 in the morning. It was the new CO on the other end.

"Hey, Sergeant Augi, this is Captain J. You have a Private So-and-so? Well, he just got pulled over and charged with a DUI and is being held by the MPs, and you're required to sign him out. He actually got pulled over on Ardennes in somebody's car driving over eighty miles per hour. Need you to go in along with his squad leader and meet us there before PT. The command sergeant major and battalion commander will want to talk to you and Lieutenant So-and-so, whom I already called." That lieutenant was my new platoon leader.

I replied, "Roger, sir. I'll sign him out, take him back to the company, and will be waiting at battalion headquarters before PT."

It was one of the new privates that had come in after we got back from deployment. The stupid shit had met a girl at the enlisted club on Long Street. He had taken her car "for a ride." I remember getting to the MP station and showing my ID card in order to sign this kid out for his release.

On the way back to the barracks, I gave him the typical, "What the fuck were you thinking? You really fucked-up." I told him he was also on my shit list, which I think hit him worse than the Field Grade Article 15 he was about to get. When we got back to the company, his squad leader was already waiting for him. I went to the command post and made a pot of coffee because I knew it was going to be a long morning.

The new platoon leader came in, and I poured him a hot cup and said, "Well, here we go, our first alcohol-related incident in our platoon." I told him what the dumb shit had done and how he'd gotten busted. No, he didn't get busted driving back on post from Fayetteville, like most people get caught. He decided to get into a new Mustang and see how fast he could get it up to a hundred miles per hour on Ardennes. "When the cops pulled him over, they had him at eighty something."

The lieutenant just shook his head and said, "What a dumbass." He said, "Sergeant A, this ain't the way I wanted to come into this company."

I could tell he was afraid about going to see the battalion commander. I assured him, "Don't worry, sir. We didn't do anything; he's the one that's in trouble. I don't like this shit any more than you do." I also told him that our platoon had a pretty good reputation with no incidences up until now. "All right, sir, we'd better get over there."

As we walked down the hallway to the stairwell, we passed by his room where his squad leader and team leader had him with his feet elevated on the wall, so that he was in an inverted push-up position. We went downstairs first and linked up with the first sergeant and commander. We all walked over to Battalion together. The first sergeant and I went into Command Sergeant Major Z's office and Captain J and the platoon leader went into the battalion commander's.

The command sergeant major started off with, "Hey guys, this is fucking bullshit. We've been back a little over two months from Iraq and this battalion already has two DUIs." Yeah, two. Apparently there had been one the previous weekend in another company as well. "Well, what are you going to do about it, Sergeant A?" the command sergeant major asked me.

I remember his question caught me off guard and honestly, I really didn't have an answer, so I attempted to wing it.

"Well, Sergeant Major, that soldier is going to get his ass in serious trouble with the punishment he's going to get from here. I'm going to recommend max punishment, that he be restricted to the barracks for two weeks and forfeit half his pay for two months."

The command sergeant major came back at me and asked again, "No, no, Sergeant A. What are you going to do to prevent this shit from happening again?"

Again, I was kind of stuck. "I guess I don't have the answer you're looking for, Sergeant Major. Other than locking these guys in the barracks and not allowing them to leave, I don't have the answer of preventing these guys from going out and getting stupid."

He didn't like that answer. *"No,* Sergeant A! You need to put the living fear of God into that platoon of yours, so that your soldiers will be petrified to even think about drinking and driving."

I responded, "Oh, *that's* gonna happen, Sergeant Major. I'm gonna get them all in the hallway this morning and they're going to hear it from me, and my squad leaders are going to have to get tighter on their guys."

Command Sergeant Major said, "All right then. That's it, you guys go back to your company, and this better not happen again anytime soon. Division is tracking this shit now on each battalion on the street and shit's rolling downhill. Me and the battalion commander are going to have to go see the division commander and the command sergeant major this morning about that piece of shit you got in your platoon, Sergeant A. Do you really think I want to spend my morning talking to Command Sergeant Major X?"

The first sergeant and I simultaneously replied, "No, Sergeant Major."

When we left battalion HQ, I remember feeling sympathy for him having to get his ass chewed by Command Sergeant Major X up on the hill. That would suck! You make it all the way to the rank of E-9 and still had to put up with an ass-chewing from another E-9, just at two levels higher. Remember what I said earlier, everything is two levels up in the Army. The battalions manage platoons, and the division level manages battalions.

Back in Division, when I was living in the barracks, we were wild and crazy, but I don't remember any of us being stupid enough to be drag racing down Ardennes drunk. We had our share of DUIs and soldiers coming up "hot" on piss tests for smoking pot, and those soldiers got busted by the same thing this kid was going to face.

The difference in those days was, the soldier's chain of command wasn't dragged into it and almost held responsible like what was starting to be noticed more in Division. What the reality had become was that the Army began tracking individual units' drug and alcohol-related incidences as the combat deployments began to increase across the Department of Defense. The Army was holding commanders at the higher levels, such as Division, more accountable than back the way it had been a decade or two before.

I remember talking to my next-door neighbor Staff Sergeant D about how it seemed it was getting different in Division. He agreed and he told me, "Yeah, it's not just about going a million miles per hour in this place twenty-four seven, but now we have to throw in watching what these kids do on their off time too."

I also went to lunch in Fayetteville with two old friends from back in the day—Shaky and S. They were still over in 2nd Brigade. I think by now, Shaky was done with his platoon sergeant time and S was still doing his. We didn't talk about our Operation Iraqi Freedom experiences, instead we laughed about the old "P Regime" and how we had dealt with the hardships of that time. Of course, we always think and say that "Nobody had it as rough as we did, back in our time." I believe all leaders in the Army and military as a whole have that mentality.

I remember mentioning the DUI that had recently occurred in my platoon, and how surprisingly involved we were in it. Shaky said to me, "Oh that ain't nothing, Nate dog. Wait until you have a soldier make an IG complaint about being abused and hazed because one of your team leaders made him do push-ups in the barracks."

I said, "What? I don't follow you."

S told me that in his battalion, you could only make a soldier do ten push-ups as corrective training and then he had to be allowed time to recover before you could do it again. The leader also had to ensure the soldier had a canteen of water with him while he was being corrected as well. I couldn't believe what I was hearing from my old buddies. Shit was definitely changing. They wanted you to train your soldiers to be warriors and kill the enemy, but you better not get caught making him do more than ten push-ups at a time for punishment. Well, that was a disturbing, but educational lunch with my old friends.

Our battalion was hitting the training, and we started hitting it hard. Weapons qualification ranges both day and night were of priority for a week straight, every day. After PT and morning chow, the companies would load up on the LMTVs (light medium tactical vehicles) parked out in the center of Gela Street. We would get all our soldiers zeroed on their assigned weapons first and then, the next day, move them down the road to the qualification ranges.

Most weapons qualification ranges on Fort Bragg were on Gruber Road, down past Pike Field. After all weapon systems were zeroed and qualified, the next week after that would be dedicated to the quick-fire range and room-clearing house that were part of the same facility. We would send the paratroopers through them by the fire teams. Of course, everything was in sequence of blank fire and then live fire, especially the room-clearing house. The teams would go through room by room, and the platoon sergeants and platoon leaders could monitor them by an upper-level deck above them to observe their progress. After fire teams were certified, we'd have them clear the house at squad level both blank and live.

This facility was pretty new at the time, very up-to-date and efficient because this is how we were fighting in Iraq: urban warfare, building to building, room to room. The squad leaders were all over it and very proficient at room clearing. We were not seeing bunker and trench warfare training like we used to all the time in the past. The soldiers within these squads were trained and trained well. Most of us leaders knew it was a matter of time before our brigade would be coming down on orders for our next deployment. At this point in the military it was imminent. The closer it was getting to 2005, the word was already going around that all combat deployments were going to be increased to a minimum of twelve months for both Afghanistan and Iraq.

Now for these ranges during the first couple of weeks of training, the companies would move to and from the battalion area. We would complete the range for the day or night, get on the trucks and head back to the company, turn equipment in, and go home for the night. Then come in the next morning, do PT, and go back out to train. We liked it because we'd knock out our training and go home to our families for the evenings.

Once we started getting to the level of actual Intensive Training Cycle, where we conducted team, squad, and platoon-level live-fire certification ranges, of course, it was continuous staying out and sleeping in the field. It had to be because the units would go day and night, nonstop. There was also a different mentality during this period than I had seen from past cycles. Leaders seemed more involved, and I mean platoon sergeants and platoon leaders, along with commanders and first sergeants, and we were, right down to every minute of training. Most of the senior leaders by now had already served in Operation Iraqi Freedom and Operation Enduring Freedom. There was a new reality that maybe hadn't existed a decade earlier. You wanted to be involved, you needed to be involved because we were in a time of war, and we knew every soldier and NCO that was out training for that particular timeline was going to go to war with us.

One thing the other two platoon sergeants and I noticed over those couple of weeks of training was that the new first sergeant wasn't around out on the ranges with us. When we would get back to the company at the end of the day, he would be there in his office at his desk. Even when we had to get dinner chow out on a later range, it was the XO or supply sergeant who would bring it out to us. It wasn't really that big of a deal, I guess, for qualification ranges, but when we were doing quick-fire and room-clearing live fires, we were kind of puzzled by his absence, especially since he was pretty new to the company and battalion.

The following week was the actual beginning of Intensive Training Cycle. We were going to break it down into team and squad live-fire certifications for the first Monday through Friday, go in for the weekend, and the last week was totally dedicated to our three rifle platoons. The next Monday when I got to the company, the CQ handed me a note from the first sergeant telling me to hold the company formation for PT. I was there early, usually around 0500 to get my shit done I needed for the platoon before we had to be in the first sergeant's office by 0600.

When Captain J came in, I went to his office and told him the first sergeant wasn't going to be in and that I was taking the formation. He asked me where the first sergeant was, and I couldn't answer because I didn't know. Anyway, I asked him if he had anything for me to put out to the company and he didn't. I already knew that the company had to be ready to load up on Gela Street at 0930 to go out to the field for the week. That was about it.

For formation, I had Staff Sergeant K take over my spot for the platoon. After Reveille I said, "All right, after chow this morning, be back down here on the rocks, we'll say 0930 with all your gear for the week. Order of weapons draw this morning will be First, Third, Second. Platoon sergeants, take charge of your platoons and conduct PT."

We saluted each other and I went back to my platoon, stretched them out, and took them on a four-mile run. Later on that morning, I found out that the first sergeant had gone to sick call.

After about two days of day-and-night team blank and live fires, the platoon leader and I were getting a little tired of walking up and down the lanes and giving after-action reviews. Our fire teams were doing well, and the soldiers were learning and getting better. I had great squad leaders who were experienced and very proficient. Staff Sergeant K was my weapons squad leader, and he definitely was my right-hand man. He helped me and the platoon leader by getting the next teams ready to go and ensuring we had water on the lanes and our AAR site. I remembered when I was a weapons squad leader on this very same range, doing the same thing for my platoon sergeant and platoon leader.

Captain J was also walking with us, evaluating the teams as well. He was that type of commander. Two levels up, he evaluated and conducted the AAR for squads, but it didn't matter; he was always present for any level of training. I remember being in the range tower on night qualification a couple of times, and he'd be right there cracking jokes with me until we would get the last soldier in the company qualified.

Going into squad live fires toward the end of the week, my platoon was going through pretty smoothly. None of the three line squads had to run through the blank portion twice because their safety precautions were met all the way through the range. After our last night iteration, the CO still had another platoon to get through with their blank and live. Again, there was no first sergeant around to help him. After I briefed the squad leaders on the next day's timeline and they went off to the platoon with the platoon leader, I finally asked Captain J, "Hey, where's the damn first sergeant at?"

He replied, "He's in the building asleep, last time I checked."

"Asleep?" I had finally had enough and had to get the shit off my chest. "What the fuck is he doing sleeping when we're in the middle of live-fire certifications? Who is this guy and what the fuck is his readout?"

"That's a good a question."

The next squad from Rambo's platoon came up for their first blank iteration. Rambo came up to me, and we started shooting the shit. I asked him if he had seen the first sergeant all day. He said, "Hell no, maybe at dinner chow earlier, and that's fucking it, dude."

"Yeah, I guess he's in the building sleeping right now and your three squads still have to go through," I said to him.

Rambo said, "Whatever. Let me get these guys ready to go down the lane."

I stayed with the CO. What else was I going to do? I was the senior platoon sergeant in the company, and he needed help and an extra set of eyes for these maneuver live fires. We went into the wee hours of the morning finishing up Rambo's platoon. We were both smoked, and by the time the last squad went through, we were droning as if we were both back in Ranger School. As we walked behind the last squad as they maneuvered down the lane, he took a sip out of his canteen.

I asked him, "What are you drinking sir, water?"

He replied, "It ain't fuckin' soda."

We both started laughing uncontrollably over that. It was so stupid and not even funny, but at the time, it was hilarious. Years later, we still laugh about that night.

As the sun came up, we got our platoons up and received our personnel and equipment reports and got them ready for the trucks to come get us and take us back to the battalion. The first sergeant came out of the building he had slept in all night and asked all three of us (platoon sergeants) if we were "green" on personnel and equipment, like he gave a shit.

"Roger. We're up, First Sergeant," we told him.

When we got back to the company, we had the company ground their equipment on the rocks with a weapons guard per platoon and had them all go eat breakfast in the mess hall. Me and the other three platoon sergeants went to the first sergeant's office to have our meeting on upcoming events and other issues. There were always other issues, such as who needed to go to the dentist and get an exam, who was going to an upcoming school, who was a "pay hurt" or a potential "pay-loss" from losing parachute pay for not jumping within sixty to ninety days. We already knew that we were going back out Monday morning for platoon live certifications for the week.

The first sergeant then told us what was going on with him, finally. Apparently he had a herniated disc in his neck and it was getting worse, to the point where he was losing feeling down one of his arms.

"So bear with me guys, I'll get this fixed and I'll be as good as new. I know I've been absent for a lot of shit since I came on board a couple of months ago, and I'm going to ask for your help, especially you, Sergeant A, being senior here."

We left his office when he was done with us and went to the chow hall ourselves. The three of us line platoon sergeants had our own little opinions of what was about to come onto the company minus a first sergeant.

I said, "Here we go guys. He basically told us to cover down on him and his duties until whenever he gets surgery and can come back to duty."

The other platoon sergeant stepped in and said, "Here's my problem with this whole thing: he didn't just get hurt when he got to this battalion. He accepted the position knowing he was broke and wasn't going to be able to perform his duties."

"Yep. Spot on," the two of us replied. That was the whole thing that had pissed us off once we started noticing him not being around, especially during field training, which was the core of our jobs and purpose in the Army—train up and go fight wars. You get hurt in this line of work, there's no arguing that point. The problems we had, to include the CO, was that he took the job knowing he had a herniated disc and that he was going to have to eventually have surgery. The next question was how long it would be before Command Sergeant Major Z found out. And that was right around the corner.

When we came back in Monday morning, the first thing that was going around was that there had been two more DUIs throughout the weekend within the battalion, but not our company—thank God. I remember telling my squad leaders it was going to get to the point where we were going to just stay in the field the entire time during

Intensive Training Cycle, like it used to be. Our battalion was actually trying something new that we all thought was awesome: going out and training for the week and letting everyone come back, get some downtime during weekends with their families, and then go back out the following week, like we were doing with this training cycle. Before the deployments overseas began to increase, it was nothing to do two or three solid weeks in the field during the cycle. We feared, though, that if soldiers were going to continue to get in trouble with drugs and alcohol on weekends, the battalion commander and command sergeant major would nix coming back in and just start keeping us out there straight through, simply to keep dumbasses from getting into trouble back in garrison.

So later on that afternoon, out in the field, here came Command Sergeant Major Z and the battalion commander to begin their walk through and evaluations for our company getting ready to begin platoon level blank- and live-fire exercises. I was over at my platoon area off in the woods going over our plans with the platoon leader.

"Sergeant Augi!"

I turned around, "Yeah, what's up?"

"Command Sergeant Major Z wants to see you up at the company command post."

As I walked up there, I sort of had a good feeling of what he was going to ask me or talk to me about. "Hey, what's up, Sergeant Major?"

He was pissed off, and rightfully so, because I'm pretty sure he and the battalion commander had just gotten back again from the division commander's office about this weekend's recent DUIs. "Sergeant A. Oh, I've had better Mondays. Where's your first sergeant, Sergeant A?"

I didn't sugarcoat it. "He's not out here, Sergeant Major."

"Well where the fuck is he?"

"He's back in the rear with an injured neck," I admitted.

I didn't say anything else because he turned around and went straight for his vehicle and I'm sure I knew where he was going. By dinner chow, the first sergeant had mysteriously showed up and was out in the field with us, face painted and all.

That shit lasted about another month and eventually, and mysteriously again, the first sergeant ended up on PCS orders to Fort Benning. The last time I saw him, I was walking from battalion HQ back to the company from a first sergeant meeting I had just attended with Command Sergeant Major Z. Damn, it was too bad I wasn't promotable at the time, I would have had that shit. Anyway, he was approaching me from the company on the sidewalk. I thought to myself, *Fuck, I should have stayed at Battalion about a minute longer.*

He'd already had his diamond taken from his rank. As we approached each other, I said hello and had every intention of continuing walking toward the company.

"Hey, Sergeant A, check this out, can you believe this fucking shit?" He was showing me his PCS award, which was an ARCOM (Army Commendation Medal—something he considered just a "participation ribbon"). He then said to me with anger as a so-called victim, "I've busted my ass in this Brigade for five fucking years and this is what I get, a fucking ARCOM?"

I replied with an uncaring tone, "Yeah, tough break, Master Sergeant. Good luck to you."

As I walked off he yelled back at me, "Oh, you gonna turn your back on me too?"

That was it. I turned around and gave it back to him. "Hey, Master Sergeant, you tried to buck the system and the system wasn't having it! Had you just gone to Brigade or Division staff until you had surgery and healed up, you could have been a first sergeant anywhere on the street later on. You came here and thought you were just gonna sit back and be hurt while me and the other platoon sergeants had to cover down for you and do your fuckin' job."

I turned around and headed back toward the company for the second time. I didn't hear shit from that crybaby again. Like I said, he had come from being 2 Panther scout platoon sergeant. He was Mr. Ranger, recon, had all the bells and whistles, pathfinder, all that shit.

He was injured, which could happen to any of us, but in Division, it's sink or swim. You are either a performer or a nonperformer; there is no in-between. He knew that, but he'd tried to cheat at the game and lost.

The next month, we got a platoon sergeant from our battalion that had recently made the E-8 list. He was a great guy, and everybody liked him. I went to his frocking ceremony up at Brigade and it felt good to have a first sergeant again so that our company could function smoothly without me or any of the other platoon sergeants running back and forth from our platoon duties to company functions. He was "First Sergeant M," and we were relieved to have him.

The division also got a new commander and command sergeant major. Yes, Command Sergeant Major X finally had retired from the Army. I believed he had thirty-three years and as I mentioned in one of the earlier chapters, he had spent all of it in the 82nd Airborne except for a tour in Korea and two years as a drill sergeant. He had an excellent career and is still talked about today—as you can see.

Later on there was a large-package, brigade-level jump on the training schedule. If there was a time I thought I was going to get fired, it was this particular jump. I was primary jumpmaster for a C-130. It was a brigade-level airborne operation, and the division commander was slotted to jump with our battalion because we were the Division Ready Force 1, which means we had been designated as the first unit to deploy. He was not on my chalk, and I was okay with that. I didn't need all the limelight drama of having a general officer command team on my aircraft. While at Green Ramp, we had just finished conducting mock door training and were in the middle of rigging parachutes.

The next thing we knew, there was a message that came over the intercom, "All primary jumpmasters, please report to the control desk immediately."

I started heading in that direction and was thinking that maybe they were going to delay or even cancel the jump because the weather was getting bad and there was a storm in our forecast around the time-on-target timeline. No, it was better than that. The division commander's aircraft had gotten grounded for mechanical difficulties and Command Sergeant Major Z was putting him and the division command sergeant major on my chalk. Joy!

So we changed up the manifest and made the correct changes. I needed their full names and social security numbers. Of course, nobody had them. We were told that his aide would have all that information when they arrived. When was that? Nobody knew, but when he showed up to Green Ramp after we were done with the jumpmaster personnel inspection portion for all jumpers on our chalk, everybody knew. We were getting close to station time, and he had just shown up. He was over talking with the brigade commander, and I wasn't going to interrupt them for shit. Fuck it, if I missed station time tonight, it was because I was patiently waiting on the division commander. Who was going to say anything to me about that? He and the division command sergeant major walked up to me. Major General C. was his name and he hollered out, "Where do you want me, Sergeant?"

I saluted him, shook his hand and introduced myself, and then told him, "Right door with me, sir." I figured the command sergeant major was going to be the number one jumper on the other door. Nope, he was right behind the commander as the number two jumper on my door. He had his aide with him, who had his parachute and reserve. That was the first time I discovered that the division commander got his own parachutes separate from the unit's draw. Actually, it was a main parachute with toggles so that he could control it easier and have a smoother landing.

"All-American 6's" (the division commander's call sign) aide is usually a captain who is also jumpmaster qualified in order to be able to give him his own sustained airborne training. Or maybe, in reality, they just show up with him and rig and JMPI him, like the aide did here. He and the command sergeant major were jumping Hollywood.

I guess they didn't get the memo that this was a combat equipment mass-tactical jump. Above my pay grade. I just needed to get him out of the aircraft safely.

We sat down on the aircraft, and he started talking to me. "What do you do in Division, Sergeant?"

I said to myself, *fuck it*, grabbed my balls, and replied, "Sir, I'm the best and baddest platoon sergeant you got in this division!"

He started laughing, "Oh. Well, that's good to know!"

The command sergeant major was looking at me and shaking his head. I should have given him the finger and asked what he was looking at. He was an artillery guy. As a matter of fact, he was the only division command sergeant major that came from division artillery that I ever heard of.

"This will be my first jump in Division since I've been back, Sergeant," he said to me.

"Oh yeah? How long has it been, sir?"

"Fifteen years!"

I started thinking to myself, *Jesus Christ, that's as long as I've been in the Army.*

We were airborne over Fayetteville, and I started my jump commands. When I gave the commander "Stand by!" He handed my safety his static line, turned into the doorway, stepped onto the parachute platform and planted both hands outside of the aircraft. I immediately said, "Heeeyyy!"

I went to grab his parachute pack-tray and bring him back inside the plane, but the command sergeant major shouted at me, "Don't fucking touch him, he'll fucking go!"

I remember thinking, *Don't fucking say that word "Go" too loud, motherfucker. I don't want the division commander exiting over Bragg Boulevard.*

He had gone old-school on me, executing the old jump command of "stand in the door." Back in the day that is what the number one jumper did. They turned and stood with both hands outside the plane, and when the command go was given, they would thrust themselves up and out, using their hands and arms to push themselves. The Army had gotten rid of that technique about thirteen years earlier. I guess division commanders don't have to go through the 82nd Airborne jump refresher course (I'm being sarcastic).

The loadmaster gave me another one-minute warning.

I leaned over to him and said, "What the fuck? You already gave me that shit!"

He said it was difficulty due to the storm. You could see the lightning in the distance.

I just remember praying that the pilot wasn't going to bank the aircraft, which was quite normal for C-130s. If they did, All-American 6 would have fallen out for sure, landing in someone's backyard in Spring Lake somewhere. That shit would have made the *Army Times* for sure, maybe even CNN. I would be passing out basketballs at the gym the remainder of my time in Fort Bragg.

The command sergeant major hollered at me, "Oh, entirely way too long, jumpmaster!"

The light turned green, thank the Lord in Heaven. I shouted, "GO!"

That was my first and only experience with the new 82nd Airborne Division commander.

The follow-on missions that each unit had were canceled because the storms were coming in hot over top of Fort Bragg. There were mass vehicles pulling up to Sicily DZ to take us back. I wonder if they would have canceled those missions if the division commander hadn't been on this jump? Oh, well, that was the least of my worries. I had to think about reporting to the gym up on the hill tomorrow.

We went home that night and had a late first call the next morning for 0900 in BDUs. I remember waiting to go see the battalion commander and command sergeant major for having AA6 in the doorway of my aircraft for over three minutes last night. 0900 came, lunch came and went, and before I knew it, it was 1700 and time to go home. I hadn't heard a word and didn't tell anyone about it either. A few days later, when I was for sure I was clear of this matter, I told Captain J and First Sergeant M about it. They were laughing and said, "Shit, man, if we'd known about this earlier, we would have gotten the battalion commander and command sergeant major in on a little gag on your ass." Good times!

The fun didn't last long. Another soldier in my platoon got a DUI. That would be the second alcohol-related incident in the platoon within a year. My platoon leader and I both received letters of concern from the battalion commander, along with a massive ass-chewing. He told me that my leadership abilities were in question and that I had no control or discipline within my platoon. I took it and the platoon leader took it as well. At the end of the day, I knew it wasn't about my leadership. I knew what kind of leader I was. The DUIs were piling up within the battalion and he and the command sergeant major were on their final straws of this shit. I knew and felt for them as well, that they didn't deserve this shit; no senior-level leadership does.

"I'm going to take care of this, sir," I told the battalion commander. I turned my head and eyes toward the command sergeant major and said, "Sergeant Major, I'm going to take care of this shit."

He looked at me with his pissed-off stare and said, "We'll see, Sergeant A. We'll see."

When we left Battalion, the platoon leader asked me what I was going to do. I told him I was going to make all of their lives as miserable as possible for a while, to include the squad leaders too. I got everybody in the hallway and put them in the front leaning rest position. Squad leaders too. I pulled out my new letter from the battalion commander and read it to the entire platoon.

"Now, motherfuckers, do you understand? Do you understand how your fucked-up decisions can damage not only yourselves, but this whole platoon and its leadership? Well, you stupid fucks aren't taking me or the platoon leader down with you. I'll tell you that right goddamn now! So effective immediately, if any of you that live in the barracks or are married and live in government housing on post, and you've had one fucking sip of alcohol, you will not leave these barracks or your house! So help you God if I fucking find out, and I *will* find out!

"So for those of you married and your wife has a problem with you drinking and leaving your government quarters, you can tell her I said to shut the fuck up! I don't give a shit. I'll restrict your fucking ass to these barracks so fast you won't know what the fuck hit you! The bottom line is you people can no longer be trusted to do the right thing!

"Furthermore, nobody is authorized to leave this platoon area when the company is released until you receive a safety briefing from me, and you will then sign a roster that you received and understand everything I told you. I don't give a fuck how late it is; nobody will leave until my roster is signed. If someone does leave without signing it, the whole platoon will wait for them to come back! I don't care if we have to stay all night. I was a drill sergeant for two years—do you think I give a fuck whether or not I go home at night? Let's get this straight now, motherfuckers: I ain't here to be anyone's friend! I challenge any of you to test me on our new rules in this platoon!"

That was it. Every night before they went home, I had them sign the new safety briefing roster. Now within the regulations, I couldn't keep them restricted to the barracks unless they were under UCMJ punishment, and I definitely couldn't keep guys restricted to their living quarters. When we got back in the command post, the platoon leader shut the door and asked me if we could get away with what I just put out.

"No, we can't, and the team and squad leaders know that too, but they'll go along with it. The bottom line: it's not *them* getting in trouble, it's the fucking new kids living in the barracks."

We never had another incident.

By January and February of 2005, the word was going around that our battalion was being reflagged to another unit with another mission.

The old 73rd Armored Cavalry Regiment was the 82nd's Airborne Cav unit that used to use the Sheridan armored reconnaissance airborne assault vehicles back in the day. The unit had been deactivated back in the nineties. I remember they used to be headquartered near the 505th, just down from 2 Panther. The confusion around our battalion and the regiment was growing. The question was at the time, *How could Division reflag an infantry battalion to an armored cavalry squadron?*

The answer turned out to be pretty simple: they were going to bring the armored cav scouts into our battalion and combine us all. We would become two companies of dismounted reconnaissance (the infantry) and two companies or troops of armored reconnaissance (the cav scouts). The concept would become known as a RSTA (reconnaissance surveillance target acquisition) battalion or squadron size unit. The 73rd Cav had three Squadrons, 1st, 3rd, and 5th. The word at the time was that 3-505th was going to be 5th Squadron, 3rd was going to be 3-325, and 1st was going to be 3-504th. So all three brigades were reflagging their 3rd battalions to RSTA units, and this was to be completed and effective by the start of 2006.

Despite the DUIs that were keeping a dark cloud over our battalion, we were being highlighted for our successes. As a matter a fact, from my perspective, our reputation as a performance battalion outweighed the negatives. For example, our battalion continued to go above and beyond when it came to tactical readiness. We would conduct Intensive Training Cycle with a different expectation of what the "norm" was at Fort Bragg. Platoon live-fire maneuver ranges were being built and constructed by our battalion itself. Our S-4 would coordinate for the construction materials, such as plywood, metal pickets, railroad ties, and plenty of sandbags for us to build our own little huts and bunkers. Once built into a small urban complex, we would conduct our live-fires on these ranges.

It got to the point where each company would go out, build their own small complex for the first forty-eight hours in the field, and then spend the next seventy-two hours shooting and blowing it up.

We would dig and build our own bunkers on the range and have the engineers come out and certify, so that we could use live grenades on them. It was a little more exhausting than back in the day when platoons would go to ranges already set up with a trench complex, but it was worth the training experience in the current state of the wars we were in.

Word immediately got back to our brigade and the division headquarters of how 3 Panther was conducting our platoon live-fires and before we knew it, we were giving demonstrations to corps- and Army-level leadership. The Army chief of staff came from the Pentagon to see a platoon live-fire demonstration upon which our battalion was selected to present. It was another platoon from another company that got selected for it. I remember thinking, *Those poor bastards are going to be smoked because of the repeated times they'll have to execute it for the demonstration.* They went through the live-fire without a hitch. So at the end of the day, our combat readiness outweighed a few rotten apples getting into trouble. That was the positive way most of us leaders looked at it during that time.

The summer of 2005 was a busy time for the battalion because the reality of changing over to 5-73rd CAV was upon us. It seemed as if it was just a rumor one day with an inactivation ceremony the next. Our battalion was also going through a change of command at the same time as well. Our battalion commander had finished his command time and headed up to the hill to work at Division staff until his next assignment. We had received a new commander who had a history in 3 Panther himself. He was actually a commander in one of the other companies when I was there in '94. Now, eleven years later, he was commanding the same battalion. What a small Army. I've said that a hundred times during my twenty years serving.

Other soldiers were being moved around to other duty stations. It was a very hectic time of change. As sad as it was, you didn't have time to sit back and worry about it, you just had to make it happen. 3 Panther was being inactivated and it was happening now. We had to make it happen, and we did. Staff Sergeant K was put on assignment for recruiting duty and another one of my squad leaders got put on drill sergeant duty. I told him, "Been there, done that."

Another transition in the battalion was that soldiers had to be selected and moved over to 3-325 to be part of their upcoming RSTA unit, the 3-73rd CAV. I remember it being a big deal at the time, because nobody knew who was staying and who was moving out. It was like a big surprise who made the list to remain in the old battalion and who was being pushed out. That wasn't the reality of what the mission was to reallocate troops over to the Falcon Brigade, but with Command Sergeant Major Z conducting the selection process, it kind of seemed that way.

With troops leaving the battalion and Panther Brigade, also meant new soldiers, NCOs, and officers were coming in as well. There was something different about it though—they were not infantrymen but cavalry scouts.

Our outgoing battalion commander had even put together a formal dinner and celebration for the leadership of the two branches coming together. I believe it was E-6 and above and held at a fancy ballroom at Pope AFB. It was fun, with plenty of drinking and live music. We all got along with few if any dick-measuring contests. The two branches were converting fast into one squadron of reconnaissance.

In the middle of all these reassignments and moving around within the battalion, word came down we were to send about twenty of us to McCord AFB for a week to be part of an Air Force rodeo competition. They needed about ten jumpmasters and ten jumpers to be part of the personnel point of impact competition. In other words, the Air Force would drop us over the drop zone and the jumper had to land within his or her marker on the ground.

This was what I had done every year that I was part of All-American Week competitions on Bragg. It was a good tasking, and I didn't mind going back to that area after all these years either. McCord AFB is adjacent to Fort Lewis, as Pope is to Bragg. Fort Lewis had been my first duty station for two years before Germany and I was actually excited about seeing it again. While doing the competition that week, I made about three jumps, which was enough for me to earn my master wings. Master wings have a long set of qualifications, most of which I had. I just needed sixty-five jumps. During this TDY trip to Pope AFB, I hit my sixty-fifth.

Also during this trip, I called back to the battalion S-1 shop at Fort Bragg, because I, along with the other platoon sergeant I was with, was curious whether or not we had made "the list" of remaining in the battalion. We had both made it, but not where we wanted to go. He was getting sent to the S-3 shop and I was going to the S-2 shop. We were not happy.

So I called Command Sergeant Major Z. "Hey, how are you guys holding up at Fort Lewis?"

"Are you ready to come back yet?" he asked.

"Roger that, Sergeant Major." I then added, "Hey, Sergeant Major, how come you got me and Sergeant First Class So-and-so going to Battalion Staff? Why are you taking us off from the line?"

He replied, sarcastically as usual, "Because your asses are done with your platoon sergeant time. It's time to let someone else step in and start theirs."

I said, "Okay, understood, but why did you put me in the S-2 shop, for Christ's sake?"

"Hey, asshole, I put you in an E-8 position. The battalion S-2 NCOIC is an 11Z position" (making it E-8).

I said, "Oh, shit! I didn't know that, Sergeant Major."

Sarcastically again he said, "Oh you feel better now Sergeant A? I can change that shit if you want me to."

"No, I'm good, Sergeant Major. Thanks!" I got off the phone, saying to myself, *Damn! He squared me away again!* I went back inside and told the other guy that he was going to the S-3 shop and me the S-2 shop. I left out the E-8 position thing. I bet he didn't know, just like I didn't.

When we got back to Fort Bragg, I went upstairs to my command post and started taking my shit off the wall and packing up my regs and other stuff. I remember thinking, *Wow, I did it—I completed over two years solid platoon sergeant time and now it's time to go to Staff until I come down on the E-8 list.*

I had cleared everything out of the command post. My platoon leader left shortly after to report to the 82nd Military Intelligence Battalion down the street because, again, he was an MI officer branch detailed to the infantry. He was an incredible platoon leader, and he and I had been through a lot together—everything from numerous field exercises to disciplinary problems within the platoon.

We were having our first awards ceremony with the new battalion commander, "Lieutenant Colonel P." It was hot out—I mean Fort Bragg summer hot. We were all in our Class B uniforms. I was standing out there, receiving my new wings that I had long awaited. The command sergeant major and battalion commander approached me with them. The command sergeant major took the backings off them, placed them onto my oval backing, pinned the wings through my shirt and then punched them into my chest, giving me my "blood wings." The battalion commander then gave me his punch, which drove them deeper into my chest. On August 1, 2005, I was awarded the Master Parachutist Badge.

CHAPTER 16

DEPLOYMENT TO NEW ORLEANS
MY FINAL "HURRAH IN THE 82ND AIRBORNE

IT WAS A good time in our battalion and squadron. At first the new "birth" of the 5-73rd CAV was very hectic, as it would have been for any organization tasked to a massive changeover with new personnel of different combat arms jobs combining. Everything started running smoothly, and personnel were getting put into place with their new duty positions and additional duties as well. Like I said, I went to Headquarters and Headquarters Company (HHC) along with most of the other platoon sergeants from 3 Panther. We had done our time as line platoon sergeants and were hoping and waiting for the day when we'd make the next promotion list. We went out, took our updated Department of the Army photos, and made sure our records were also up to date as well.

I was happy to find out that Captain J was selected to be the HHC company commander too. That was cool, having my old buddy from the old company with me again. I believe First Sergeant M stayed where he was at or perhaps changed companies, but he remained as a first sergeant.

As the new S-2 NCOIC, I pretty much didn't have a major contribution to the military intelligence spectrum, at least in garrison. Command Sergeant Major Z also selected me to have an additional duty of being the squadron's Pre-Jumpmaster School instructor. So a couple days a week, I would have access to the squadron's conference room and teach Jumpmaster School procedures out of the study guide to NCOs and officers that were trying to get into upcoming jumpmaster classes. I'd usually have one or two other jumpmasters help me test them on nomenclature, written exam questions, and sustained airborne training. We would also take them to the mock door setup within our squadron area and teach them actions in the aircraft procedures. The S-3 Air even got two slots for the 82nd Airborne master jumpmaster course, and me and another E-7 got selected to attend it.

I hadn't even known such an animal existed until that point. "Master Jumpmaster School? What the hell is that?" I remember asking. "What the fuck are they going to have us do, JMPI ten jumpers in ten minutes or some shit?"

No, it was more of an administrative course that lasted two days at the School House. They covered the senior-level decision-making process at the division and corps levels on airborne operations. On the last day, they gave us an open-book exam and we received our certificates. It wasn't about shit, but it damn sure sounded good in the Airborne community—master jumpmaster, for Christ's sake!

How well our soldiers back in our squadron did on our tests would be the result of who attended the next jumpmaster classes. During this time period, there were more slots being allocated to the units because of the deployments within Division. Obviously, more units gone meant more opened slots for schools at Fort Bragg.

There seemed to be quite a few jumps during this transition period of our new squadron too. I think they were trying to get these new NCOs from the cavalry current and up-to-date on their jumpmaster duties. Either way, the airborne operations were coming in big time. One night at Green Ramp, I received another good surprise. No, not the Division commander again, this time it was a chalk that had Egyptian paratroopers on the opposite door of mine. Apparently their original chalk was grounded for whatever reason and Command Sergeant Major Z had told the S-3 Air to move them to my aircraft.

"Hey, Sergeant A, you got your foreign jump wings?"

I said, "No, Sergeant Major, not yet." Up until that point, I had my German Schutzenschnur, or German Marksmanship Badge, but not foreign parachute wings. In the Army, you're only allowed to wear one foreign military badge on your dress uniform.

He said, "Well, you will after tonight. I'm putting an Egyptian jump team on your aircraft. They have their own jumpmaster who will interpret your assistant jumpmaster's jump commands."

That was it. Once I got my orders, I took off my Schutzenschnur and put on the Egyptian Parachute Badge on my Class A's. I haven't mentioned this until this point, but yes, it is common for many foreign armies to deploy and train at Fort Bragg, as we do in their countries. So you'd see foreign military paratroopers at Bragg quite often. The units at Bragg would jump together with them, which qualified both armies to exchange jump wings. It's a tradition that dates back to World War II.

The good times and positive vibes would soon come to a—I won't say *halt*, but a *slowdown* for sure. For me, anyway. My wife filed for divorce and moved to Michigan with our two children. My world fell from underneath my feet immediately.

It was a common theme in this place and happens more often than people think. When you move a hundred miles per hour, twenty-four seven and are married to the lifestyle and your unit, eventually your spouses have enough and go back home to their families. I had seen it time and time again throughout my nine years in Division. I had seen it happen to my buddy Shaky when we were squad leaders. When he found out his wife was leaving, he'd ridden his motorcycle over my house in Raeford and hung out for a while. When it happened to me, I went over S's house and had a cookout with him and his family. We were sitting around his grill drinking beer, and he started singing, "You picked a fine time to leave me Lucille . . ."

I looked at him and said, "What the fuck?"

We both started laughing. Only military buddies could get away with shit like that.

The unit was real supportive of my situation, especially Captain J. He was close with my family too. We used to go to each other's houses and he'd play with my kids. Hell, he'd even babysat one night for us during our anniversary one year. I remember finishing up PT one morning and walking to the S-2 shop, and here came Lieutenant Colonel P and Command Sergeant Major Z. They had just finished a run themselves and were walking down the sidewalk. "Hey, Sergeant A!"

"Yes, sir." I saluted him as they approached me.

Lieutenant Colonel P asked, "You doing okay Sergeant A?"

"Oh yeah, I'm good, sir, I'll be all right."

He asked me again, "You sure, man?"

"Yeah, I'm good," I replied to him.

Command Sergeant Major Z said, "I saw you walking down the sidewalk the other day from my office, and it looked like you were feeling bad, with your head down and shit."

"Oh, yeah, I'm doing a lot better now, Sergeant Major," I assured them both. "I'm good gentlemen; I got this shit."

Command Sergeant Major Z said, "Okay. You need anything, you come see me, Sergeant A."

"I will, Sergeant Major."

"Thank you both." I then saluted and went into the shop. It meant a lot to me because I could tell they were being sincere and concerned as well.

The next day after that, I remember we had another jump for which I was primary jumpmaster. Mysteriously, the squadron chaplain was on my aircraft. So during manifest, I came right out and asked him. "Hey, sir, you wouldn't happen to be on my aircraft because of my current situation, would you?"

He replied, "Oh, just here if you need to talk, Sergeant A."

I said, "Well, thank you sir, but I won't have time for that. The Airplane Game doesn't slow down or get put on hold for marriage separations."

A few days after our jump, this whole thing was truly getting to me. It was going to happen; there was no coming back and working things out. I had to make a decision, and it was going to be a tough one. As a matter of fact, it was going to be the hardest, but easiest decision I was going to have to make throughout my military career.

I had two options: I could stay there with my kids seven hundred miles away and maybe see them once or twice a year, or I could attempt to move duty stations to be closer to them, possibly right in Michigan. The real choice was *Do I want to be a part of my children's lives or not?* That's why I said it was an easy decision as well.

I knew the first thing I would have to do was to get the okay from the command sergeant major. So I walked to the squadron HQ building and went straight to his office. I remember thinking, *He did say if I needed anything, to come see him.* Well, there I went.

I took a seat on his couch and began telling him what I was thinking about doing and if it were clear for me to leave Fort Bragg. I remember him telling me, "Okay, Sergeant A. That's fine. You've been here three years now, and you've done everything I've asked of you." He then added, "The only problem you're going to have is finding a duty station in Michigan."

"I thought the same thing, but with all the universities in that state, I may be able to land an ROTC instructor position, or an AC-RC trainer and evaluator position." Active component to reserve component positions were given out to help train up and prepare National Guard and reserve units that were preparing for combat deployments.

Command Sergeant Major Z then told me to go back and call Ranger Branch at the Department of the Army and see what they had to offer for me. So, I called the Ranger Branch Manager and asked him for a reassignment position somewhere near my kids. He immediately began asking me questions, such as, "How long have you been on your current assignment? Do you have a combat deployment with them yet? Do you have at least two years of successful platoon sergeant time?" The answers were yes to all the above.

At that point in our conversation, he told me I was authorized to leave Fort Bragg and PCS somewhere new. He did say he had nothing available in Michigan, but then gave me hope for somewhere near the border. "Have you ever heard of Bowling Green, Ohio?"

I said, "Yeah, I drive past it when I go home on leave to Michigan."

He told me they had an ROTC instructor slot opening up at Bowling Green State University, and that it was mine if I accepted it. I took it in a heartbeat. BGSU was only about two and half hours from where the kids were, so I could do that easily. He then told me that I would be coming down on assignment officially through the Department of the Army, and that I had a tentative report date of January 2006. That was it. It was a done deal. I walked back over to Command Sergeant Major Z's office and told him what I'd gotten.

Mysteriously, a few days later, I got a phone call at my house one evening. It just so happened to be the professor of military science at BGSU Army ROTC. "Is this Sergeant First Class Aga-naga?"

"Yes, it is," I responded.

"This is Lieutenant Colonel B calling you from BGSU."

I remember wondering how he had gotten my phone number, but I didn't take an issue with it either. "Yes, sir, what can I do for you?"

He said, "Well, glad you asked. When you get up here in a couple of months, I want you to bring the 82nd Airborne mentality to this place. We have a handful of cadets that can definitely use the discipline."

"Okay, sir. I'll do my best when I get up there in January." Lo and behold, he was the older brother of the Ranger branch manager I had just talked to a few days earlier who had got me the BGSU assignment. What a small Army it was.

At the end of that month, I turned on CNN, and there it was, one of the worst weather catastrophes our nation has ever seen.

Hurricane Katrina had slammed into the Gulf Coast. It was all over TV for that entire initial weekend that it hit, even after it had come and gone. The entire city of New Orleans, Louisiana, was underwater because their levees got destroyed from the hurricane. Thousands of people were trapped in their homes and the Superdome in downtown New Orleans.

When everyone showed up to work Monday morning, the word was already out that our brigade was going to join the rescue operation underway down there. Now, at this point, our 1st Battalion was deployed to Afghanistan, so our brigade consisted of 2 Panther and our newly assembled 5-73rd. It was becoming more common by this time that certain battalions were supporting other brigade task forces on the street during their combat deployments to Iraq and Afghanistan. Now I remember we were not on DRB-1 at the time, that the 325th was. However, they were slotted to deploy soon, so that left us, the 505th.

It was a weird alert status situation because the initial point of Katrina was just a standby mode for everybody in the brigade. *You can go home at night, but don't leave too far from Fort Bragg,* was the word that we got in the units. We stayed in this mode well into September and there still wasn't an official word of whether or not we were going.

We all watched the situation in New Orleans deteriorate into more disaster and death. By this time, the looting in the stores and violence was in full effect down there. There was even an incident where a National Guard soldier was shot by a gang. We were definitely wondering what the holdup was on getting us down there to help.

I remember it was a Sunday afternoon and the phone rang. It was the CQ calling from the unit. All companies were being alerted and were to be in on Lindsey Field by like 1600 or something close to it. We all showed up in BDUs and began to receive our briefing from Lieutenant Colonel P. We were going to New Orleans on a humanitarian mission, which included emergency response and conducting rescue operations for displaced citizens. The first sergeants received the packing list within an hour from operations. We were told to send everyone home to pack up, say goodbye to their families, and be back in three hours to begin our movement to New Orleans.

Once back at the squadron, each company was responsible to provide their Humvees with a driver and a truck commander and have them parked and lined up on Lindsey Field. Our company would be in charge of the squadron convoy that would take all vehicles down to New Orleans, led by Captain J. The first sergeant would stay back and was in charge of getting the rest of the company personnel down there with the squadron. We were to make it down there with the convoy around the same time that the rest of the Brigade Task Force would make it down via C-17 aircraft.

About nine hours after our alert and initial briefing from the squadron commander, Captain J and I left with the squadron convoy and started making our way down to Louisiana. On or around September 10, 2005, approximately twelve days after Hurricane Katrina hit, Task Force Panther deployed to New Orleans in support of Operation Helping Hand. This would be my last major event with the 82nd Airborne Division, and it was definitely one that I will never forget.

It took us just under two days to get down there with the convoy. We had minimal trouble with our vehicles making the trip. I believe only one vehicle had to be removed from service out of all thirty-five or forty. Overall, the mission of getting the squadron's vehicles down to New Orleans was a success. It had just turned dark when we hit the outskirts of the city. Our destination was the Naval Reserve and Recruitment Center, just about a mile or so north of the French Quarter.

As we came over the Mississippi River on the Crescent City Connection Bridge, everything was blacked out. There were no lights at all in the city. The only illumination was the little bit of moonlight we had. As we came over the bridge and could finally make out the skyline of the city, an eerie feeling came over me. It reminded me of the movie *Escape from New York,* when Kurt Russell flies into Manhattan and the entire New York City skyline is blacked out.

When we got into the city, the only lighting came from our headlights on the vehicles and the lights from emergency workers who had their generators on. We had received directions from one of the workers on the street we were on to the Naval Center, so we headed in that direction. Once we arrived, all the vehicles remained in the parking lot and the drivers and TCs just stayed in them for the remainder of the night. I want to say the commander, command sergeant major, and the staff were already at the complex awaiting on us to arrive. Our first sergeant came out and met Captain J and took us inside, where they had established our squadron headquarters.

The next morning, when the sun came up, we linked up with our soldiers that had arrived a day earlier. We were quartered in the offices on the first, second, and third floor. We each just found a space on the floor next to a desk, placed our ruck and equipment down, including our weapons, and that became our new homes for the next month. The electricity was down all over the city. The entire complex was completely abandoned except for our squadron, and we had just moved in less than twenty-four hours ago.

The building reeked to high heaven of rotted meat. The meat cooler for the mess hall had been rotting for the past two weeks in the heat. There was a crew cleaning and sanitizing it out as we were moving in. I'm not quite sure who they belonged to, but I wouldn't have wanted that job if it came with a million dollars. It was at least ninety to a hundred degrees when we got down there. Air conditioning was obviously nonexistent as well.

The rest of the brigade was across the river in an old National Guard facility staying in tents. Once the entire unit was on the ground, there was no time to waste. We immediately began rescue operations with other entities down there with boats. Captain J, the first sergeant, and I rode around at first and started going down to explore some of the nearby neighborhoods. Most of the streets off the main boulevard that connected to our facility were still underwater with no vehicle access except by boat. We made our way downtown and began making connections with FEMA representatives to see how we could help them or if they could assist us. Later on that first day, the first sergeant found a Humvee on the facility. It was painted blue. He actually signed for it from a representative on the compound. That blue Humvee became our primary means of transportation for the remainder of our time in New Orleans. Every day, we drove around and checked on all areas where our soldiers were. We made sure they were being taken care of with food and water. Most of them reported to the FEMA rescue teams deployed throughout the city. Each day they would cover areas marked off on their maps. They cleared house by house and street by street by watercraft. A company each day from 2 Panther was tasked to patrol dismounted through the French Quarter and the Bourbon Street area to maintain a show of presence for the prevention of criminal activity. Looting had become common since the hurricane hit two weeks prior. The water around the downtown area had begun receding, but very slowly. Around Bourbon Street, it was still ankle or even knee-deep in some parts. All the northern portions of the city, where the levees had broken from Lake Pontchartrain, were completely underwater. This is where primary rescue operations were.

As we were driving through the 9th Ward District, as far as our blue Humvee would take us without getting too submerged in the water, we came across our first dead body. There was a male corpse lying on top of the roof of a car with his arms slung out over the windshield. At this point the water was up to the bottom of the windshield, just over the hood of the car. We took note of his location, turned around, and headed back toward our facility, but through a different route. We drove along a wall that ran alongside the river heading north to where we were staying. We stopped and found our second body. This body was wrapped up in a white sheet and placed next to the wall. Above it was a spray-painted message on the wall that said, "Fuck You Katrina," with an arrow pointing down at the body. I'll admit it: I was a little creeped out by it, especially because it was so close to where we were staying.

As the sun went down that first night, everything got quiet and all you could hear were abandoned dogs in the distance. Knowing the bodies were outside our compound, with the dark silence in the city, it felt like a fucking zombie movie. We had some bad dreams at night trying to sleep in that stinking smell and the heat—and we hadn't seen the worst yet.

One of our companies was responsible for patrolling around and maintain a presence at the convention center. This was a primary point of pickup that buses took the displaced citizens out of the ravaged city. There was a walkway that connected from the rear of the center to the Superdome where thousands sought refuge during and after the hurricane.

The mess outside the convention center was unexplainable. Diapers, MRE trash, shopping carts, clothing, you name it, was piled up outside and scattered all over the place. The state had just evacuated these people just a day prior to our arrival. I remember wondering how this was ever going to get cleaned up to where people could come here again without the chance of disease. It was disgusting.

Captain J, the first sergeant, and I thought we had seen the worst until we decided to walk over to the Superdome. From the point we entered into the stadium from the walkway of the convention center, we had come out into the parking garage, and it was like the second or third floor. The first floor was underwater. It was real dark inside, so I turned on the tac-light on my M4 for lighting.

The smell was terrible. The floor underneath us was flooded, and all you could see were the roofs of the vehicles. "Oh, shit!" I shouted out. There was a body floating face down in the parking lot underneath us. His face was peeled back on both sides of his head from lying and rotting in the water for at least a while, we predicted from the hurricane itself two weeks ago.

I shone my light further down. He had a perfect water bottle in his back pocket of his jeans.

"Oh, look, a water bottle. He couldn't keep his face on, but that damn water bottle is in perfect condition," one of us said—I can't quite remember. "That's Bobby Boucher, from *The Waterboy*." We shook our heads and the name stuck with us.

When we entered the Superdome itself, it was the same scene that was at the convention center. Diapers piled up and trash everywhere. I'm sure there were some dead bodies in there too, but we didn't stick around too long because it was so hot. We looked down on the football field, which was covered in water and had trash floating on top of it. I remember thinking, *The city of New Orleans is going to have to tear this place down and rebuild it for sanitation reasons, if they ever want people to come back to this place.*

When we got back to the convention center, I told a FEMA guy about "Bobby Boucher" floating in the parking garage of the Superdome. Captain J also told them about the other two bodies that were over by the naval complex. He told us that the team they had with them couldn't do anything about the bodies, that it wasn't their jurisdiction, that it was for a different FEMA team that had not made it to the city yet. That made no sense to any of us. As a matter of fact, nothing about this disaster relief was making sense.

We asked the first sergeant there at the convention center if his soldiers needed anything from us that we could bring back for them. He said he needed more batteries for his radios.

"We'll be back with some for you, First Sergeant, no problem," I told him.

When we left in the blue Humvee, I had to ask, "Do either of you find it completely fucked-up that there are bodies still lying out in this city two weeks later?"

The first sergeant said, "Yeah, because the correct department for body disposal isn't here yet . . ."

The next day or so, we traveled north as far as we could on I-10 to check out a boat launch area that FEMA had designated as a launch and recovery point. They were launching the boats from an exit ramp off the interstate.

As we were driving to the site, we drove past another body. This one was wrapped in black trash bags. The body had bloated so much that it was popping through the bag and had one arm hanging out. Just lying on the side of the interstate. You can't make that shit up.

Captain J said, "That's 'Chester.'"

I said, "What the fuck?"

"Yeah, that's "Chester, Chester, the I-10 Infester."

Me and the first sergeant looked at him and said, "Okay, that's his name."

It's how we were making ourselves deal with what we were seeing in the streets of the United States. Hell, bodies in Iraq didn't stay out in the open this long—only in America . . .

The more we went out into the neighborhoods, the more paranoid I got. Not about people coming after us, but the dogs were becoming violent. They had been swimming in this shit for weeks now, starving, eating who knows what, and I could only imagine. We would be driving through one of these neighborhoods, and all of a sudden, a dog would jump out barking and acting all crazy. I started locking and loading my M4, which we weren't supposed to, but like I told Captain J and the first sergeant, "I'll be damned if I'm gonna get bit by one of these pit bulls or rottweilers."

Neither one of them said shit to me. Our blue Humvee didn't have doors on it, so I could see one of those wild, ravaged bastards trying to jump in our vehicle like Cujo or some shit.

We would sit outside at night at the Naval Center and shoot the shit about some of the craziness we'd seen that day. Some crazy stuff would come out of our mouths too. "So we have 'Bobby Boucher' and 'Chester, Chester, the I-10 Infester.'"

The first sergeant said, "Yeah, but what about the guy on top of the car a block down the street?"

Captain J suggested that we refer to him as "Blue."

I asked, "Why Blue? What's the significance of the name Blue?"

"I don't know," he replied. "From the movie *Old School*. 'You're my boy, Blue!'"

"Okay, his name is Blue from here on out." Captain J said, "Are we three in agreement? Because we can't fuck this up."

"Oh yeah, Blue it is."

We never did name the body that had been behind the complex against the wall.

I went upstairs through the dark-ass stairwell, waiting for a zombie or some shit to jump out at me. The smell of the rotted meat was dissipating. I made it to my rucksack, pulled out my wooby, went back downstairs to the open outdoors, put a cot together, and slept outside. I tried to fall asleep, but it took a while with the dogs barking in the distance. I kept my weapon snuggled up to me as I laid on my cot, trying to fall asleep. A couple hours went by, and a soldier came up to me and said, "Sergeant Augi."

I woke up and replied, "Yeah, whatcha need?"

"Here you go Sergeant. I found this in the parking lot—I thought you might want it."

"Found what?" I replied. "This had better be good since you woke me up out of a dead sleep."

He reached into his pocket and handed me a piece of a jawbone. It was the soldier from Iraq. I sat up quickly, and realized I'd had a nightmare of that kid handing me that on the side of ASR Jackson a year earlier.

As the water was receding downtown, many of the business owners were coming back to clean their restaurants and bars. The streets were dry by now, and the owners were asking for help taking down the plywood off their windows. We started noticing life slowly coming back to the city, at least downtown. Up north was still a ghost town, and some parts were still underwater.

The French Quarter had a large portion of tents set up for emergency responders. There were grills constantly going, cases of water, sodas, veggies, you name it. I remember running into two police officers from my hometown of Lapeer, Michigan. We sat down and had lunch together and talked about life back home, high school, etc. It was funny because, the next day outside the Naval Center, there was a police car from Davidson, Michigan, the town next to mine. The cop was taking a catnap, and I didn't want to bother him. Everybody down there was exhausted, hot, and nasty.

About halfway through our deployment down there, a Navy ship pulled up on the river in front of the convention center. We were authorized to take showers on the ship, not just the soldiers, but all emergency responders too. We ran our soldiers through there like an assembly line. It wasn't the Hilton Inn, but we always made the best of what we could.

I remember running into the guy I had gone to ANCOC with a couple of years earlier, the Ranger honor graduate. He was the NCOIC of operations during that day at the convention center. He and I sat down and started shooting the shit. I was telling him some of the stuff we had run across throughout the city.

The mayor of New Orleans was making a speech not too far away from where the FEMA teams were headquartered near the French Quarter. The three of us showed up to listen in on what he had to say. Trust me, we didn't stay long. I remember hearing him say, "I'm tired of hearing all these helicopters! I want to hear some jazz again!" I was thinking he ought to be worried less about listening to jazz and more about taking care of the dead bodies along his streets.

"Blue" wasn't looking too good. The water in the neighborhood he was in had all receded. One of his arms was gone from the elbow down. We were arguing in the vehicle about whether it had rotted off or a dog had chewed it off. He had a green slime running from his head down the windshield of the car. He'd seen better days.

We took note on what day it was from our arrival, which was about two weeks at this point of the deployment. So we figured Blue had been on top of this vehicle going on a month by now.

We drove around the backside of our complex again to see if that body wrapped in the sheets was still there. Lo and behold, he was. What pissed us off at this point was that there were two neat piles of brush that had been bulldozed on both sides of him. So the trees and branches were being cleaned up before the bodies were. I guess those FEMA body cleanup crews hadn't made it to New Orleans yet.

A couple of days later, when President Bush came and flew over the city, every body that we had been reporting and complaining about for the past two weeks had mysteriously vanished.

We were getting close to the end of our deployment. The paratroopers had pretty much finished up operations. The city had electricity back on and most of the streets were not flooded anymore. The neighborhoods or parishes in the northern parts of the city were still ghost towns. Many of those homes had to get destroyed and later, they were. Many families left Louisiana altogether and never came back.

Today, we know the failures of the government on the response to this crisis and have learned from the mistakes. State governors no longer hesitate to declare a state of emergency and ask for federal assistance. That was one of the biggest problems in Katrina. That's why we stayed so long back at Fort Bragg before getting down there. The Louisiana governor hadn't declared an emergency, and by the time she did, it was too late.

However, probably the biggest problem that happened in the beginning of the storm was that the citizens didn't take the warnings given by their local officials to get out of the city. Lessons learned from this catastrophe range from the citizens to the highest levels of our government.

We were down to the last couple of days in New Orleans, and the chain of command was letting everybody relax and have a little bit of fun. Wayne Newton came to perform for our squadron at the Naval Center we were staying at.

At first everyone was like, "Wayne Newton? We want some Linkin Park!"

The paratroopers were all gathered around the parking lot and up in the different decks of the parking garage. Wayne came out on a cargo ramp where he was going to perform, and we all cheered like it was a 1960s Beatles concert. I guarantee three-quarters of the soldiers didn't know who this guy was unless they had spent time in Vegas. I was nervous for him at first, thinking he was going to get booed or some shit like that. Nope! He was cool and he knew how to work a crowd of soldiers.

He brought his wife out on stage, and she was like a model. The troops were whistling and cheering for her. He got on the microphone and said, "Yeah, baby! That's my wife, and those titties are real, boys!" That was it, he had captured and earned the admiration of the entire squadron.

Some of the troops were screaming, "I want to fucking hear 'Danke Schoen!'" He sang it, and everyone went apeshit! Who knew?

Later that evening, some of the business owners downtown brought out food and cases of beer for all of us to show their appreciation.

During our month deployment to Operation Helping Hand in New Orleans, Task Force Panther evacuated more than five thousand displaced citizens and rescued almost one thousand people trapped and stranded at their flooded homes. The task force also assisted in the refurbishment of key facilities throughout the city, such as the Saint Louis Cathedral, the Superdome, medical facilities, housing projects, and schools.

When we got back to Bragg, Captain J had a party and cookout at his house. It pretty much lasted the whole weekend—at least it did for him and me. We had our first sergeant from HHC and First Sergeant M over. Most of the other officers and section NCOs from the company came over, and so did the squadron XO, Major C.

He was a great guy and funny too. He used to ride his bike over on weekends since his neighborhood was across the street from J's. We all sat around and talked about the experience we had just gone through in New Orleans and where most of us would be taking off to in the near future. Captain J had been selected to be the commanding general's aide. Command Sergeant Major Z had been picked up for brigade command sergeant major at Fort Riley, Kansas. Major C was off to Fort Leavenworth for his next Officer's Career Course. My other buddies back from our squad leader days were moving on as well. Shaky eventually made E-8 and went to Fort Jackson to be a first sergeant. So did S, if I'm not mistaken. S actually went all the way to E-9 before he retired. I believe Javier ended up finishing his platoon sergeant time in Bragg and PCS'd back down at Benning where his family was. My next-door neighbor, Staff Sergeant D, PCS'd to Fort Drum and took his family up to New York.

The Panther Brigade was on orders to deploy back to Iraq in early 2006. They would deploy as part of the Army's new modular force: instead of deploying as division elements, units would be deploying as brigade combat teams or basic combat training teams.

As for me, I had a house to sell and had to find a place to stay while I finished up my time at Fort Bragg.

The word going around our unit was that the squadron reenlistment NCO had his own real estate business. So I went to his office and started talking about needing to sell my house in Raeford. After he put the for-sale sign on it, he had it sold in less than a week. Military installations always have a huge turnaround rate on homes with all the people always coming and going. So by age thirty-three, I had sold my first home. Too easy.

Now I just needed a place to stay while I cleared the unit and the installation. So I asked Captain J, and we became roommates for my last few weeks there.

On my way out of Fayetteville, I wanted to go through Fort Bragg, so I drove on post and went to the drive-thru at Burger King on Reilly Road. I got a couple of breakfast sandwiches and a coffee. I looked at the clock on my dash and it read 0610. It took me about one second to make my next decision on what I was going to do.

I drove up Ardennes Street and went to the Airborne PX parking lot and parked my vehicle facing the street. I had about five minutes left before morning PT was going to start across the entire Division. It was December, so it was dark out, with the streetlights and the lights from the 325th across the street shining. All of a sudden, I could hear over the loudspeakers, "Here we go, all the way, every day, Airborne!" It was the famous PT recording of the 82nd Choir conducting run formation cadences that echoed down the street every Monday through Friday. I ate my breakfast sandwich as I watched all the paratroopers running up and down Ardennes Street. Of course, it wasn't as packed as it used to be because, at this point in time, there was at least one brigade always deployed to combat.

I sat there eating my sandwich and began thinking back to the young man walking up the sidewalk along Ardennes for the very first time, heading to the very place I was parked at right now. I had been so excited to get started here and was very proud to be here as well. It seemed like a hundred years ago.

What an incredible journey of my life and incredible people that I had the honor to serve with. I thought about wanting to come back some day during All-American Week and watching the parade on Pike Field where that big painted double-A sign faces the crowd. I would love to hear that big old "Aaahhhh" come from the paratroopers in the formation when the Division commander says those famous words, "Pass and review."

Maybe someday I'll be that old man asking a young man how many jumps he's got.

From trying to throw that grappling hook into the concertina wire, to being told "Flip to the flap to the floop," to being called "motherfucka" for a year and a half straight, to meeting "Bobby Boucher" down in New Orleans, I wouldn't change any of it for one minute. It defines some of the hardships I had to overcome in order to be the person I am today. We all have them, and sometimes sitting back, remembering and laughing about them, can help us get by in life.

The 82nd Airborne Division is a sink-or-swim environment twenty-four seven. I chose to swim. I still choose to swim every day of my life and will continue to do so until my days are over here in this world.

As PT was finishing up, I wondered if I'd ever be back here again during my military career. Probably not. Not if I were going to be part of my kids' lives. I made the right choice and wouldn't change it for anything. No, I knew at that time that in about four more years, I'd be retiring. I was going to do twenty years and get out, which I did, and it paid off for me and my family.

After Ardennes Street was cleared to drive on that morning, I pulled out and headed down toward the Advanced Airborne School. I took a right onto Long Street and headed off post. I even thought about driving past Green Ramp one last time but told myself it was time to go. When I got to the intersection of Bragg Boulevard, I took a left on it and headed north toward Sanford, then Greensboro.

As I drove out of Spring Lake, I thought about what the Army had in store for me next, both for my career and my personal life. I was about to embark on a different and final chapter of my military career. Seven months later, I was selected by the Department of the Army for the E-8 promotion list. After two years of serving as an ROTC instructor, and meeting the wonderful woman who became my wife, I PCS'd to Fort Riley, Kansas. There, I was assigned to a combined arms battalion in the 1st Infantry Division, where we deployed to Iraq for a year. After returning back to Fort Riley, I retired as a master sergeant with twenty years active duty service. My wife and I built a house and live happily in Northwest Ohio.

That's how this book came to be. I was telling my wife one morning a story about back in the day in the 82nd, while we were drinking coffee in the kitchen. As we were both laughing about it, she suggested that I should write these stories down as memoirs or a book someday. So here I am.

MASTER SERGEANT AUGI IN KUWAIT. PREPARING FOR THE FINAL YEAR-LONG DEPLOYMENT TO IRAQ IN 2008.

ACKNOWLEDGMENTS

I would like to thank all those who have served, and are serving, in the great military of the United States.

www.ingramcontent.com/pod-product-compliance
Lightning Source LLC
LaVergne TN
LVHW091702070526
838199LV00050B/2254